SOCIAL MOVEMENTS

Social Movements: The Key Concepts provides an insightful, contemporary introduction to some of the frequently encountered terms and groups that are central to the study of collective action and social and political activism. Following an A–Z format, the entries defined and discussed are drawn from the following areas:

- the 'old' social movements of the nineteenth century
- the 'new' social movements of the 1960s and 1970s
- the rise of contemporary 'network' movements

Key American, European and global social movements are addressed, with each entry related to contemporary developments and emergent tendencies within the field. Including helpful references for further study, this concise and up-to-date guide is of relevance for those studying a range of disciplines, including sociology, politics, cultural studies and human geography.

Graeme Chesters is Senior Research Fellow in Peace Studies at Bradford University, UK. His books for Routledge include *Complexity and Social Movements: Multitudes at the Edge of Chaos* (2006) with Ian Welsh.

Ian Welsh is Reader in Sociology at Cardiff University, UK. His books for Routledge include *Mobilising Modernity: The Nuclear Moment* (2000).

ALSO AVAILABLE FROM ROUTLEDGE

SOCIAL MOVEMENTS

The Key Concepts

Graeme Chesters and Ian Welsh

Routledge
Taylor & Francis Group

LONDON AND NEW YORK

First published 2011
by Routledge
2 Park Square, Milton Park, Abingdon, Oxon OX14 4RN

Simultaneously published in the USA and Canada
by Routledge
270 Madison Avenue, New York, NY 10016

Routledge is an imprint of the Taylor & Francis Group, an informa business

Typeset in Bembo by
Book Now Ltd, London
Printed and bound in Great Britain by
TJ International Ltd, Padstow, Cornwall

British Library Cataloguing in Publication Data
A catalogue record for this book is available from the British Library

Library of Congress Cataloging in Publication Data
Chesters, Graeme, Ph. D.
Social movements: the key concepts / by Graeme Chesters and Ian Welsh.
p. cm.—(Routledge key guides)
Includes bibliographical references and index.
1. Social movements. 2. Globalization—Social aspects. 3. Social networks.
I. Welsh, Ian, 1954– II. Title.
HM881.C443 2010
303.48'403—dc22   2010016754

ISBN10: 0–415–43114–X (hbk)
ISBN10: 0–415–43115–8 (pbk)
ISBN10: 0–203–84068–2 (ebk)

ISBN13: 978–0–415–43114–9 (hbk)
ISBN13: 978–0–415–43115–6 (pbk)
ISBN13: 978–0–203–84068–9 (ebk)

CONTENTS

ACKNOWLEDGEMENTS

We would like to thank all the editorial staff at Routledge for their professional support and patience in seeing this project into print. Thanks also go to all the anonymous referees on both sides of the Atlantic. Many of the suggestions have found their way into the text and have added value that underlines the fact that authoring has an important collective element to it. To all the students and colleagues who have helped us to test some of the material here we have a debt of gratitude. Particular thanks are owed to Michal Osterweil for her enthusiasm for this volume and her willingness to contribute time and words to the introductory essay.

To our families we owe our thanks for all the times when we have been present but not quite there and the times when we have been absent during the course of writing and editing. Without your support and inspiration, such tasks would be much harder, if not impossible to complete.

We hope that this volume will be useful to students in sociology, politics, cultural studies, geography and other disciplines as they work with the notion of social movement in the early years of the twenty-first century. Our approach to the key concepts and key movements covered here melds the definitional with the contextual. We have endeavoured to combine accuracy with our understanding of the development and trajectory of this field of study.

The selection of entries reflects both our shared priorities and the limitations imposed by a project like this. We are painfully aware that there are thousands of movements in countries of both the North and South that could have featured here. Our selections are strategic and illustrative and also confined to areas where we feel we can be legitimate codifiers of knowledge. We will have inevitably erred and have to accept this inescapable aspect of authorship.

Graeme Chesters, *Department of Peace Studies, Bradford University*
Ian Welsh, *School of Social Sciences, Cardiff University*

ACKNOWLEDGMENTS

LIST OF KEY CONCEPTS

Alternative Globalisation
  Movements
Anarchism
Antagonistic Movement
Anti-Movement
Anti-Nuclear Movements
Anticapitalism
ATTAC
Autonomy
Biographical Availability
Black Power Movement
Capacity Building
Civil Rights Movement
Claimant Movement
Cognitive Praxis
Collective Behaviour
Collective Identity
Computer Mediated
  Communication
Counterculture
Countermovements
Culture
Cycles of Contention/Protest
  Cycles
Defensive Social Movement
Direct Action
Disability Rights Movement
Disobbedienti
Earth First!
Ecology of Mind and Ecology of
  Action
Emergence

Emotions
Environmental Justice Movement
Environmental Movement
Feminist Social Movements
Frame Analysis
Free Rider Problem
Friends of the Earth
Global Civil Society
Global Social Movement
  (Transnationalism)
Green Movements
Greenham Women
Greenpeace
Health Social Movements
Identity Politics
Indigenous Peoples' Movements
Indymedia
Knowledge-Practices
Latency Period
Leadership
Lesbian, Gay, Bisexual and
  Transgender (LGBT) Movements
Lifeworld
Marxism
Moral Action
Movement as Media
Multitude
Network Movements
New Social Movements
Offensive Social Movement
Old Social Movement
Peace Movement

Peoples' Global Action (PGA)
Political Movement
Political Opportunity Structure
Poor Peoples' Movements
Power
Precarity
Protest and Disorder
Reclaim The Streets
Repertoire of Action
Resource Mobilisation Theory

Scientific Social Movement
Situationist International
Social Movement Organisation
Social Movement Society
Social Movement Unionism
Students for a Democratic Society
Subvertising
Urban Social Movement
World Social Forum
Zapatismo (Zapatistas)

INTRODUCTION: THE CONCEPT OF SOCIAL MOVEMENT

The concept of social movement has been around for almost one hundred years now and remains a contested concept within sociology and other disciplines. Despite this, use of the term social movement has spread across disciplinary and sub-disciplinary boundaries in recent years. This suggests that the importance of social movement as a category for describing and analysing the contemporary milieu has a renewed prominence. Like any area of study with a hundred-year lineage, the relationship between contemporary developments and established approaches results in a dialogical process of claim and counter claim. The relevance of different established positions to contemporary developments is one major theme that sits alongside debates between new interpretations and theories. This is an important part of the process through which knowledge is socially negotiated and consolidated within and between disciplines.

In an area as diverse as social movement studies some sort of thematic ordering device is essential to make sense of the richness that we are confronted by through the term social movement. The established terms 'old social movement' and 'new social movement' are valuable in terms of a sequential understanding. Old social movements originate in the social, economic and political dynamics of the nineteenth century whilst new social movements originate within the dynamics of the latter part of the twentieth century. However, the terms are analytically problematic on a number of grounds. Many of the surrounding processes, methods of organisation and intervention found in old and new movements are very similar. Many of the 'new' social movements had broadly equivalent counterparts in the nineteenth century or even earlier. This certainly applies to feminism, the environment and animal rights. An internationalist or global level of engagement has also been a feature of both old and new movements, as has the use of networks for organisational purposes. Irrespective of this, we would argue that after the old and new there has been a significant rise in the importance of 'network movements' as physical mobility and instantaneous electronic communications have transformed the mobilising capacity of social movement actors.

Approached in this way old, new and network movements can be thought of as historically and spatially located expressions of social and cultural responses to prevailing political and economic dynamics. Put another way, in each epoch key aspects of social, sexual, cultural, racial, political and economic equality and equity are contested by social movements utilising the range of resources available in a given place and at a given time.

THE BACKGROUND FOR SOCIAL MOVEMENT STUDIES

Although people have always protested, resisted and pursued action for social change, the use of the term 'social movement' as we know it today is a relatively recent phenomenon. In fact it was only in the late 1960s, with the emergence of increasingly visible and for many, surprising, forms of collective action, specifically in Europe and the USA – i.e. student, environmental, and women's movements – that social movements began to be recognised as empirical objects of study worthy of scientific research.

Notably, even though there were some *global* similarities in the movements or mass social uprisings, especially around the year 1968, approaches to studying social movements differed radically in Europe and the USA. How they were understood, theorised, or whether they were in fact considered *new* varied by context: for example, while in the USA the paradigmatic referent was the Civil Rights Movement, precursors in Europe included labour and suffrage movements with much longer historical lineages. The differences in these movements, at least as they are traditionally conceived, are multiple. Whilst the US Civil Rights Movement demanded inclusion and rights within the existing framework of state and society – i.e. equality before the law, desegregation, etc. – European Labour movements, and their precursors, had pursued more systemic and ideological challenges questioning the very way state and society were organised. European labour movements raised issues around whether there should be a socialist or capitalist state far more prominently than their American counterparts. These multiple differences, many of which continue to be relevant today, are important reminders that specific issues and histories in particular places (i.e. the particular condition of African–Americans in the USA in the 1950s, the US constitution, etc.) have shaped the field of Social Movement Studies. This shaping has taken place through the prioritisation of different theoretical and epistemological frameworks constituting particular societies' understanding of 'the political', 'the social', 'the economic' and 'the cultural'.

The multiple differences between the European and North American approaches were largely products of contextual factors, especially the different intellectual traditions and political cultures of the countries in which both social movements and the social scientists studying them were located. European approaches contain significant Marxist and post-structuralist lineages that contrast with the influence of Liberal pluralism prominent within North American approaches. These contextual differences underpin to a considerable extent the different questions and analytical problems addressed by European and North American researchers and the prioritisation of different levels or scales of analysis. These differences can be summarised in terms of *Why* and *How* questions and the relative importance of structural explanations in comparison to human agency.

Consider some of the different kinds of questions or problems researchers have been interested in solving:

1   Why do some *individuals* participate in protest – or other forms of collective action – while others do not?
2   What are the *structural* or societal conditions that cause or at least tend to accompany social movements? (Economic factors? Political factors? Technological Changes? Alienation? Repression?)
3   What do social movements do and *mean* and how do they reconfigure our understandings and notions about society, and how society can be organised?
4   What do social movements want and in what ways do movements pursue their goals in ways that are different from protest or lobby groups?

These questions are not only concerned with fundamentally different parts of the mobilisation process – i.e. micro-level concerns with individual psychology, versus more macro levels like the economy, political system, etc. – they also employ very different research methodologies and theoretical frameworks. These different methodologies and theories in turn enter into fundamental debates within sociology and the social sciences more broadly, such as structure versus agency; and quantitative versus qualitative analysis. For example and schematically speaking, a focus on individuals usually carried out through interviews, questionnaires, and specific empirical studies will probably be accompanied by social theories where human agency, rather than structural determinism, are seen as primary. Alternatively, those primarily interested in structural causes tend to come from social theoretical traditions where human actions are considered to be influenced by where they are situated in relation to social structures and the divisions that flow from them (i.e. gender, age, race, class, sexuality etc.). Others, coming from a more hermeneutic or interpretive approach to the study of humans, will treat meanings and cultural products as mixed outcomes of both structures and human will. For the most part, social movement studies doesn't choose one side of the structure versus agency debate (one with a long history in sociology and other social sciences), but rather research on social movements becomes key sites from which to gather empirical evidence and either interrogate or develop new social theories. These different question areas or levels of focus continue to characterise and differentiate different approaches within the broader field of Social Movement Studies (SMS).

Despite the theoretical and empirical focus upon the differences between North American and European approaches it is also important to remember that there are many important contemporary movements beyond the borders of the 'Global North'. When studying movements it is important to pay attention to how certain phenomena can quickly become seen as original or paradigmatic because of other blindspots. Something important to keep in mind is that at its inception SMS, as a sub field, was predominantly centred in North America and Europe, in terms of both the movements researched, and where the researchers and authors came from. While this has changed and there is a growing body of work on movements in other parts of the world, we should remember that when using concepts and approaches from the SMS field, this gap in knowledge remains a very real and troubling one.

Today, while the SMS field has become more consolidated and interconnected, remnants of these initial differences of context and interest remain in the *kinds of questions asked*, the *methodologies used*, the *aims and objectives of the research*, as well as the *theoretical and political framework* of the author or researcher.

PREDECESSORS TO SOCIAL MOVEMENT THEORY IN THE USA: THE COLLECTIVE BEHAVIOUR SCHOOL

In order to understand the different schools or trends in research and theorisation of social movements it is important to be aware of the theories and traditions which SMS authors responded to in developing the concepts of social movement studies and the political culture and context within which they wrote. The next section addresses the theories and debates in Europe and the USA that directly preceded the emergence of a more directed field of study on social movements.

In 1930s' North America mass movements were viewed negatively. Contextually, during the period 1935–1945, the Wall Street crash, the ensuing Great Depression and worldwide recession linked to the rise of European fascism and the Second World War of 1939–1945 created a climate where populist expressions of dissent were approached with suspicion. Rather than people mobilising for rights and social change, they were seen as spontaneous eruptions coming from aberrant, deviant or mob-like behaviour. As such they were generally viewed as dangerous and threatening to order and stability. Mass society theories (Adorno and Horkheimer 1976; Arendt 1958; Kornhauser 1959) argued that people were likely to join mass movements – often viewed as 'extremist' – when they felt atomised, insignificant and socially detached. Mass societies, in these views, were seen as antithetical to intelligent government and the contemporary notions of democracy.

Despite the predominance of these negative views of collective behaviour, sociologists became interested in understanding different forms of such behaviour and discerning whether they were in fact so dangerous and altogether negative. In 1934 Harold Blumer's *Outline of collective behaviour*, shed a slightly different light on collective action, even if fundamental presuppositions about their negative or unruly nature remained in place (Blumer 1946, 1951). Looking at empirical phenomena ranging from spontaneous and emotional crowds to the more sustained types of collective behaviour associated with social movements, Blumer coined the term symbolic interactionism and argued that collective action, even that of crowds, should be understood as purposive, meaningful and potentially creative action capable of introducing new norms, behaviours and skills among participants and within society.

This symbolic interactionist approach was consolidated by Turner and Killian in 1957, with their book *Collective Behaviour*. Dealing mainly in the 'micro' or individual and psychological levels of collective action – i.e. understanding what compelled an individual to join in collective action – symbolic interaction formed one half of what became known as the *Collective Behaviour* school – one of the most important strands of sociological thinking in what would later become the field Social Movement Studies.

The second half of the *Collective Behaviour* school, known as structural functionalism, was more concerned with the broader picture of how social order was maintained. Continuing in the tradition of classic questions about social order originating with Emile Durkheim, Talcott Parson's structural functionalism underpinned an integrated theory of collective behaviour central to the emergence of SMS, and articulated by Smelser in his *Theory of Collective Behaviour* (1962). As the name implies, structural functionalists were less interested in the micro or social-psychological unit of analysis and more concerned with structural or societal-level factors – i.e. not what led people individually to join movements, but what kinds of changes in the political, economic, social context accompany/lead to the emergence of a mass movement. The basic premise of this school of thought was that because societies tended toward equilibrium, collective action by social movements could be understood as a natural mechanism reacting to structural strains or changes in society. According to structural functionalism then, things like the fascist movement were not simply a case of alienated or duped citizens being manipulated by a dictator, but rather, structurally caused phenomena that worked to bring a society hit by economic and other 'traumas' back to a new state of equilibrium.

While there were important differences between structural functionalism and symbolic interactionism, including the political and personal opinions of its key authors, there were certain notable commonalities. If nothing else, these commonalities mark them off from the later developments in the field that move away from the centrality of strain. Both were premised on a) common commitments to the all-seeing power of an objective, empirical scientific approach, and b) the assumption that there are two types of behaviour: 1) institutional and conventional – i.e. normal – and 2) non-institutional collective behaviour. The latter is clearly associated with the 'abnormal', or with reactions to breakdowns in the 'normal' institutionalised ways of doing things (Eyerman and Jamison 1991). Cumulatively then, while collective behaviour might possess positive aspects at times, i.e. creativity, norms of self-regulation à la Blumer (1951); Turner and Killian (1987), it had to be studied and understood as qualitatively different from the 'normal' and 'rational' behaviour of everyday life and politics.

The tension between rationality and deviancy, as well as structure and agency, continued to characterise approaches to making sense of collective action though the early 1970s. Even relative deprivation theory (Gurr 1970) and accounts of 'mass deprivation' that explain violent rebellion as occurring when there is a discrepancy between what one has and what one thinks one can get – i.e. seeing a certain amount of rational calculation and perception in extreme forms of collective action, remain characterised by these presumptions. While they do grant more *agency* to individual and collective actors, and as such, counter certain strands of structuralism by arguing that there is no objective level of structural or material strain that immediately yields collective action, such approaches clearly remain within the view of collective behaviour as something negative, i.e. caused by strains, dysfunction etc.

The massive mobilisations during the 1960s, including the US Civil Rights Movement, women's movement, and student movements against the Vietnam war forced important ruptures with these ways of thinking. The idea that collective action necessarily emerged at moments of breakdown or dysfunction was challenged by the mobilisation of women, students, environmentalists, and others in both significant numbers and innovative ways. These events took place in societies where post-war prosperity rather than hardship and dysfunction prevailed and many of the activists were not drawn from the most deprived or marginalised classes. Explanations of movement based in 'objective' structural conditions underpinned by economic causes struggled in the face of such diverse movements. More broadly, these theoretical models could not explain how or why collective struggle emerged, instead the events of the 1960s *appeared* as spontaneous eruptions of collective protest compared to more formally organised movement interventions.

One response to these theoretical and methodological shortcomings was the introduction or invention of resource mobilisation theory (RMT), an approach that regarded collective action as rational and organised action dependent not on structural strain, but on contextual resources. The creation of RMT arguably marked the founding of the contemporary North American School of Social Movement Research.

RESOURCE MOBILISATION THEORY

During the 1970s a number of sociologists produced studies that pointed to the qualitative difference between *organised* political action and *deviant* or irrational collective behaviour. Whereas deviant forms supposedly arose spontaneously as a response to ambiguous or irrational grievances, organised movements engaged within a rational framework requiring a lot of prior work and co-ordination (McCarthy and Zald 1973, 1977; Oberschall 1973). These arguments formed the basis of what came to be called the Resource Mobilisation approach.

Arguing that grievances and strain were always present, the proponents of RMT wanted to understand *how* social movements emerged at particular moments. In taking the 'why' of social movements for granted, they focused mainly on the organisational resources and the rational orientation of political actors to explain the emergence of the phenomena. Put another way, resource mobilisation theorists (McCarthy and Zald 1977, 1987; Oberschall 1973; Tilly 1978) argue that instead of trying to discover *what* grievance gave rise to *which* movement, the focus of theorists' attention should be upon *how* social movements mobilise successfully:

> The resource mobilization approach emphasizes both societal support and constraint of social movement phenomena. It examines the variety of resources that must be mobilized, the linkages of social movements to other groups, the dependence of movements on external support for success and the tactics used by authorities to control or incorporate movements.
>
> (McCarthy and Zald 1977: 1213)

In moving the emphasis from 'why' movements mobilise – i.e. deprivation, strain, interest – to 'how' they mobilise, resource mobilisation theorists shifted the emphasis of movement analysis away from structural factors and towards organisational questions.

This shift has been attributed, in part, to the growing importance of economics and business cycles within the US academy at the time (Tarrow 1998). RMT has had a large impact upon social movement theory, and many familiar terms and concepts originate in this body of literature. Reflecting the influence of economic theory McCarthy and Zald (1977, 1987) introduced the idea of 'movement organisations', 'movement entrepreneurs' and 'movement industries'. The development of a set of analytic terms laid the foundations for an extensive research programme which consolidated the place of RMT as the dominant paradigm for social movement analysis in the USA. The process of consolidation was further enhanced by the pursuit of a certain kind of empiricism within American sociology that sought to produce objective and generalisable knowledge about social and human phenomena broadly equivalent to that of the natural sciences. A 'how' focus combined with an analytic vocabulary readily applicable to empirically measurable phenomena, such as organisational size and membership composition for example, was consistent with the prevalent Mertonian (1942) view of science. Merton regarded the scientist as a professional practitioner engaged in a process of knowledge formation independent of personal views, preferences and cultural codes. The empirical programme mounted through RMT resonated with Merton's thesis and was influential in securing it a prominent place in the prevailing US context.

The initial notion of 'resource' central to the consolidation of RMT referring to financial and material assets has since been extended to include abstract resources such as ideology (Moaddel 1992) or culture (Johnston and Klandermans 1995). The development of RMT thus operates at two levels:

1 First at a mezzo level, 'the analysis emphasizes how social movement organisations (SMOs) and cadre combine money, materials, people and technology into strategic and tactical action' (McCarthy and Zald 1987: 45).

2 Second at a macro level, the level of 'infrastructure', RMT theorists analyse 'the set of roles and facilities that are generally available to people in a society or social segment' (McCarthy and Zald 1987: 45).

This second level positions social movements within a 'sector' comprised of competing social movement organisations vying for generalised institutional and societal resources. In keeping with the US system of pluralist political interest representation, this is approached as an effectively open competition between equals operating on a level playing field. Success is primarily approached in terms of effective organisation and deployment of resources.

Overall, RMT posited three main areas of attention that can be seen to constitute some of the core questions, areas of research and contentions of social movement studies:

1 Participation: why people do or do not participate in movements – RMT argues that there is a more or less rational process of assessment, i.e. a cost/benefit analysis even if costs and benefits are not necessarily always immediately economic or monetary.

2 Organisation: there are differences between the organisations that make movements possible, and those that serve as a resource for broader social movements that by definition exceed one organisation. Part of the empirical work of social scientists is to study these.

3 Political success – as part of the rational calculation for participation, RMT theorists suggested that movement organisations and individuals assess the 'political opportunity structures' (POS) and their chance for making political impacts, usually within the established political sphere. Moreover, it was presumed that the primary motive for social movements were political, rather than social, cultural, semiotic. (This became the basis for a later evolution from RMT to political process theories [PPT].)

CRITICISMS, QUESTIONS AND FUTURE DIRECTIONS

Since its inception, there have been numerous critiques of RMT. Criticisms revolve around four main points:

1   Ideological Indifference. Critics have suggested that RMT is 'indifferent to the political or ideological content of a movement' and is 'applied in an almost mechanistic way to organisations of widely different political and ideological scope, without incorporating these factors within the workings of the model' (Dalton *et al.* 1990:10).

2   Overly rationalising. RMT is also criticised for overemphasising economic, rational calculation either in terms of personal interest in participating, or in terms of chances of institutional political impact.

3   Overemphasising the politico-institutional. RMT is criticised for being politically reductive, that is of neglecting or subordinating social and cultural factors such as identity and meaning in explaining the importance and occurrence of social movements (Welsh 2000).

4   Politically Reductive. This is, in turn, related to another form of political reductionism, i.e. the assumption that movements necessarily move within the given politico-institutional terrain without allowing for the possibility that they might offer more systemic critiques, i.e. of capitalism, modernity and the cultural codes that underpin them (Melucci 1996).

Many of the most astute criticisms came from Europe, where a different approach to studying movements was developing, almost simultaneously alongside RMT: new social movement theory.

'NEW SOCIAL MOVEMENTS' APPROACH

At around the same time that the resource mobilisation approach was being consolidated in the USA, European sociologists (and philosophers) including Alain Touraine (1981, 1983), Alberto Melucci (1980, 1985, 1989), Claus Offe (1985), Jurgen Habermas (1976, 1985), Ernesto Laclau and Chantal Mouffe (1985) began to write about what they provisionally titled the 'new social movements' (NSMs). The European experience of 1968 challenged theories of change predicated in class conflicts arising within the process of production. The long-standing European tradition of class radicalism by 'Old Social Movements' pursuing systemic ideological change was confronted by the same constellation of radical actors that mobilised in the USA. Whilst Marxist commentators such as Raymond Williams wrote of the emergence of a 'New Left', the term New Social Movement became more widely, if cautiously, adopted.

The term NSM was used in part literally to refer to *new* struggles – i.e. women's, student, environmental, anti-nuclear – and in part to refer to the emergence of new struggles organised around new grievances and changed aspirations. This element of NSM thinking extended to considering that there had been a fundamental change in the trajectory of enlightenment, modernity and the capitalist system.

In contrast to the American RMT approach these researchers asked 'why' and looked for structural reasons *why* non-traditional social movement actors – rather than the workers and peasants from the nineteenth and early twentieth centuries – initiated a set of struggles at this particular moment and in these particular ways. Unlike their American counterparts, these theorists assumed that the change in practices and actors necessarily corresponded to a change in the grievances experienced, and thus required new political analyses to comprehend a changed political system. As a result of this focus on the systemic and political nature of *why movements mobilised*, these authors paid far less attention to the specific organisational and mobilisation processes themselves.

Very different understandings of social movements arise when one adds or emphasises the question of *why* social movements and resistance practices emerge as they do, rather than simply *how* they function. Although it might seem like a semantic difference at first, the emphasis on system and cause ultimately corresponds to a radically different vision of the role of scientific or 'expert' knowledge, as well as the role and nature of theory and social science more broadly.

Beginning in the late 1970s, debates over how 'new' these social movements were – whether they indeed followed new logics, or perhaps made visible dynamics that had also been present in the old workers' movements – abounded. The debates, in turn, helped produce a lively exchange between various European and American sociologists throughout the 1980s and 1990s. However, before discussing the claimed 'convergence' between North American-based theories and the European ones, it is important to outline some of the key contextual factors underpinning why movements were considered new in the first place.

WHAT MAKES THESE MOVEMENTS NEW?

The European experience of the bi-polar post-war period was significantly different from that of the USA. Whilst sharing in post-war prosperity, key European countries experienced significant welfare state provision *and* proximity to the then USSR. Germany was divided into East and West, placing Europe on the front line of the ideological cold war. Soviet military intervention against reforming Soviet Republics, notably Hungary and Czechoslovakia, posed major questions for theorists with a Marxist lineage. American foreign policy, strategic nuclear weapons doctrine and military intervention in Korea and Vietnam raised the prospect of nuclear armageddon and echoes of imperialism in Europe. The cold war was simultaneously a local and global phenomenon for Europe. US military deployments in Europe and pressure to participate in wars against communism in Indo-China underlined the vulnerability to conventional and nuclear attack and gave rise to the Campaign for Nuclear Disarmament (CND) and European Nuclear Disarmament (END) movements. Pressure to participate militarily in Indo-China coincided with the end of empire and the assumption of independence in former European colonies and raised echoes of imperialism.

The massive mobilisations of the 1960s and 1970s added to this, posing theoretical and political challenge, which neither Marxist nor Weberian paradigms could address adequately (Touraine 1977). Whilst RMT had embraced economic, business-orientated theory, European theorists, particularly Herbert Marcuse, conceived these developments as the extension of subliminal control over individuals that fundamentally undermined the potential for radical social change (Marcuse 1964). Following events in 1968, Marcuse published *An Essay on Liberation* (1969) arguing that marginal social actors, students, women, black and ethnic minorities, young people, lesbians, gays and bisexuals, and the unemployed represented a new radical constituency with the capacity for systemic social change. Endorsements such as this made the epithet 'new' an irresistible force and a term that led to some intense debates within SMS.

Bert Klandermans's (1991) argument that the novelty of the 'new' movements can be understood by looking at three elements: *constituencies, values* and *forms of action* is a useful way of engaging with this area.

1   Constituencies – *constituencies were new* in that rather than the proletariat, participants in movements had shifted to groups that had been newly marginalised by the contemporary phases of capitalist development, and those who had begun to experience shifts in values and needs as a result of the general changes brought about by industrialisation and modernity. According to some authors (Inglehart 1977, 1990) this meant NSMs were largely comprised of middle-class constituents whose basic needs were already met. (However, empirical research showed that this was not always the case.)

2   Values – the NSMs were understood as a challenge to the enlightenment *values* underpinning modernity, the key institutions of political representation, and economic development based on technological progress. Combined, these forces were perceived to be undermining quality of life. Growth in environmental, and subsequently, anti-nuclear

activism across Europe were prominent examples associated with such a value shift.

3   Forms of action – *new forms of autonomous action originating outside established groups within civil society and frequently involving coalitions between emergent and established groups* became increasingly common. These movements were often anti-hierarchical, attempting to embody alternative values and principles within their organisational practices. The NSMs were often antagonistic towards institutional politics and the State, rather than seeking inclusion.

Others reflecting on these new movements pointed out that the new issues were indicative of new ways of doing and challenging politics, often focusing on problems and conflicts considered part of private or cultural life, rather than the 'political' organisation of the country. In the context of welfare states, the private sphere became subject to incursions by state institutions and their professionals (Habermas 1981; Offe 1985).

In other words, the movements were considered *new* in both content and composition because they were comprised of actors that had not pre-viously mobilised and because they organised around issues and demands that were not previously politicised or contested. These changes required empirical and theoretical modifications both in how academia thought about social movements as well as within the movements themselves.

SOCIAL MOVEMENT STUDIES AND THE EUROPEAN ACADEMY

Whilst SMS was firmly embedded in the empirical programmes of soci-ology and political science in North America, European engagement involved a much broader spectrum of disciplines. As previous sections have demonstrated, in Europe debate on the significance of 'new' move-ments involved not only sociologists and political scientists, but philoso-phers, political theorists, feminists, anthropologists and geographers. This had serious implications for the nature of the knowledge desired and produced by research on social movements. In Europe, those studies of social movements informed by established approaches, such as Parkin's Weberian study of CND (Parkin 1968), sat alongside a range of work which was interested in the macro-theoretical (philosophical) and/or sys-temic (politico-theoretical) understandings of the *meanings and implications* of movements rather than their sociological make-up, or the mechanisms by which they mobilise.

These interdisciplinary and more philosophical approaches included the contributions of Herbert Marcuse and Jurgen Habermas, developing themes established by Horkheimer and Adorno in the Frankfurt School. For example, one of the most cited explanations of these new social movements comes from Jurgen Habermas who argues:

> In the last ten to twenty years, conflicts have developed in advanced Western societies that, in many respects, deviate from the welfare-state pattern of institutionalized conflict over distribution. These new conflicts no longer arise in areas of material reproduction ... and they can no longer be alleviated by compensations that conform to the system. Rather the new conflicts arise in areas of cultural reproduction, social integration and socialization ... In short, the new conflicts are not sparked by problems of distribution, but concern the grammar of forms of life.
>
> (1981: 33)

> I would like to support at least cursorily ... that these conflicts can be understood as resistance to tendencies to colonize the life-world.
>
> (1981: 35)

Chantal Mouffe, a political theorist, argued that the new social movements emerged in response to new antagonisms resulting from the 'contemporary development of capitalist societies', 'societies [that] have been transformed into extensive market places'. This development, she contended, manifested itself in the 'commodification' of social life; the increasing presence and intervention of the State into daily life – what she terms 'bureaucratization' – as well as the destruction of collective identities via 'cultural massification' (Mouffe 1984: 141). According to her, then, not only were there new actors and issues, the very fact of these new elements meant that capitalism's recent developments had produced new forms and experiences of subordination, politicising spaces that had previously been seen as private or apolitical. The new social movements, subsequently, emerged to resist these new experiences in newly politicised spaces. 'What is new,' Mouffe sums up, 'is the diffusion of social conflict into other areas and the politicization of more and more relations' (Mouffe cited in Slater 1985).

POST-MATERIAL VALUES, NEW ANTAGONISMS AND A NEW SYSTEM

As such, the new values posited by these movements were considered important in that, whereas the working class had always been primarily concerned and motivated by material conditions (or so went the assumption) – i.e. wages, food, housing, what we might call 'bread and butter issues', many of these 'new movements' were characterised by their support of demands and values that were described as 'post-material' (Inglehart 1977, 1990) because they were concerned with questions of culture, power and identity. Traditional Marxism addressed such themes as 'super-structure', whilst emphasising instead the importance of the economic 'base'.

The debate over new values as a reaction to new grievances in society opened the way to academic engagement with 'grievances' originating within the cultural sphere and arising within the subjective experience of those affected. In the United Kingdom, Raymond Williams and subsequently Stuart Hall were key to the development of a critical cultural studies approach. Whilst the debate over 'post-material' values implied a rejection of Modernist values, others argued persuasively that there was a mobilisation for the 'selective modernisation' of Enlightenment values (Offe 1985). Commenting on German mobilisations over nuclear power and the environment, Offe pointed to coalitions between a residual peasantry (small farmers), students, citizens' action groups and federal authorities, suggesting that former class boundaries were confounded by the 'new' conflicts. These conflicts marked the rise of large-scale and sometimes prolonged direct actions, including occupations. Following practices developed in the occupation of universities, potential reactor sites became centres for 'teach-ins' and meetings organised on non-hierarchical lines as a means of embodying the 'new' political values and ideals pursued by the movement (Offe 1985; Rudig 1990; Welsh 2000). Similar actions took place in America with the Clamshell Alliance being a prominent example. Whilst these events were theorised in terms of significant transformations in capitalist modernity in Europe (Offe 1985, Touraine 1983, Welsh 2000) US accounts remained primarily focussed on the 'how' (Nelkin and Pollack 1982).

These contrasting academic approaches illustrate an enduring tension within SMS between social movements as agents of functional accommodation and social movements as agents of systemic transformation. Whilst we have presented this as a tension between a US and European tradition this is not to claim that all US or European social movement scholarship falls neatly within this categorisation. RMT and POS approaches are used widely within Europe and North American scholarship, whilst scholars from Anthropology and other disciplines raise significant 'why' questions. The important point for present purposes is that in the critically important formative period between the early 1960s and mid 1970s the very different intellectual traditions and orientations present in Europe and the USA engaged with 'new' movements in the ways we have outlined here. In the next section, we rehearse some of the key transformational claims made within the European tradition.

SOCIAL AND CULTURAL THEORY AND THE NEW SOCIAL MOVEMENTS

We have suggested that the European social movement milieu expressed key conflicts over technological innovation, a process driven by state and commercial enterprises, environmental and ecological issues as well as a diverse range of social and cultural conflicts with significant 'lifestyle' and rights dimensions. The structure/agency issues outlined earlier thus become central in a 'new' context. Key questions of how the effervescent eruption of new social movements related to structural changes in the political, economic and social spheres became a prominent theme in European work. Throughout the 1970s and into the 1980s this work was done in the context of the postulated transition to a 'post-industrial society' (Bell 1973) accompanied by a postulated shift from Fordism to post-Fordism (Mayer and Roth 1995).

These transitions were envisaged as transforming the occupational structure of industrialised and industrialising nations. Manufacturing employment would be increasingly automated; a new international division of labour would accompany the globalisation of production. Technocratic management, albeit in different forms, would prevail in both the USA and Europe and be extended to the developing world. This envisaged future can be thought of as the extension of the economic and business cycle approaches underpinning RMT to an increasingly global level. First multi-national corporations (MNCs) and then trans-national corporations (TNCs) began to displace 'domestic' industries in terms of economic significance.

These macro-change debates were addressed within social theory and social movement studies, with the French writer Alan Touraine assuming a prominent role. In *Post-Industrial Society* (1971) Touraine questioned the Panglossian approach of Bell (1973) and others on the grounds that this concealed a technocracy which would permeate all areas of private life and give rise to 'the programmed society'. State, science, technology and business would combine to subordinate the social in the pursuit of an elite-led, expert-driven trajectory. *Post-Industrial Society* laid the foundation for his subsequent corpus of work, emphasising that in any particular epoch there is a prevailing dominant social movement; that social change occurs via social movement; and that in each epoch there is only one prioritised social movement capable of producing systemic change.

Touraine developed this schema in work on anti-nuclear struggles in France throughout the 1970s (Touraine 1983) in the context of his insight that the historical dependence of science upon the State for basic funding was coming to an end. The implication being that 'the technocracy' was increasingly autonomous and dominant, making anti-nuclear struggles a prioritised movement. Within this theatre of mobilisation, he recognised instrumental ends, affective ends and an innovative cultural sphere constituting ideological and symbolic challenges. The combined product of mobilisation included models of knowledge, economic activity and ethics, all with a social content absent in a technocratic system-planning approach. To achieve this dynamism required *not* the most unified movements but the *most divided* (Touraine 1983: 189).

Touraine is clear that the movements he engages with are derived from the 'political ecology' that began to be formalised in 1968, the movements are new but also engage with and include elements of organised labour such as trade unionists that could be termed 'old' movements. Methodologically, his work contrasts markedly with RMT approaches by emphasising the *difficulty* of identifying social movement within a particular field of conflict, the importance of working as closely as possible with a social movement rather than using secondary sources (e.g. newspaper reports) and the status of the researcher as an active agent in the recognition, constitution, maintenance and development of a social movement.

In the tradition of European social science, a number of macro-theoretical approaches had evolved to account for and document this structural re-ordering, and a proliferation of terms were used to describe and analyse the emerging society. Originally these included 'post-industrial' (Bell 1973), 'technocratic' or 'programmed' (Touraine 1971) and latterly 'post-Fordist' (Murray 1989), and 'postmodern' (Lyotard 1984), all of which were contested and some of which, particularly 'postmodern', have been subsequently stretched to the point at which their utility as explanatory terms is questionable. However, all of these terms chart similar territory in their exposition of a more differentiated, complex, technologically advanced, aestheticised and pluralistic society; a society where the new movements are conceived both as symptoms of change and as increasingly important actors, in upholding, defending, contesting or withdrawing from those forces, frictions and fissures which are uncovered by structural change (Castells 1997; Chesters and Welsh 2006; Urry 2003).

SOME PROBLEMS AND FUTURE AREAS OF RESEARCH

Critiques of NSM theory can be organised around three major axes, and in fact were often asserted by some of the approaches' key authors:

1 overemphasis on macro-social theory;
2 lack of attention to empirical complexities and micro-level factors, i.e. individual motivation etc.
3 an over-investment in the notion of newness distracts from recognising continuities.

The Europeans were aware of empirical shifts such as new constituencies and new forms of action, including groups that challenged modern forms of political organisation and experimented with decentralised, directly democratic forms of organisation, and often sought to affect culture and lifestyle more than laws and macro-institutions. However, unlike their North American counterparts, the European propensity to explain collective action in such macro-political and social-theoretical terms often left them unable to explain why particular movements emerge to prominence at particular times, through reference to the availability of resources, and the opportunities for action offered by a political structure.

In addition, and as Alberto Melucci (1995) the originator of the phrase was keen to point out, the concept of 'newness' has to be recognised as both relative and as an analytical tool, rather than corresponding to an empirical or ontological reality. He worried that any 'hard' definition of a movement, or newness, would encourage scholars and activists to think of social movements reductively almost as persons, or unitary actors on a political stage. This way of thinking and studying them would neglect the complexity of these movements, including how they are formed, their historical antecedents, and the processes and meanings of their action. Notably, Melucci, a psychologist and sociologist by trade, was very concerned about reducing the complexity of social movements – which he came to define as multi-level 'systems of action' (1996: 4) that work simultaneously at several different levels of the social system. As such social movements not only function within their given politico-institutional spaces to demand change, more rights, etc., they are also an important source of identity and meaning for participants (Melucci 1989), as well as an important part of the processes of challenging the historical trajectory of a society or for the creating of new cultural codes (Melucci 1996).

Melucci's teacher and mentor Alain Touraine was also interested in the ways that social movements challenged the dominant codes through which a present was read and contested. However, while ultimately Melucci turned to RMT and the North American school in efforts to create a synthetic approach that focused on the how and why, the macro and micro simultaneously, Touraine continues to focus upon the articulation between the macro-theoretical and systemic, and the micro or empirical realities on the ground. Moreover, his belief in the role of the sociologist as ultimate truth-teller or adjudicator of the potential efficacy of a movement raised many questions about method, and how a sociologist or researcher was to situate him/herself vis-a-vis the movement.

INTERACTIONS BETWEEN NORTH AMERICAN AND EUROPEAN SOCIAL MOVEMENT RESEARCH

In the late 1980s, there was increasingly more engagement between North American and European theorists. While Melucci, Touraine and other New Social Movement theorists continued to do research and write on social movements, in many ways the subsequent developments in their work can be understood to be largely reactions to criticisms of the limitations of each approach, and appreciation of the validity of the other approach. However, many who had written about NSMs did not limit themselves to research on social movements, while others studied movements, but did not participate in the field being created. While the field continued to develop, and along with it a repertoire of analytical categories, methods and concepts, there remained an important difference between those interested in movements as empirical objects in and of themselves, and others more interested in movements because they believed they pointed to key antagonisms in society, who were more broadly interested in understanding how processes of social change might, or did, happen.

As we will continue to see throughout the book, the study of social movements takes place both within a self-conscious field that recognises itself as 'Social Movement Studies' and through more variegated interdisciplinary spaces and traditions – including political theory, feminist theory, cultural studies, geography, peace studies and many others. The latter contribute to our understanding of social movements and social change without always referring to the repertoire of categories and concepts that have become dominant in the sociological and political science literature.

19

CONCLUSION: NEW DIRECTIONS

During the past decade social movement studies has continued to flourish, taking a number of new, diverse and fruitful directions and increasingly beginning to acknowledge the role of social movements as producers of knowledge rather than as mere objects of knowledge for academics. Amongst the more recent social movement approaches have been those that emphasise emotions at both macro (causal) and micro levels (collective action dynamics) (Goodwin *et al.* 2001; Jasper 2003), those who see networks as the new paradigm (Diani 2000; Diani and McAdam 2003) and those working on self-organisation and complexity approaches to social movements (Chesters and Welsh 2006; Escobar 2009). There have also been important contributions based upon conceptions of embodiment and experience (McDonald 2006), those that emphasise cultural perspectives drawing upon movement narratives and storytelling (Johnston 2009; Polletta, 2009) and a wide array of important developments in social and political theory that have impacted upon social movement studies. These include the work of political theorists such as Hardt and Negri (2000, 2004) and their concepts of empire and multitude, the work of actor network and theorists who challenge the way we understand the 'social' (Latour 2007) and the growth of interest in social movements as examples of an increasingly mobile society (Urry 2007) or as an antidote to the failure of institutional politics (Badiou 2005).

This growth of interest also reflects attempts to respond to and theorise an important wave of social movement mobilisation that began in the early 1990s (Notes from Nowhere 2003) and which focussed around resistance to the globalisation of neoliberal capitalism, the promotion of 'social justice' and the elevation of climate change as a new horizon against which all collective action and public policy should be judged. This cycle of mobilisation has produced activist-researchers who have sought to challenge the epistemological premises of social movement studies. To theoretically and methodologically operationalise long-established critiques of positivist and Cartesian epistemologies, by blurring the boundaries between the subject and object of knowledge and pursuing practices of co-producing knowledge with, rather than on, movements (Casas-Cortés *et al.* 2008; Conway 2004; Cox and Fominaya 2009; Esteves 2008). This has led to some interesting and innovative work, including that on the specificities of local and indigenous knowledges and their implications for understanding the 'global' (Burawoy 2000; Escobar 2009), as well as a variety of attempts to develop 'knowledge-practices' (Casas-Cortés *et al.* 2008) that bridge academic and movement domains (Graeber and Shukaitis 2007; Sen *et al.* 2004).

CONCLUDING COMMENTS – OUR APPROACH

In reflecting upon these new directions it is perhaps also worth reflecting upon our own approach in this book, which is to provide a guide to some of the many concepts, schools of thought and disciplinary frameworks that animate social movement studies. Inevitably, our selection is just that – selective, we have not made any attempt to be comprehensive, believing that such an attempt would be as futile as attempting to list the many thousands of movements that have changed the social and political in immeasurable ways. Instead, we hope that by tracing the evolution of social movement studies through this introduction, and in picking a range of concepts drawn from distinctive approaches, illustrated here and there with concrete examples of prominent and not-so-prominent movements, we are providing the beginnings of a map for those as yet unaccustomed to the breadth and possibilities of this field of study. Our sense is that many of those who are actively involved in social movements look at some point for a guide to what, if anything, the study of social movements can offer them, in terms of reflection, inspiration, strategy or tactics. We also believe that for many students encountering the study of social movements as a route to understanding social and political change, there is a value to identifying an issue, idea or movement that might help them develop both a scholarly and practical engagement. From this position, we have sought to present both an accurate reflection of the field *and* a description of the concepts that we believe are most conducive to intellectual and material mobilisation.

SOCIAL MOVEMENTS

The Key Concepts

ALTERNATIVE GLOBALISATION MOVEMENTS

The alternative or alter-globalisation movement (AGM) came to prominence through its capacity to mount large-scale protests and interventions during summits of international governance and finance organisations (World Trade Organisation/International Monetary Fund/World Bank/ G8) during the late 1990s and early 2000s. This capacity was one outcome of networking processes that were underway for a considerable time before the AGM came to public prominence in events during 1999, such as the June 18th Carnival Against Capitalism in London or the massive protests and shutdown of the Seattle meetings of the WTO in late November and early December of the same year. These protests were amongst the first to explicitly articulate a link between Northern movements and the backlash against neoliberal globalisation that had found previous expression in the resistance to structural adjustment policies and free-trade agreements by movements in the Global South during the late 1980s and early 1990s.

There were many catalysts for these links, but perhaps the most significant for the emergence of the AGM were the actions of the Zapatistas – the EZLN (Ejército Zapatista de Liberación Nacional, see **Zapatismo**), an insurgent movement in Mexico who had militarily occupied parts of the Mexican state of Chiapas on 1 January 1994. They timed their actions to coincide with and protest the introduction of the North American Free Trade Agreement (NAFTA). The Zapatistas were crucial to the emergence of the AGM because they were amongst the first to publicly articulate and communicate the potential for a global resistance movement to neoliberalism. Their conception and realisation of the 'First Intercontinental *Encuentro* for Humanity and Against Neoliberalism' in Chiapas in 1996 gave a form and expression to a network of previously disparate actors and provided the inspiration for a movement that was to subsequently animate protests globally.

The AGM is not a social movement in the traditional sense of the concept. The AGM is best defined as a **network movement**, with significant nodes and clusters consisting of social movements, **social movement organisations**, groups and individuals, expanding across a multidimensional space with both material and virtual manifestations. Coterminous with this network is a series of what are referred to as 'plateaux' (Chesters and Welsh 2006): protest events, campaigns, gatherings of one type or another (see **World Social Forum, Peoples' Global Action**) which allow for a brief manifestation and stabilisation of the network, facilitating processes of identity building, the exchange of ideas, and the planning of protest actions etc.

The AGM's use of globally co-ordinated days of action has proven a significant innovation in mobilisation and the network architecture it produced was highly significant in the development of the movements against the Iraq war, culminating in the global protests on 15 February 2003, the single largest co-ordinated protest in history. The suggestion for this emerged from the assembly of social movements held at the end of the first European Social Forum in Florence in 2001. In many ways, then, the AGM represents a confluence of different conflictual currents originating in diverse regions of the world that have identified a common opposition and sought a shared field of action. Consequently, any neat or linear explanation of origins and context is likely to be problematic and reductive, leaving the debate as to whether this complex phenomenon is correctly identified as a movement, network movement or movements to remain open.

References and resources

Chesters, G. and Welsh, I. (2006); McDonald, K. (2006); Mertes, T. (ed. 2004); Marcos, Subcomandante. (2001). Notes from Nowhere (eds. 2003); Tormey, S. (2004).

ANARCHISM

Anarchism is the collective term for a diverse range of philosophical, political, social and cultural theories originating in the nineteenth century and subsequently revised and reinterpreted. Whilst anarchy is commonly understood in terms of the absence or breakdown of social order, advocates of anarchism promote voluntary forms of association constitutive of social order independent of a state. Independence from the state can also be consistent with support for capitalism and neoliberalism. Forms of collective anarchism which argue for forms of sociality involving justice in dealings and respect for difference challenge all state forms whether capitalist or communist.

Nineteenth-century European anarchism emerged within the International Working Men's Association, better known as the First International, and had counterparts in Russia, Latin America, America, the Philippines and Pacific Rim. Anarchism was a prominent response to what Anderson calls 'early globalisation' (2005: 3) as the first wave of industrialised economies became colonial powers. Whilst the relationship between historical and contemporary forms of anarchism is beyond the scope of this text it is important to be aware of key continuities and disjunctures.

In terms of political expressions of anarchism, syndicalism – the self-organising process of voluntary association between workers, formalised in nineteenth-century anarchism – remains important. Syndicalism retains a contemporary significance and was a prominent part of the philosophy of the 1970s advocate of *Post-Scarcity Anarchism* Murray Bookchin (1974). Community and communitarian expressions of the nineteenth-century European anarchist tradition emphasised the capacity for self-organising, collaborative interaction within human societies. Mutualism, the propensity towards co-operation, was advanced by Kropotkin (1998) as more important than competition in terms of evolution and survival and is a prominent underpinning of the contemporary work of Noam Chomsky.

Michael Bakunin (Dolgof 1972) is best known as a nineteenth-century insurrectionist drawn to conflicts throughout Europe as the industrial revolution transformed societies and sharpened class antagonisms. He was a prominent figure within the First International where he clashed with Marx and Engels, arguing that the peasantry rather than the emergent industrial proletariat represented the true revolutionary social force. Whilst the revolutionary catechism written with Nachiev has made him famous for advocating the uncompromising use of violence in the pursuit of revolutionary change, there are more important aspects of his work for the contemporary conjuncture. Two in particular stand out. First, Bakunin argued for the importance of what he termed 'invisible pilots' to guide and facilitate the revolutionary process. Anarchist groups throughout Europe fulfilled this role, representing a pre-cursor of contemporary network actors. The use of cells as an organisational form became widely used by a wide range of movements on several continents. Second, Bakunin wrote at a point when science and technology were becoming dominant drivers of economic and social change. Whilst Bakunin mourned the fact that the introduction of modern rifles using manufactured ammunition ended the ability of revolutionaries to make lead shot for muskets, he also theorised the role of the emergent 'savants of science'. Within this work lay key elements of an anarchist theory of science (Thorpe and Welsh 2008).

After a prolonged period of apparent decline anarchism achieved a renewed prominence with the emergence of the **counterculture** and **new social movements** during the 1960s and 1970s. The US writer Murray Bookchin was a prominent exponent of struggles based outside the workplace, prioritising **autonomy** and voluntary association coupled to the rejection of authoritarian behavioural norms. Combined with the liberatory potential of 'alternative technology' capable of capturing the energy of the sun, tide and wind Bookchin's work resonated with the emergent green and environmental movements (Dobson 1997). The emphasis on decentralised social forms based on consensus decision-making in Bookchin's work was influential within a wide range of activist networks in the USA, the United Kingdom and beyond.

In Europe anarchist influences were prominent in and around the student-led Paris rebellions of 1968. Drawing on a range of left-orientated thinkers, events in Paris contained many currents. Those most closely associated with the anarchist canon included the **Situationist International** (SI) and the work of Guy Debord. Debord and the SI prefigured many elements of postmodernism with their emphasis on spectral and iconic practices (Stephens 1998). By creating situations and spectacles revealing the sterility and emptiness of everyday life associated with consumer capitalism the SI prefigured a diverse range of social movement repertoires (e.g. **subvertising**) which have increased in prominence as **computer mediated communications** have developed. The founding editor of the journal *Anarchist Studies*, Tom Cahill, argues that the New Social Movements of this era were all examples of anarchist praxis. Irrespective of the veracity of this argument, anarchism and anarchist influences were key sources in the upwelling of citizens' initiatives and action groups that took place across the industrialised nations of the world at this time.

Towards the end of the twentieth century, anarchism was a prominent element within the social, political and economic transformations that accompanied the end of the post-Second World War bi-polar world order. The end of Soviet Communism was accompanied by a series of revolutions across Central and Eastern Europe within which anarchist groups played important roles (Kenney 2002). In a similar manner the consolidation of neoliberalism within industrial economies such as the United Kingdom was also accompanied by innovative, anarchist-inspired interventions (McKay 1996, 1998). As the global stakes associated with neoliberalism became increasingly prominent with the advent of US neoconservatism, anarchism played a prominent role in constituting the **alternative globalisation movement** (Chesters and Welsh 2006; Graeber 2002; Tormey 2004). Compared to previous decades this upwelling has achieved global reach with anarchist principles of self-organising, autonomous initiatives rooted in the contradictions of everyday life appearing all over the world (Notes from Nowhere 2003). At the start of the second decade of the twenty-first century it is clear that the historically significant anarchist traditions of non-violent direct action and violent confrontation remain active. More importantly, the digital commons and ease of physical mobility have added a range of modalities to the anarchist tradition and ended the isolation associated with small-scale anarchist interventions.

The contemporary significance of anarchism continues through an engagement with post-structural thinkers such as Foucault and Deleuze and Guattari (Call 2002; May 1994) leading to the introduction of the term postanarchism. Whilst the theoretical bases of this work are complex it is also informed by, and engaged with, emergent forms of cultural and political agency within a highly mobile and electronically connected world. **Zapatismo, Reclaim The Streets,** the **alternative globalisation movement** are amongst the widely dispersed, horizontally structured, network actors around which postanarchism builds. Postanarchism is a self-conscious attempt to reposition anarchist theory and praxis through a critical engagement with the existing canon of anarchist thought and post-modernism to formulate modes of collective political engagement based on diversity and hybridty rather than collective identity (Newman 2007). Anderson's discovery of **Indymedia** via a traditional paper leaflet headed 'Organize Without Leaders!' led him to speculate about the arrival of 'Late Globalization' (Anderson 2005: 234). The persistence of anarchist theory and praxis through space and time suggests that anarchism will continue to play a significant role in social movement studies.

References and resources

Anderson, B. (2005); Bookchin, M. (1974, 1982, 1986); Bookchin, M. and Foreman, D. (1991); Call, L. (2002); Chesters, G. and Welsh, I. (2006); Dobson, A. (1997); Dolgoff, S. (1972); Graeber, D. (2002); Kenncy, P. (2002); Kropotkin, P. (1998); McKay, G. (1996, 1998); May, T. (1994); Newman, S. (2007); Notes from Nowhere (eds. 2003); Stephens, J. (1998); Thorpe, C. and Welsh, I. (2008); Tormey, S. (2004).

ANTAGONISTIC MOVEMENT

Concept derived from the work of the late Italian social movement theorist Alberto Melucci (1989, 1996) which constitutes one of four analytically distinct types of behaviour that Melucci argues can be identified in social movements, the others being conflictual networking, **claimant movement** and **political movement.** An *antagonistic movement* is one that challenges society and politics in the most fundamental of ways. It not only questions the allocation of resources between social groups or classes, but challenges the ideological and organisational basis for the production, distribution and exchange of crucial social and economic goods. Examples might include radical environmentalists' critique of economic growth and the incommensurability of growth and environmental protection, or the growth of explicitly anticapitalist movements whose choice of **direct action** is for ideological (against representative liberal democracy) rather than for instrumental (influencing policy) purposes.

Whilst no movement is ever completely antagonistic, that is, without recourse or relationship to existing formal systems of social and political representation and decision-making, an antagonistic orientation may be empirically observable within certain movements in certain contexts and might become increasingly apparent in circumstances where organisational or political systems attempt their repression through a process of criminalisation.

Melucci makes this argument through his description of the criteria for determining an antagonistic social movement:

1   The way in which the system affected by the collective action responds. Melucci argues that a movement's opponents, having greater access to resources, will not allow a significant margin for error when threatened. Consequently, if a movement exhibits an antagonistic orientation (i.e. it is, or has the potential to become, a significant challenge to existing organisational, administrative and/or political systems), the response might include action that occurs at a systemic level higher than that which is immediately affected. The inclusion of specific social movement organisations/networks or particular forms of collective action within the discourse of security or terrorism by states is indicative of such a response. In both Europe and the USA, radical ecologists, animal rights and social justice activists have been targeted by anti-terror legislation where public order statutes would suffice. One difficulty for political elites is that this form of public recognition of potentially antagonistic movements can, itself, provide a platform around which previously unconnected groups can discover common cause, and potentially realise that which the state intervention was designed to prevent.

2   The way an antagonistic movement uses the language of its own culture to cast the conflict in terms of those who produce crucial social and economic resources and those who appropriate them. An example here would be the transitions in the discourse of social movement activists campaigning on trade, environmental and social justice issues, who rejected externally imposed labels such as anti-globalisation, preferring instead terms such as alter-global or anticapitalist as a self-description.

3   The mechanisms by which the actions of a movement pass along a spectrum, comprising increased symbolic content, a decreasing reversibility of conflict, a decreasing negotiability of goals and an increased clarity of the ratio between costs and benefits, coupled to a tendency towards a zero-sum solution (Melucci 1996: 38–39). Whilst many movements exhibit these tendencies in contexts of prolonged or acute

confrontation, the danger according to Melucci is that movements moving into an antagonistic phase can lose contact with any form of mediation and end up either sanctioning violence or retreating into countercultural ghettos.

References and resources

Melucci A. (1989, 1996).

ANTI-MOVEMENT

Anti-movements are defined in relation to their object of opposition by the insertion of the prefix 'anti'. A prominent example of a contemporary anti-movement can be seen in the use of the term 'anti-globalisation movement' whilst **'anti-nuclear movement'** was widely used in the 1970s. Anti-movement is used when there *appears* to be a clear-cut adversarial relationship between opposing forces. This can lead to some counter-intuitive uses such as the notion of anti-environmental movements developed by Greenpeace. As we note elsewhere anti-movements commonly include elements articulating alternatives to their object of opposition. This leads into a consideration of the implications of the 'anti' prefix.

Dialectically, an anti-movement can be approached as part of the necessary social conflict required to achieve a synthesis resolving a particular contradiction. In this case the use of the 'anti' prefix denotes a distinct phase of mobilisation. In some cases anti stances are only adopted after all the opportunities available within a prevailing **political opportunity structure** have been tried and exhausted. In cases typified by deeply embedded stakes and asymmetries of power, such as those associated with slavery, 'anti' stances can be adopted from the start.

Dualistic use of anti-movement opposes competing social forces in a reductive manner that formalises 'pro' and 'anti' stances. Whilst this is an analytically clear-cut approach it is one which *can* oversimplify underlying relations. The centrality of a singular collective identity as a defining feature of a social movement has tended to reinforce this sort of approach. The consequences of this include a failure to engage analytically and empirically with the ambiguity and ambivalence of movement participants.

Anti-movement is frequently a fast frame applied to heterogeneous movements by academic commentators. The term reduces the complexity of movement actors by foregrounding their object of opposition as a category of absolute refusal.

301 563

ANTI-NUCLEAR MOVEMENTS

Anti-nuclear movements became prominent features of advanced industrial societies in the 1970s as the use of nuclear power for electricity generation expanded. Anti-nuclear activity coincided with the consolidation
of environmental social movement organisations, such as **Friends of the
Earth** and **Greenpeace** and the wider growth in environmentalism. They
are widely regarded as one of the most prominent 'anti-movements' within
social movement studies (see 'anti-movement') and the impact of their
campaigns on the policy process is the subject of an extensive literature
(Flam 1994; Rudig 1990). The potential for 'dual use' of a nuclear fuel
cycle to produce weapons-grade materials led to significant tensions
between anti-nuclear movements and anti-nuclear weapons movements
such as the Campaign for Nuclear Disarmament.

Anti-nuclear movements have been widely analysed as movements
opposed to the use of nuclear power within a prevailing set of political
opportunity structures and resource mobilisation constraints. From this
approach attention is focussed upon the formal channels through which
opposition can be mounted, such as public inquiries, and the kinds of
resources opposition movements can bring to bear. Alan Touraine (1983)
attributed a wider role to the French anti-nuclear movement, analysing it
as a prominent component of a wider social movement struggle contesting
the imposition of a pervasive technocratic social order. From this perspective anti-nuclear struggles were also attempts to redefine democracy and
participation in the face of changing circumstances.

Whilst anti-nuclear movements typically contested nuclear expansion
within a range of institutional settings including court hearings, tribunals and
public inquiries, it was the use of direct action repertoires which distinguished these movements from pressure groups and defined them as social
movement actors. A wide range of direct action techniques were used. In
Germany, France and Japan violent confrontations between protestors and
riot police accompanied the occupation of designated nuclear sites. In
America campaigns of non-violent civil disobedience, inspired by the **civil
rights movement**, featured prominently (Nelkin and Pollack 1982; Joppke
1993). These included the passive occupation of potential reactor sites, resulting in the mass arrest of protestors. The American emphasis on non-violent
direct action against nuclear power also influenced interventions in countries
such as the United Kingdom (Welsh, 2000, 2001).

American and UK direct action was typically the product of diverse
alliances, with the Clam Shell and Torness Alliance being prominent 1970s'
examples in the respective countries. Alliance activities extended beyond
narrowly defined 'anti' campaigning, promoting a range of alternative

energy sources, for example. The diversity of these alliances also questioned the prominence given to collective identity in defining the presence of a social movement. Such alliances pursued a wide range of social and political campaigns through the nuclear issue, including feminism (Nelkin 1981), native American rights, and civil liberties. This campaigning extended to the implications of nuclear power for the 'South' such as the mining of uranium in Namibia by Rio Tinto Zinc. The alliances' politics thus extended far beyond technical debates over nuclear reactor safety or the environmental and health impacts of the nuclear fuel cycle.

The activities of both social movement organisations and these wider alliances played an important role in gaining public prominence for a range of critical experts on nuclear safety and radiation hazards. Through publications and public platforms for debate this added 'social force' to issues confined to inquiry halls and closed expert debate within formal **political opportunity structures**. The expansion of nuclear power envisaged in the 1970s did not come to fruition in most countries. Anti-nuclear movements contributed to a rise in public scepticism and recognition of the importance of public acceptability within political and policy circles. The substantive decline in the nuclear industry was driven by internal constraints such as the technical difficulty and cost of nuclear waste disposal, compounded by major reactor accidents at the US plant at Three Mile Island in 1979 and the Soviet Chernobyl reactors in 1986. The hot-cold war accompanying the modernisation of US theatre and strategic arsenals diverted the campaigning energies of many anti-nuclear activists towards the **peace movement**, particularly in Europe.

Since the reduction of carbon dioxide emissions became a major priority of climate change policy, numerous States have turned to nuclear power as a bridging technology in the twenty-first century. The anti-nuclear movements of the 1970s and early 1980s currently resemble movements in abeyance and it remains to be seen whether the return to nuclear new build will herald a further period of anti-nuclear activity.

References and resources

Babin, R. (1985); Flam, H. (ed. 1994); Joppke, C. (1993); Kitschelt, H. (1986); Nelkin, D. (1981); Nelkin, D. and Pollak, M. (1982); Rudig, W. (1990); Touraine, A. (1983); Welsh, I. (2000, 2001).

ANTICAPITALISM

From its inception and throughout its history, capitalism has produced oppositional movements that have engaged in analytical critique and practical struggle against it. Some of these movements were revolutionary and seized power with the aim of destroying capitalist relations (Bolshevik Revolution, 1917) before subsequently becoming institutionalised as part of the ideological and organisational functions of the state. Others became left/socialist political parties and some continued to exist as intellectual currents with varying levels of engagement in social or political activism. Due to the success of the Bolshevik (Russian) Revolution, anticapitalist movements of the mid and early twentieth century were presented, often by proponents and adversaries alike, as ideologically and symbolically synonymous with state communism. This only began to break down after the events of 1968 when the normative presentation of a clear-cut opposition between capitalism and its 'opposite' – communism – began to fracture in response to multiple and conflicting demands, made by movements in both capitalist and communist countries.

Anticapitalists have traditionally objected to three core principles of capitalism: first, the private ownership of the means of production – land, machinery, property; second, the exploitation of labour for the purposes of generating surplus value (the profit created by the worker over and above his/her pay); and third, the privileging of markets as the primary means of distributing economic goods. Struggles around these issues have typically involved trade unions, civil society organisations, socialist and leftist political parties. They continue to find outlets in the context of globalisation by addressing the global divisions of labour that result in new inequalities and forms of oppression, including those that are facilitated by the free movement of capital and the restricted movement of labour, and through challenges to the new precariousness of employment across white- and blue-collar sectors of the economy.

However, a further and profound critique of capitalism concerns its impact upon the finite ecological resources of the planet and the inability of the earth to provide the conditions of production for continuous economic growth, a situation accelerated by the despoliation of the environment caused by capitalist enterprise. This 'contradiction' (O'Connor 1998) – the destruction by capital of the means through which it can reproduce itself, was a key factor in the re-emergence of anticapitalism as a concept for social movements in the late 1990s. Until that point, as Simon Tormey notes (2004: 1), anticapitalism had 'meant looking mostly at the events of the past, sometimes the far-flung past', despite the relevance of such a framework for understanding many of the problems highlighted above.

The fall of the communist regimes of Eastern Europe and with it the monopoly of claims to the mantle of anticapitalism, the continued rise of ecological movements committed to direct action and the rise of new libertarian and autonomist movements in the Global South, particularly the **Zapatistas**, created a context in which anticapitalism could find new forms and expressions. In its first articulation on 18 June 1999 the City of London encountered a 'Carnival Against Capitalism' that brought together radical greens, anti-corporate and anti-globalisation activists and many others who had been developing a systemic critique rooted in their own experiences of challenging ecologically damaging road and runway building in the United Kingdom over the previous ten years. Whilst these events attracted considerable local attention, it wasn't until sustained resistance to the World Trade Organisation meetings occurred in Seattle in December 1999, prompting a local state of emergency to be declared, that the re-emergence of anticapitalism as a key concept for contemporary social movements began to become widely apparent. Since then a plethora of new work on the subject has emerged, most notably Simon Tormey's (2004) excellent 'Anti-capitalism: a beginner's guide', which is complemented by activist overviews and analysis (Harvie *et al.* 2005; Notes from Nowhere 2003) and academic and intellectual commentary (Saad-Filho 2003; Schalit 2002; Starr 2000). The re-emergence of anticapitalism as a signifier, rather than a signified (communism) means it is once again open to being invested with meaning by movements, commentators and opponents alike. As such, it is difficult to speak of a specific and empirically discrete anticapitalist movement, but it is possible to observe the opportunities the discourse of anticapitalism opens up – whether that involves the renewal of a critical lens, a starting point for building **collective identity** or the calling into question of the unquestioned and normative basis for capitalism by others within civil society.

References and resources

Harvie, D., Milburn, K., Trott, B. and Watts, D. (eds. 2005); Notes from Nowhere (eds. 2003); O' Connor, J. (1998); Saad-Filho (2003); Schalit, J. (2002); Starr, A. (2000); Tormey, S. (2004).

ATTAC

This movement originated in France through Le Monde Diplomatique staff and their engagement with neoliberalism in the late 1990s. A central part of this engagement was the call for the imposition of a tax on international financial activity to fund social goals. The call for a 'Tobin Tax' and the prioritisation of social needs over market needs resulted in a deluge of interest. Staff at Le Monde responded by assuming an organisational role in 1998. This started from co-ordinating the organisations responding to their initiatives, including trades unions, civic associations, social movements and a range of newspapers (Cassen 2003). The formation of a national executive committee was rapidly followed by the formation of two hundred local groups as the Association for the Taxation of financial Transactions for the Aid of Citizens (ATTAC) cascaded through French society. ATTAC groups were also formed in most major European countries and spread to the Americas, Africa and Japan.

ATTAC's goals expanded from the narrow advocacy of a Tobin Tax based on the French tradition of a campaign of public education, to the impact of neoliberalism on the lived experiences of citizens. The international, national and local agendas of ATTAC centred on the renunciation of unregulated global neoliberalism and the advocacy of a socially and environmentally sustainable globalisation. This platform included abolishing tax havens, asserting social control over transnational corporations, cancelling the developing world's debt, and a reformed world trade order based on social and natural sustainability. In terms of France and the European Union ATTAC campaigned against the privatisation of public services, promoting a new political settlement establishing a form of social wage for citizens sufficient to secure health, education, care and housing. This programme was to be pursued through non-violent means and included a commitment to peaceful conflict resolution with other parties.

ATTAC's commitment to a federal structure of educative initiatives in pursuit of this programme within France combined with the international connections of Le Monde Diplomatique was influential in the formation of the **World Social Forum**. ATTAC was central in the campaign against the EU 'Nice Treaty' in 2005. The Nice Treaty included a range of constitutional changes and increased the role of the market within the EU. France was one of the countries that rejected it in a referendum in 2005, delaying ratification of a derivative treaty until 2009.

ATTAC is an example of a distinctly national network actor that has made significant impacts at a national and global level. In the wake of the 2008–2009 crisis in capitalism, advocacy of a Tobin Tax has increased in prominence with substantial backing from the then British Prime Minister, Gordon Brown.

References and resources

Cassen, B. (2003, 2005). ATTAC web resources: http://www.attac.org/

AUTONOMY

Autonomy is a Greek term meaning 'self' plus 'law'. Philosophically, it is at the heart of the liberal theory of justice and central to political values such as freedom of speech and movement and is advocated by commentators and theorists across the political spectrum. Understood radically, it is a concept that has had a significant appeal for revolutionary social movements throughout Europe (Katsiaficas 1997) and is defined as involving self-organisation and self-determination outside political parties, institutions and structures. In this sense, autonomy is the desire to allow differences to develop at the base of an organisation or movement without trying to synthesise them or impose a particular line. Instead, common attitudes and dispositions are encouraged where they emerge, with the idea of unity in and through diversity being held up as something to aspire to politically.

This idea was most dramatically manifest during the mass mobilisations in Italy during the 1970s and 1980s. 'Autonomy at the base' was the core principle of Potere Operaio (Workers' Power) the influential group and magazine that was at the heart of social unrest in Italy during the late 1960s and early 1970s, dissolving itself in 1973 to become part of a broader movement known as *Autonomia* (Autonomia Operaio) a mass movement involving students and workers (Wright 2002). *Autonomia* never unified and as a series of fluid organisations and shifting alliances, it refused to separate economics from politics and politics from everyday existence. This approach led ultimately to the idea of refusing waged labour and to the extension of struggle from the factory, where occupations, sabotage and strikes were commonplace, to the cities in which 20,000 buildings were squatted between 1969–1975. As an active political force *Autonomia* was finally crushed by the Italian state beginning with the 'April 7th' arrests in 1979. This began a process leading to the arrest and imprisonment of over fifteen hundred intellectuals and militants within a year, many of whom were held under charges for anti-State activity that were introduced into Italian law under the fascist regime of Mussolini. Notable amongst those arrested were militants and theorists such as Toni Negri and Paolo Virno, both of whom are now prominent in debates concerning resistance to global neoliberal capitalism (Hardt and Negri 2000, 2004; Virno 2004).

Autonomy is also a key idea and departure point in debates amongst sections of the **alternative globalisation movement** who have drawn upon the experiences of previous autonomist movements, indigenous peoples, peace communities and experimental communities in order to develop theories of autonomy in a networked and informationalised era.

A common inspiration for this re-working of autonomist theory has been the discourse of the **Zapatistas** in Chiapas, Mexico, and the 'Asambleistas' and 'piqueteros' of the Argentinean uprisings in 2001 (Sitrin 2006). Similarly, autonomist theory and the idea of a politics that seeks to avoid taking power (Holloway 2002) has grown in influence alongside the prominence of anticapitalist and alter-globalist movements as activists and commentators alike have sought to find a theory to express their practice.

References and resources

Hardt, M. and Negri, A. (2000, 2004); Holloway, J. (2002); Katsiaficas, G. (1997); Sitrin, M. (2006);Virno, P. (2004);Wright, S. (2002).

BIOGRAPHICAL AVAILABILITY

This term (McAdam 1988) is used to denote and discuss an individual's ability to participate in social movement activity. It is useful in terms of addressing differing degrees of involvement and the social composition of social movements. Constraints associated with employment, child care, family commitments, physical ability and so on impact on biographical availability. At an interpersonal level factors like these shape the social composition of social movement actions. An occupation, for example, requires a very high level of biographical availability and participation is limited to those with sufficient freedom. Occupations thus typically exclude those in full-time employment or with parental responsibilities whilst a protest march can be attended by many more people.

At a more structural level different societies have different levels of socially necessary labour time – the number of hours in a week which it is necessary to work to conform to the norms of a particular economy. In countries where long working hours are a norm this represents a systemic constraint on movement participation. The spread of flexible labour markets associated with neoliberal deregulation starting in the 1980s increased this kind of constraint. European Union legislation on work time seeks to limit the number of hours worked in any one week.

References and resources

McAdam, D. (1986, 1988).

BLACK POWER MOVEMENT

The Black Power Movement developed in the context of the US **Civil Rights Movement** but diverged from the non-violent stance adopted by Martin Luther King. Stokely Carmichael consolidated the term whilst he was head of the Student Nonviolent Coordinating Committee (SNCC) and Black Power became a rallying point for a diverse range of African-Americans. The emphasis on racism and the importance of consciousness-raising to promote black pride were distinctive features of this movement. Malcom X and the Nation of Islam were key in arguing for the importance of racial self-determination that had to be part of equality. The emphasis on autonomous black associations and political organisations was a key part in the pursuit of self-determination.

The Black Panther Party for Self Protection (BPP) was a prominent expression of this movement. Established in late 1966 to monitor acts of police violence the Black Panthers spread widely throughout urban centres in the USA but the Black Power Movement was a diverse movement engaged on multiple social, cultural and political fronts. There were many factional disputes within the movement revolving around the degree of autonomous self-determination that could be sought without running the risk of reproducing a divided society. The use or threat of violence was another divisive issue. In many cities the majority of Black Americans lived in run-down ghettos where they struggled to get landlords to carry out maintenance work. The Black Panthers were one of the groups which spread support for the Black Power Movement by exercising persuasive force to get heating systems and roofs fixed. The emphasis on action targeting concerns associated with day to day life rather than the pursuit of more abstract rights secured wide support amongst sections of the most deprived members of the black community.

Cultural initiatives were also important in re-appropriating links with Africa and African culture. Black artistic, performance, dance and musical genres specifically aimed at black audiences affirmed the significance of black culture. Some sections of the Black Power Movement adopted a militaristic salute in the form of a raised right fist clad in a black leather glove. In 1968 this generated some controversy when medal-winning black American athletes, Tommie Smith and John Carlos, gave the salute during an Olympic medal ceremony as the American national anthem was played. The Olympic committee imposed a lifetime ban on the athletes and after returning from Mexico they were subject to a range of threats. The case illustrates how the Black Power issue divided America.

The movement continued into the 1970s but as the more formalised elements declined it lost cohesion as a presence within the public sphere. Despite apparently minimal enduring impacts the importance of the Black Power Movement as a consciousness-raising force should not be underestimated. In 2008 the Olympic athletes Tommie Smith and John Carlos received an Arthur Ash Courage Award in recognition of their action in 1968.

References and resources

Carmichael, S. and Hamilton, C. V. (1967); Cross, T. (1984); Van Deburg, W. L. (1992).

CAPACITY BUILDING

This term refers to the cumulative ability of social movement actors to collectively intervene in social conflicts drawing upon established and novel repertoires of action and a diverse network of participants. The term originates in an analysis of non-violent direct action against nuclear power in Scotland which drew on a UK-wide anti-nuclear alliance which was, in turn, influenced by the activities of anti-nuclear alliances in the USA (Welsh 2000). It has been used more widely in relation to the green movement (Doherty 2002).

Capacity building is a property of network interactions which have become an increasingly prominent feature of the contemporary movement milieu. The critical aspect of these network interactions lies in maintaining open boundaries that enable interaction with other networks. An analytic emphasis upon capacity building is sensitive to the interactions between apparently discrete networks with a range of declared objects of opposition. Forms of direct action that create temporary autonomous zones (TAZ), typically through an occupation with a reasonable duration, create spaces of interpersonal debate, negotiation and exchange. These spaces become crucibles within which identity and meaning are forged (McKechnie and Welsh 2002). A TAZ becomes a nodal point within a network within which a number of discrete though linked processes result in capacity building. Three key processes are: innovation involving techniques of self; the symbolic declaration of societal stakes; and processes of network extension and network amplification.

Techniques of self include learning individual capacities for action; these can include training in techniques of non-violent direct action. Techniques of self are typically adapted to the specific situation confronted by participants through a process of discussion and debate that is often intense.

Examples of techniques of self include the use of comedy and parody to diffuse potentially violent confrontations, the ability to adopt a variety of role-play personas as well as practical capacities. There is thus a process of innovation and refinement of techniques of self that are appropriate to a particular context and object of opposition. This process of refinement typically seeks to identify and highlight key symbolic stakes associated with an action.

Meaning within complex societies is coded in terms of symbolic registers and Melucci's (1996) notion that social movements declare the stakes to society raises issues of the symbolic resources used in this process. Female activists dressed in pink and silver carnival costumes dancing up to Kevlar-clad riot police during street protests juxtaposes symbolic registers of frivolity and repression, for example. Other iconic examples juxtaposing symbolic stakes include women inserting flowers into the rifles of US Guardsmen and a lone protestor standing in the path of an oncoming tank in Tiananmen Square. Occupations using non-violent direct action techniques that place the bodies of protestors between a site and the agencies that threaten it represent a particularly powerful set of symbolic registers. UK resistance to road building programmes became prominent within the public sphere following the publication of photographs of activists locked into tunnels in the mainstream media. Media images and support networks within local communities become channels which engage with the stakes and meanings forged within the crucibles of movement.

Movement activity and the wider declaration of societal stakes contribute to a process of network extension and amplification that typify a contemporary movement milieu understood as a network of networks. The techniques of self originating within these sites become embodied within activist networks and circulate as communicable forms of knowledge (see **knowledge-practices**). Individuals and collective resources, including movement literature, video and electronic sources, disseminate techniques of self, arising within particular nodal events. These resources become distributed more widely within the initial network (network extension) but are also taken up within adjacent networks (network amplification) where they give rise to further unintended consequences (Welsh *et al.* 2007).

A capacity-building approach recognises the importance of such 'weak ties' in the process of innovation within movement networks focussing upon the cumulative process rather than the declared objectives of a particular movement. Methodologically, attention to capacity-building processes requires longitudinal, qualitative work to follow the iterative interactions involved. This is quite distinct from approaches emphasising the success or failure of movements in terms of their direct impact upon the decisions of political systems.

References and resources

Doherty, B. (2002); McKechnie, R. and Welsh, I. (2002); Melucci, A. (1996); Welsh I. (2000); Welsh I., Evans R., and Plows A. (2007).

CIVIL RIGHTS MOVEMENT

A civil rights movement campaigns for the extension of recognised rights to groups that are excluded within a particular political system. The American Civil Rights Movement is the best-known and documented example of this kind of movement within social movement studies. This movement campaigned for the civil rights of black citizens in America in the 1950s and 1960s when the majority did not have the vote and when segregation was widespread. Civil rights continue to be a focus for social movement interventions as the process of democratic state formation continues in the twenty-first century. The American case demonstrates how a wide variety of actors and modes of intervention contribute to the process of change and is summarised here.

The American Civil Rights Movement developed from its origins in a legal campaign under the auspices of the National Association for the Advancement of Colored People (NAACP). The NAACP's Legal Defense and Educational Fund was created to promote civil rights for African-Americans through court cases and educational outreach work. In 1954 it achieved a significant legal victory in the Supreme Court (*Brown* v. *Board of Education* 1954) which ordered the end of *de jure* racial segregation in public education. The case paved the way for a civil rights bill in 1957.

Racial segregation and the disenfranchisement of Southern blacks continued into the 1960s as most Southern states refused to effectively implement the *Brown* decision. In Southern states, including Alabama, Mississippi, and Arkansas, governors openly resisted federal injunctions to integrate public schools and state universities. In Northern states de facto segregation persisted in public schools, housing, public buildings and transport systems. Civil rights campaigners and activists were subject to violence from citizens and police, making mobilising a challenge (McAdam 1986).

Acts of conscience by individuals refusing to recognise segregation played a significant part in initiating wider campaigns. Rosa Parks, a black seamstress arrested for violating the segregated seating of bus passengers in Montgomery, Alabama is one of the better-documented cases (Parks and Haskins 1992). Her case was supported by the Southern Christian Leadership Conference (SCLC). The SCLC was founded by Martin Luther King Jr whose potential as a movement figurehead had been spotted by a trade union organiser. Martin Luther King Jr was influenced by the pacifism of Gandhi, and SCLC used non-violent civil disobedience to mount a blockade of the buses in Montgomery in 1955 which lasted into 1956.

Televised images of these disputes, coverage of Martin Luther King's speeches, and cases involving the murder of black citizens and the use of federal US forces to break segregation on campuses raised the national profile of civil rights issues throughout the early 1960s. The involvement of **Students for a Democratic Society**, particularly the Student Nonviolent Coordinating Committee (SNCC) and the Congress of Racial Equality (CORE), increased the potency of civil rights campaigning. The Montgomery bus boycott inspired similar peaceful protests elsewhere in the South, such as the sit-in protests by black college students seeking service at lunch counters and the Freedom Riders seeking to racially integrate Greyhound buses and passenger facilities on an interstate basis. National rallies in Washington provided platforms for high-profile speeches including Martin Luther King Jr's 'I Have a Dream' speech delivered in Washington in 1963. The following year SNCC members and others organised Freedom Summer, a campaign to secure the mass registration of black Americans' votes in the Southern states.

King's pacifism was challenged by Malcom X, a black Muslim, based in New York, who argued that black African-Americans should take up arms to protect themselves against attacks by whites. Malcom X questioned the goal of integration, adopting a separatist stance based on economic independence and an African-based cultural identity amongst black Americans. His murder by a rival faction in 1965 brought the exchanges with King to an end but his influence continued through the Black Panthers and the wider **Black Power Movement**. As the 1960s progressed King opposed the war in Vietnam and increasingly campaigned on the economic rights of black people issues emphasised in Malcom X's stance. Martin Luther King Jr was assassinated on 4 April 1968. By the end of that year federal legislation had established the electoral rights of black Africans, abolished segregation, and made discrimination in the sale and rental of housing illegal.

The Civil Rights Movement created repertoires of action and inspiration to waves of successor movements pursuing rights. These included the womens' movement, gay rights activism and Latino rights, championed by the United Farm Workers of America. The Environmental and Social Justice Movement of the 1990s can also be linked to the Civil Rights Movement.

The US Civil Rights Movement provides a clear example of a **political movement** within a particular advanced Western nation. The case underlines the historical significance of individuals (e.g. Rosa Parks), trade union organising, charismatic **leadership**, **direct action**, movement networking and media coverage. The acceptance speech of Barack Hussein Obama, the first black African President of the USA, evoked the enduring significance of the Civil Rights Movement declaring that America could begin to realise 'the Dream'. An estimated 2 million people attended the ceremony, with many black African-Americans travelling to Washington from the Southern states.

References and resources

Eyerman, R. and Jamison, A. (1991: Chp. 7); Gitlin, T. (1980); McAdam, D. (1986, 1988); Parks, R. and Haskins, J. (1992).

CLAIMANT MOVEMENT

A *claimant movement* is one of four analytically distinct types of behaviour that Melucci (1989, 1996) argues can be identified in social movements, the others being conflictual networking, **political movement** and **antagonistic movement**. This typology distinguishes social movements according to 'the field of their action' (Melucci 1996: 34) a phrase that describes the system in which the movement acts. Therefore, in establishing this four-part classification of social movements Melucci is also describing the systems of social and economic reproduction that movements challenge. At the same time, Melucci (1996: 37) stresses that his typology is a conceptual instrument and cannot reflect the complex characteristics of movements that often invest a number of systems (political, administrative etc.) simultaneously.

A claimant movement seeks a different distribution of resources, roles, and rewards within an organisational system or struggles to make an organisational apparatus more efficient and responsive to its constituents. It might be mobilised to seek, or defend, a set of conditions and rewards that it has internally defined as appropriate and in doing so it will clash with the power that imposes the rules and decides the division of labour. In doing so it pushes the conflict beyond the operative level to the level at which norms are produced, challenging both the reproduction of roles within the system and the system's limits of variability. Examples of such movements include mobilisations of underprivileged workers, campaigns for equal access to public buildings and transport by the disabled, or the campaign to lower the age of consent for homosexual sexual relations.

References and resources

Melucci, A. (1989, 1996).

COGNITIVE PRAXIS

This concept was introduced to social movement studies by Eyerman and Jamison (1991) as part of a methodological means of studying social movements that bridged American and European traditions. Cognitive praxis refers to the collective knowledge-making activities of social movements. The approach emphasises the importance of identifying and understanding the spaces which specific movements create within which the formalisation of knowledge can take place. Whilst emphasising that this is a collective activity the theory attaches importance to movement intellectuals as key resources within the process of knowledge formation. The formulation of knowledge becomes a central resource in shaping the core identity of specific social movements. This is an ongoing and evolving process shaped by wider social, political and economic forces over time.

Following earlier work on environmental movements (Jamison *et al.* 1990) three dimensions of cognitive praxis are developed. Together, these three elements are involved in the negotiation of a social movement identity. The three dimensions are termed cosmological, technological and organisational. The cosmological dimension of a social movement consists of a prevailing world view and particularly the relationship between nature and society. The importance of ecological systems, networks and niches are emphasised as key in understanding the nature/society relationship. The technological dimension of a social movement defines the specific focus around which knowledge is formalised. The development of clean, alternative technologies are used as examples of this dimension of social movement activity. Finally, the organisational dimension of cognitive praxis refers to the form of social organisation adopted by a movement.

Whilst drawing on the environmental movement to illustrate these terms cognitive praxis is advanced as an analytical approach which can be applied to the field of social movement studies. For Eyerman and Jamison this is a key theoretical and methodological means of *differentiating* between social movements and understanding the *relationship* between movements.

By approaching social movements as processes involving the continual work of cognitive praxis their theory offers an approach capable of relating the specific form of particular movements to both historical precursors and other contemporary movements.

Attention is given to nineteenth century **old social movements**, environmentalism, American Student and **civil rights movements** and **feminist social movements**. Eyerman and Jamison argue that feminism and environmentalism would have been inconceivable without the emphasis on liberation and anti-authoritarian forms of organising during the 1960s, particularly by **students for a democratic society** (Eyerman and Jamison 1991: 91). The 1960s thus defines a wide ranging and heterogenous cosmology of liberation which specific social movements consolidate through defining particular knowledge stakes and modes of engagement.

Within this approach the cyclical trajectory of movements results in the knowledge stakes defined by the new social movements being transferred into more established forums. The movement spaces dedicated to the formalisation of the transferred knowledge are then available to other social forces embarking on the process of cognitive praxis. This can lead to the definition of new knowledge stakes and new movement identity formation (Eyerman and Jamison 1991: 92). Social movements are thus seen as transitory phenomena associated with periods of transition within which they define key issues of meaning and knowledge stakes which transform mainstream debates and practices.

In terms of environmentalism, Jamison (2001) has argued that the historic acceptance of 'green knowledge' can be seen in 'the environmental activities of the World Bank' (2001: 127) whilst seeing 'signs that the old crap of the 1960s' is coming back in the name of anti-globalism' threatening 'the new wave of environmental politics' (2001: 148). This position appears to neglect the movement cosmology of *social justice*, which became increasingly prominent from the 1980s onwards.

References and resources

Eyerman, R. and Jamison, A. (1991); Jamison, A. (2001); Jamison, A. Eyerman, R., Cramer, J., with Laessoe, J. (1990).

COLLECTIVE BEHAVIOUR

This is the term applied to the North American school of social movement studies that developed through the 1950s and 1960s. This school established the importance of studying collective behaviour for understanding the emergence and significance of social movements as agents of social change. The collective behaviour school approached forms of behaviour, such as those associated with the crowd and the mob, as socially meaningful responses to the prevailing social structure associated with social change. The three most prominent thinkers associated with the collective behaviour approach are Herbert Blumer (1946), William Kornhauser (1959) and Neil Smelser (1962). The collective behaviour school drew upon two quite different approaches, with Blumer drawing on symbolic interactionism whilst Smelser draws upon the structural functionalism of Talcot Parsons. The two approaches resulted in differing emphases. Symbolic interactionism focussing upon the negotiation of meaning between individuals and structural functionalism emphasising the ways in which structural factors, such as the economy, shaped the individual.

Blumer was part of the influential Chicago School of Sociology which applied aspects of ecology to the sociology of the city. The Chicago school emphasised the analytic importance of recognising urban zones in terms of social composition and activity. Ruggerio and Montagna (2008) suggest that Blumer's work provides a way of analytically explaining how the marginalised, deviant and dysfunctional inhabitants associated with twilight zones become organised as forces of social transformation. Blumer emphasised the way in which gradual but pervasive changes in values led to cultural drifts involving psychological changes as individuals' aspirations and self perceptions diverged from their material circumstances.

Cultural drifts led to general social movements from within which specific social movements could form. In this way, Blumer understood the anti-slavery movement as a specific expression of a general humanitarian movement. Blumer also considered the role of expressive social movements in terms of religious and fashion movements. There is an emphasis in Blumer's work on how social tensions become the basis for new social order. The balance between reform and revolution in the transition to a changed social order is a prominent theme, with reform having respectability derived from adherence to a prevailing ethic. Blumer considered that revolution does not seek to influence public opinion, but instead seeks converts and compared this to religious conversion.

The emphasis on psychological factors is continued in the work of Kornhauser (1959) who wrote at a time when the notion of the 'mass' society was particularly pronounced. Kornhauser identified a number of features characterising 'mass behaviour' in the mass society. Mass behaviour originated in events that were national or international and far removed from concrete daily experience. Distance from such events meant that codes of appropriate conduct, such as those governing day to day interactions, were not readily available. Mass behaviour characteristically sets out to directly influence events using whatever means are available. Kornhauser saw this ranging from direct lobbying to forms of direct action and discussed a range of examples, including the International Workers of the World (IWW) and Ku Klux Klan, where direct action included violence. Mass behaviour was regarded as inherently unstable and capable of turning into mass apathy – foreshadowing more recent debates on quiescence and withdrawal. Mass behaviour with a programme and a degree of continuity in the pursuit of its objectives was recognised as a mass movement usually engaging marginal sections of society.

Kornhauser thus argued that mass society was characterised by numerous mass movements which could be differentiated from totalitarian movements, such as communism, as they formed relatively frequently in open conditions that were not dominated from above or from below. The cautious argument advanced, was that mass movements could be regarded as part of a pluralist set of social relations which enabled accessible elites and non-elites to participate in the political process. This was important in distancing mass movements from forms of deviance and social pathology.

This process was developed further by Neil Smelser (1962) who noted that examples of collective behaviour tended to cluster in terms of time and social location. Smelser set out to answer the question of why episodes of collective behaviour happen where they do, when they do and in the way they do. Smelser follows Talcot Parsons in identifying the impact of structural strain in a social system as the origin of spontaneous or collectively structured action, drawing a distinction between norm- and value-originated movements.

Strains can arise from well established disparities such as wealth, status, ethnic identity which are aspects of a social structure. Smelser also recognised that strain could originate from differences and distinctions generated by social movement activity creating new social strains and divides. In keeping with other members of this school Smelser distinguished 'collective outbursts' and 'collective movements' to differentiate panics and hostile outbursts from collective efforts to modify norms and values. He proposed the existence of 'norm-orientated' and 'value-orientated' movements acting on the basis of collective belief, distinguishing these from 'general social movements' such as the labour and peace movements. The pursuit of normative and value change was set within a context of 'structural conduciveness' which shaped the kind of reception such demands met at the political level. The notion of structural conduciveness is redolent of the more recent term **political opportunity structure**.

Smelser explicitly recognised that the pursuit of value-based change was historically linked to the collective use of violence in political revolutions such as those in Britain, France and Russia. In recognising the clustering of such violent outbursts Smelser was attempting to explain forms of collective behaviour that would otherwise have been classified as deviant. In his consideration of normative movements Smelser considered that there was less potential for violence, recognising instead the importance of organised and informal channels of communication in creating agitation and demands for change. Norm-orientated movements created organisations such as political parties, pressure groups or clubs to disseminate their beliefs and their success was dependent upon their chosen organisational form.

Smelser's work contains insights redolent of more recent work in social movement studies. Structural conduciveness equates to political opportunity structures; the emphasis on informal communication perhaps prefigures network approaches whilst the importance attributed to the organisational form is evocative of parts of resource mobilisation approaches. As part of the collective behaviour school, his work is important in recognising the importance of not dismissing all forms of collective behaviour involving violence as deviant or pathological. The emphasis within his work on the place of 'strain' in social systems in evoking forms of collective behaviour does imply that structural variables are more important than agency in the pursuit of change but this has not precluded contemporary uses of his work within social movement studies (Crossley 2002, 2002a).

References and resources

Blumer, H. (1946); Crossley, N. (2002, 2002a); Kornhauser, A. (1959); LeBon, G. (1960); Ruggiero, V. and Montagna, N. (eds. 2008); Smelser, N. (1962).

COLLECTIVE IDENTITY

A key concept for explaining movement cohesion that came to prominence at the end of the 1980s through the work of Alberto Melucci (1989). It subsequently became a central concern and even a 'new orthodoxy' for social movement studies when taken on board by political process theorists (McDonald 2006: 26). The rise of **global social movements** and the contestation of the discourse of **identity politics** associated with postmodernist accounts have maintained the term in a position of central but contested prominence.

The term collective identity refers to the outcome of work conducted by movement actors to produce shared understandings of the issues at stake, the terms under which different actors, either individuals, groups or networks might work together, and the actions required to effect change. In some circumstances, the production of a collective identity might itself become *the* goal of a movement. The key question though is how the 'I' becomes a 'we' and the basis on which the collective 'we' recognises itself. Social movements often form around a shared sense of political interests that are associated with experiences derived from a particular aspect of their identity – gender, age, ethnicity, sexuality etc. (see **identity politics**). In other circumstances, however, the collective identity of a movement might emerge around a particular issue (animal rights, labour reforms, climate change) or even due to an affinity with a particular protest repertoire (see **direct action**). So whilst some form of collective identity might be present within a specific community for reasons of geography, experience or identity characteristic this needs to be differentiated from the work of collective identity construction that takes place within movements. Even in circumstances where social movements are formed and mobilised to defend a particular identity, that identity will invariably be subject to redefinition and renegotiation during the process of mobilisation. In this understanding of the term collective identity is 'a continuous process of recomposition, rather than a given' (Schlesinger 1987: 237).

In a similar way, Alberto Melucci (1996: 70) defines collective identity as the process of constructing an action system, where identity is neither static nor fixed, but remains continuously in motion, requiring active identity-work even where it crystallises into semi-permanent institutional forms. Melucci calls this process 'identization' (1996: 77) to emphasise an orientation towards solidarity over solidity and to stress the iterative process of renegotiation that occurs in social movements. The concept of collective identity therefore highlights the self-reflexive capacity of social actors to recognise themselves and the field of opportunities and constraints in which they are situated and to adapt their practices accordingly.

Another important contribution is Melucci's (1996: 73) emphasis upon the role that the recognition of adversaries plays in the process of 'identization'. Melucci argues that social movements need to locate *an* enemy amongst multiple potential interlocutors, otherwise collective action can easily atrophy into ritual, or banal equivocation. It is also important, he suggests, that this enemy's orchestration of power must be 'revealed' for the movement to remain credible within its political milieu and the wider public sphere. Confrontation is a definitive part of social movement activity (della Porta and Diani 1999; Melucci 1996; Tarrow 1998). However, confrontation in itself is not sufficient either to indicate the presence of a social movement or to sustain a collective identity, and as Tarrow suggests 'it is only by sustaining collective action against antagonists that a contentious episode becomes a social movement' (Tarrow 1998: 6). Collective identity is therefore a complex construction, which is dependent upon a high degree of reflexive work by movement actors who are required to engage in a tripartite process of recognition, which involves identifying:

- *themselves* – including their own agency and capacity to act, their commonality with other actors and a structure of opportunities for action. Elements of this recognition include phenomena described in the literature as 'solidarity' (della Porta and Diani 1999; Melucci 1996; Tarrow 1998), 'communitas' (Turner 1974) or 'structures of feeling' (Hetherington 1996, 1998);
- *their adversaries* – these are not always fixed or easy to identify (della Porta and Diani 1999: 43) and an episode of collective action will probably involve the recognition of differing adversaries at different points during a confrontation. Adversaries might include the State, either as a bureaucratic or administrative force or as a force of repression, the media, scientific or technological elites and even other social movements;
- *a system or structure of power* – recognising the operation of power is implicit in the previous two points and involves recognition of a field of conflict constituted by the social movement and its adversaries. This renders visible the operation of power at multifarious levels and produces an awareness of the way power can traverse, produce and construct collective action.

References and resources

della Porta, D. and Diani, M. (1999); Hetherington, K. (1996, 1998); McDonald, K. (2006); Melucci, A. (1989, 1996); Schlesinger, P. (1987); Tarrow, S. (1998); Turner, V. (1974).

COMPUTER MEDIATED COMMUNICATION

Computer mediated communication (CMC) refers to communication between computer users using a network connection to exchange messages or information in digital form. Such exchanges can be on a global scale via the Internet or more localised via a wireless router or Bluetooth technologies. CMC has enabled the mounting of unprecedented amounts of information in forms ranging from text, to images, video and sound files. Expanding hard drive capacities accelerating processor speeds and peer-to-peer (P2P) software have made it possible to create, download and share feature-length documentaries and films. Within the movement milieu much of this output is open access and can be freely downloaded. The increase in the information resources and communication within the movement milieu are important in terms of the capacity for reflexive framing. CMC has *asynchronous* and *synchronous* forms.

Asynchronous CMC includes e-mail exchanges, discussion forums, wikis and e-mail lists which enable one-to-one and one-to-many communications in almost real time. The maintenance of web-mounted diaries or blogs by activists are an example of asynchronous CMC which influence mainstream media agendas (see **movement as media**). Asynchronous CMC plays an important part in co-ordinating physical meetings and events. These range from political and campaigning events such as summit sieges associated with the Alternative Globalisation Movement to cultural, identity and lifestyle events.

Synchronous CMC verges on or achieves real-time communication between geographically distant individuals or groups. Textual forms of synchronous CMC include chat rooms and instant messaging, whilst new platforms for internet telephony have removed the costs of real-time conversations between activists on differing continents. Increases in computing power and the incorporation of webcams into laptops have also made mobile video conferencing more widely available. Advances in mobile phone technology mean that both forms of CMC are widely available independently of direct access to a computer, increasing the impact of CMC within both wider society and the movement milieu. Within the movement milieu web-mounted projects such as **Indymedia** can increasingly mount material approximating to real time.

The growth of CMC represents significant challenges. The ability to exert control or censorship is reduced, though the owners of search engines can exclude key search terms originating from specific countries such as China. The near instantaneous nature of images also impacts upon politicians' ability to manage news agendas, leaving them confronted with demands for responses in real time.

References and resources

De Jong, W., Shaw, M. and Stammers, N. (eds. 2005); McCaughey, M. and Ayers, M. (2003); Meikle, G. (2003); Van De Donk, W., Loader, B., Nixon, P. and Rucht, D. (2003).

COUNTERCULTURE

A counterculture can be understood as a purposive attempt to create forms
of expression and association which invert the prevailing cultural norms
of a society or social formation. A counter culture typically seeks to subvert
the dominant social order by drawing attention to the paradoxical content
of familiar terms such as 'freedom'. Within social movement studies the
term counter culture was developed and applied to a diverse range of
youth movements in the late 1960s and early 1970s. In North America, the
Beat Generation was an important precursor with a range of authors and
poets adopting stances critical of the American Dream. Jack Kerouac and
Alan Ginsberg are amongst the better-known authors and their writing
influenced the work of Bob Dylan.

In the 1960s authors like Tom Wolfe continued this strand of literary
critique with books such as *The Electric Cool Aid Acid Test* relating the
activities of Ken Kesey and The Pranksters. The Pranksters were a prominent feature of the US counter cultural milieu and Wolfe's book relates
their bus journey across America during which they set out to challenge
the American Dream. The journey was financed in part from the proceeds
of Ken Kesey's book, *One Flew Over the Cuckoo's Nest*, a trenchant critique
of mainstream psychiatric care, which was also made into a movie. The
counterculture of the 1960s and 1970s was pre-eminently a music-orien-
tated phenomenon as groups like The Grateful Dead, Jefferson Airplane,
Frank Zappa and Jimmy Hendrix contributed to an American wave of
innovation in pop music that combined psychedelic substances and
advances in technology to achieve performances that changed the rock
genre. The US counterculture of the 1960s was associated with the Hippy
movement of the San Fransisco Bay area where many of these musicians
performed. The Woodstock music festival in the USA featured acts from
the USA and the United Kingdom and became an iconic representation
of the era in a full-length movie. There were counterparts to this festival
in other industrial societies, notably in Europe.

The idea of a counterculture can only be understood in the context of
the advanced industrial societies as they moved out of the era of post-war
austerity. A number of factors combine that explain the importance
attached to counter culture. Post-war demographics produced a 'baby
boom' generation entering early adulthood during the 1960s and 1970s.

This coincided with a significant expansion of university places.
Consumer culture was becoming ascendant as mass production techniques
developed and material consumption became regarded as a social good.
Television began to be omnipresent within households as radio broadcast

channels multiplied. A vibrant music industry recorded a generation of electric and electronic artists who literally broke the mould of popular music. The onset of mobility made the 'hippy trail' to the East viable for increasing numbers of young people. Drugs, such as LSD, developed by US agencies as a possible means of enhancing the combat performance of troops in Vietnam became available on the streets. The birth control pill removed the fear of pregnancy as a barrier to sexual experimentation and played an important part in a 'sexual revolution'.

For an affluent minority of young people the availability of Eastern philosophies, mind-altering drugs, alternative publishing and broadcasting channels and the time to explore forms of self-expression far removed from the normative good life idealised in the 'American Dream' formed the basis for a rejection of Western technocracy. The Vietnam War acted as a further locus to militancy as did the civil rights record of the USA. Countercultural elements drew upon pre-existing currents of criticism and rejection, with the Beat Generation being influential in the USA whilst there was a more evident 'new left' orientation in Europe. Given these complex lineages and the diversity of countercultural forms, even prominent exponents of the term regarded it as one that 'possesses all the liabilities which a decent sense of intellectual caution would persuade one to avoid like the plague' (Roszak 1970: xi).

Despite this caution the notion of counterculture is important because it does mark a point at which the cultural premises of industrialised societies became the object of a cultural critque within a media age. To Roszak this was important because formal politics 'draws upon culture for its sanctions' requiring 'a good, a true, a beautiful' to secure 'widespread acquiescence'. Culture in his sense represented the 'embodiment of a people's shared reality' with the West generalising its scientific world view to other peoples (Roszak 1972: xxiii–xxiv).

Technocracy and expert pronouncements were widely regarded as threatening self-expression, freedom and personal integrity. The existence of a countercultural milieu represented a crucible within which social and technical experimentation and innovation was possible. The Alternative Technology movement is one example of this process as sustainable energy becomes increasingly mainstream five decades later – albeit in more centralised forms than those initially envisaged. Social experiments from this era in areas such as communal living are less prominent though many communes from the period remain active. The activities of the counterculture demonstrated the importance of the cultural domain for the legitimacy of formal politics and underlined the vulnerability of political institutions to cultural interventions. In America and Europe this political impact became explicit with the campus-based protest movements and the street riots of 1968 in Paris. These events led members of the Frankfurt School to identify students and marginal social groups as potentially revolutionary subjects. The counter cultural milieu shaped the New Left in Europe and is an important term in understanding the trajectory of social movement development within industrial societies.

References and resources

Gitlin, T. (1980); Marcuse, H. (1969); Roszak, T. (1970); Stephens, J. (1998); Yinger J. M. (1982).

COUNTERMOVEMENTS

Within social movement studies a countermovement is a response to the form and/or content of social change advocated by an existing social movement. The term originated within the USA (Mottl 1980), was developed by Zald and Useem (1987) and further developed to address issues raised by network movements by Meyer and Staggenborg (1996). Whilst the core definition is straightforward the range of countermovements discernible within what has been termed the **social movement society** requires some clear distinctions. These fall into three categories: the social movement milieu, contested state concessions to social movement actors, and state/intellectual movement initiatives.

In terms of the *social movement milieu* a countermovement mobilises against another social movement. Examples of such mobilisations abound within most countries, spanning diverse categories including the domains of politics, social order, gender, sexuality and culture. Many of these examples raise fundamental issues for liberal representative democracy associated with the development of modernity. These include the balance between freedom of speech and expressions of 'race' hatred associated with extreme right-wing politics; debates around abortion, gay rights and so on. In this domain countermovements highlight the contested nature of change brought about by social movement actors. Movements and countermovements are in a dialectical relationship contesting the legitimacy of competing positions. At times this can become reduced to confrontations between the members of opposing movements.

Contested state concessions involve mobilisations targeted directly at the political state contesting concessions attributed to another social movement. Such actions can involve the use of social movement action repertoires by groups not normally associated with the wider social movement milieu. In the United Kingdom, elements of the landed aristocracy, a decaying class fraction, used direct action on the floor of the House of Commons to protest against a ban on fox hunting. The ban was associated with both the animal rights movement and the dominance of urban political values. Again in the United Kingdom, the fuel protests of 2000 have been analysed as a petit-bourgeois countermovement contesting a fuel levy on petrol and diesel justified on the environmental grounds of reducing road-vehicle use.

State/intellectual movement initiatives such as the re-orientation of national and global agendas around neoliberal economic, social and political programmes are considered to have laid the foundations for countermovements at both a national and global level by a number of prominent writers (Bourdieu 1998/2004; Castells 1997). At this level an overarching ideology constitutes a 'common enemy' which whilst it is experienced differently in multiple locations results in sufficient common interest to permit a coalition of movements sufficiently cohesive to pursue collective action (see also **global social movement, alternative globalisation movement)**.

The increasing visibility of countermovements suggests that there has been an increase in mobilisation within mature democracies over the past two decades. This suggests that social movement engagement is in a phase of innovation and extension as national political opportunity structures simultaneously confront the internal consequences and planetary impacts of globalisation.

References and resources

Bourdieu, P. (1998/2004); Castells, M. (1996); Meyer, D. S. and Staggenborg, S. (1996); Mottl, T. L. (1980); Zald, M. N. and Useem, B. (1987).

CULTURE

Culture is a highly contested term in academic discourse and is the subject of significant debate over its relationship to social and political theory (Archer 1995). For present purposes, a key feature of this debate involves the extent to which political and social change can result from cultural interventions (see **counterculture**) rather than more formal channels. The centrality of social movements as agents of social change means these debates also feature prominently within social movement studies (Alvarez *et al.* 1998; Darnovsky *et al.* 1995; Johnston 2009). The use of culture as a lens to describe and analyse social movements has been a fruitful one, however, and can be divided into two distinctive but interrelated approaches.

The first approach focusses upon the relationship between movement and mainstream culture. It contrasts the ideas, values, attitudes and beliefs of movement participants with those of the society they wish to challenge and transform. This approach tends towards a 'commonsense notion of culture' (Johnston 2009: 4) that conceives social movements as subcultures of a larger society (Inglehart 1997; Jasper 1997) that movements aim to change by forms of 'exemplary action' (Eyerman and Jamison 1998) aimed at transforming established values. This includes frame analytical perspectives (see **frame analysis**) that seek to explain how movements engage in re-aligning activist and mainstream cultures by 'bridging' work that draws upon shared cultural resources from historical memory to the use of common symbolic registers, cultural narratives and storytelling (Polletta 2006).

The second approach concentrates upon the internal culture of social movements and aims to demonstrate how movements produce their own cultural forms, which are specific to, or emerge from, their organisation and practice. These might include values associated with democratic participation, such as integration, education and empowerment or particular aesthetic and representational forms, from clothing to music (Eyerman and Jamison 1998) and dramaturgy to literature etc. This approach augments the first by helping develop reflection on the performance and representation of movement values and beliefs for the purposes of solidarity, mobilisation and protest.

Some of the most sophisticated work under the rubric of culture and social movements has been conducted by Hank Johnston (Johnston and Klandermans 1995; Johnston 2009). His work identifies three categories of cultural factors that provide a means of exploration for both the approaches to culture and social movements detailed above. These three categories are ideations, artefacts and performances that form a 'cultural matrix' within which cultural analysis of social movements can take place.

1   Ideations are 'the traditional stuff of culture' and involve values, ideas and beliefs including specific normative forms of behaviour and speech. Johnston includes the most recent conceptual formulations of these factors, such as cognitive schemata, framing processes and grammars of action and experience (see McDonald 2006) in this category.

2   Artefacts are cultural objects, including literature, music, film, art and software that have a material existence, and which circulate beyond the individual or collective cultural work that gave rise to them. Social

movement artefacts include the production of videos of actions which are frequently mounted on sites such as YouTube.

3 Performances produce both artefacts, a CD for example, and symbolic resources through the interpretation and attribution of meaning by others present – the audience, whether this is the public, the media, elites, or political rivals.

In Johnston's schema, performances (protests, demonstrations, press conferences etc.) are the most crucial of the three cultural factors because they represent the location of human agency and the process through which 'culture is accomplished'. His argument is that 'social movements are special kinds of performance' (2009: 9), which exemplify oppositional perspectives and alternative values that are produced by a complex network of relations involving both the movement actors and their 'audience'. Consequently, 'there are two sides to the social movement performances: the collective action that constitutes the opposition and the reading of it by the audience. Together they constitute the creation of social movement culture' (2009: 9). In these ways, social movements increase the range of cultural expressions and resources through which individuals and groups can interpret events and issues confronting societies. In an era where media forms are multiplying, the generation of symbolic resources becomes increasingly important (Bourdieu 1998/2004; Schudson 1989).

References and resources

Alvarez, S. E., Dagnino, E. and Escobar, A. (eds. 1998); Archer, M. (1995); Bourdieu, P. (1998/2004); Darnovsky, M., Epstein, B. L. and Flacks, R. (1995); Eyerman, R. and Jamison, A. (1998); Inglehart, R. (1997); Jasper, J. M. (1997); Johnston, H. (2009); Johnston, H. and Klandermans, B. (eds. 1995); McDonald, K. (2006); Schudson, M. (1989).

CYCLES OF CONTENTION/PROTEST CYCLES

Social movements and the protests they give rise to often proceed through phases of increasing visibility and impact, leading to a peak of activity before they eventually decline as a result of either their successes or failures. The speed at which this process occurs, the impact of the movement and the incorporation, diffusion or suppression of its aims, values and ideas is conditioned by the resources available to it, the social and political context in which it occurs and the responses of authorities and competitors. This process is referred to in the social movement literature as a 'protest cycle' (Tarrow 1991), or as part of a 'cycle of contention' (Tarrow 1998: 141).

The latter term, however, is the more inclusive, describing as it does, the way protest repertoires and master frames can be diffused between and amongst social movement organisations to create a 'broad wave' of struggle. Tarrow was keen to emphasise the need to analyse situations that lead to the extension of contention across society, believing this to be a significant gap in research that otherwise tended to focus upon individual movements or movement organisations. The term 'cycle of contention' therefore provides more than a descriptive shorthand for a brief upsurge in protests at a particular moment. It is a concept that describes the diffusion of protest repertoires from mobilised to non-mobilised social actors, novel and rapid innovation in framing and collective action and intense periods of communication and exchange amongst movements and between movements and authorities (Tarrow 1998: 142).

Tarrow (1998: 144–150) describes a cycle of contention as having nine aspects or phases: mobilisation; conflict and diffusion; repertoires and frames (see entries); old and new movements (see entries); increased information and interaction; demobilisation; exhaustion and polarisation; violence and institutionalisation; facilitation and repression. For the most part he argues that these phases are shaped by the prevailing **political opportunity structure**, placing great emphasis upon the role of adversaries and competitors in responding to and therefore helping to determine the way in which the cycle progresses. In later work McAdam *et al.* summarised these phases as follows:

> Through publicly mounted contention, challengers' actions are communicated to, and produce political opportunities for, other groups. This leads states to devise broad strategies of repression and facilitation. Movements respond to these strategies either by radicalization or moderation. Cycles end through a combination of exhaustion, sectarianization and cooptation.
>
> (2001: 66)

The difficulties with such a concept are, as McAdam *et al.* (2001) admit, that it remains a stage theory which relies upon describing distinct periods of mobilisation and demobilisation occurring across movements and thus fails to account for patterns of mobilisation and demobilisation that might occur at differing points within the cycle and between movements. It also fails to account for the role of the actors themselves, their relationships, actions and identities, emphasising instead the political opportunities which emerge for other social movements when an 'early rising' movement proves able to challenge the status quo. Similarly, the cycles of contention described by Tarrow (1998), including the French revolution of 1848 and the wave of global protests in 1968, are of such a scale and involved so many actors in such differentiated contexts that the utility of the concept for analytical purposes becomes a lot weaker than it might when applied to more specific outbreaks of contentious politics.

References and resources

McAdam, D., Tarrow, S. and Tilly, C. (2001); Tarrow, S. (1991, 1998).

DEFENSIVE SOCIAL MOVEMENT

Defensive social movements can be thought of as movements which seek to defend established traditions, customs, practices and forms of association from changes imposed by the forces of modernisation. This may involve the renegotiation of the social relations between groups confronted by the modernisation process. The German anti-nuclear mobilisations provide one example of this sort of defensive movement, in areas where a residual class of small landholders combined with urban anti-nuclear activists to oppose the construction of nuclear power plants.

The term was introduced by German philosopher and social theorist Jürgen Habermas as a way of situating the diverse range of social movements emerging in the 1960s and 1970s in relation to both contemporary developments within industrial societies and earlier social movements. Habermas's approach develops some themes reflected in the work of the Frankfurt School of which he remains a member. His summary of the prevailing social movement milieu distinguishes between three main spheres of movement dynamics. Movement initiatives that developed in relation to the sphere of production or the economy, movement initiatives that developed in relation to the sphere of welfare provision and new conflicts arising in 'areas of cultural reproduction, social integration and socialization' (Habermas 1981: 33).

Habermas regards these new conflicts as distinct from problems of distribution (work and welfare) and centrally concerned with 'the grammar of forms of life' (Habermas 1981: 33). What Habermas has in mind here is the way in which modern technologies and techniques, including genetic manipulation, cumulatively begin to define the good or acceptable life in a capitalist free market system. Modernisation threatens tradition, traditional relations and traditional ways of being, raising the question of 'how to defend or reinstate endangered life styles' or 'how to put reformed lifestyles into practice' (Habermas 1981: 33).

Habermas argues that defensive social movements 'can be understood as resistance to tendencies to colonize the life-world' through the defence of traditional and social property *and* new forms of co-operation and community between established actors. On these grounds he distinguishes between 'old middle-class protest' (1981: 35) – examples cited include the neighbourhood impacts of technical projects, introduction of comprehensive education, tax protests and most independence movements – and '*the youth and alternative movement*' mounting a critique of growth based on '*environmental and peace concerns*' (1981: 35 emphasis in original). Rather than defending the particular, Habermas sees the youth and alternative movement mobilising against a visible attack on the '*organic foundations of the life-world*' with implications for both biological life and aesthetic needs (1981: 35 emphasis in original).

Defensive social movements can thus be thought of as engaging in spheres where the stakes involved are well delineated and defined and not subject to the problems of over-complexity Habermas associated with overarching 'invisible risks' threatening both planetary and human integrity.

References and resources

Habermas, J. (1981); Ruggiero, V. and Montagna, N. (eds. 2008: 201–205).

DIRECT ACTION

Direct action is intervention to achieve change by means that lie outside the normal channels of social or political engagement. It is often described as the 'last resort' of social movements and is frequently prefixed with 'non-violent' and abbreviated to NVDA – non-violent direct action. However, recent articulations by social movement activists have sought to widen this definition and to present it as a methodology and justification for social movements, rather than just a tactic of protest (see **Peoples' Global Action**). In this latter conceptualisation direct action is a mode of being and relating to each other – the combination of agency and participation that is required to shape the decisions that affect participants' everyday lives. The concept is therefore both descriptive and normative. In academic writing, it usually describes a repertoire of contention or protest that is likely to be confrontational and sometimes unlawful: a sit-in; an office occupation; a strike or blockade etc. However, it can also articulate a political position associated with self-organisation and autonomy and when used with the prefix non-violent it also implies a set of parameters for appropriate behaviour, usually aimed at convincing external audiences of the moral force of its proponents (see **moral action**).

Historically, direct action has exerted huge political, moral, and symbolic force (Carter 2005). Examples range from the various forms of collective action, including property destruction and the storming of parliament, that were used by the Suffragettes to achieve votes for women in the United Kingdom. Ghandi's '*satyagraha*' – meaning 'truth-force' which consisted of principled non-violent resistance aimed at achieving Indian independence and Martin Luther King's 'soul-force' which was directly influenced by Ghandi *satyagraha*. This included non-violent direct action that was designed to convey the moral position of the **Civil Rights Movement** in the USA and which helped dramatise the power relations involved in the segregation of black and white communities. Direct action was also a favoured repertoire of a number of 'anti-disciplinary' movements of the late 1960s from draft-burning anti-Vietnam war protestors to the Yippies (see Stephens 1998). It has also featured strongly in **peace movements** (Randle 1994) including the Greenham common protests against the stationing of US nuclear weapons on British territory (Roseneil 1995). More recently direct action has been a favoured repertoire of environmental (Seel *et al.* eds. 2000), animal rights and social justice movements, including the **alternative globalisation movement** (Graeber 2009; Notes from Nowhere 2003).

The use or otherwise of violence in the course of direct action is a continuous source of debate for social movements (Churchill 1998; Lakey 2001), and this tends to revolve around definitions of violence and its efficacy or desirability in social change processes. However, the potential costs to social movements of direct action that can be labelled as violent have increased considerably over the last decade. These debates have taken on a renewed importance since the terrorist attacks on the USA on 11 September 2001, which provoked a wide range of states to pass legislation aimed at identifying, controlling and punishing potential terrorists – with the use of violence, defined in some contexts to include property damage, being a key criteria for defining 'terrorism'. This has resulted in arrests and prosecutions, under anti-terrorist legislation, of animal rights activists in the USA and the United Kingdom, situationist-inspired (see **Situationist International**) writers/activists in France (Toscano 2009) and peace activists in New Zealand.

References and resources

Carter, A. (2005); Churchill, W. (1998); Graeber, D. (2009); Lakey, G. (2001); Randle, M. (1994); Roseneil, S. (1995); Seel, B., Paterson, M. and Doherty, B. (eds. 2000); Toscano, A. (2009).

DISABILITY RIGHTS MOVEMENT

Disability rights movements' campaign to improve the quality of life of people with disabilities and challenge discrimination and social stigma through collective political action. An initial emphasis on physical disability has shifted to include a wide range of developmental, psychological and chronic conditions impairing the capacity of individuals to participate fully in the full range of social activities associated with normal citizenship.

Disability rights movements have campaigned for legislative recognition within the advanced industrial economies such as the USA and the United Kingdom. Some US sources trace the movement back into the nineteenth century. Action as a **claimant movement** is accompanied by action as a **political movement**, however, as the boundaries of disabled rights are constantly contested and consolidated in the face of shifting social, political, medical and scientific stakes. There is a significant debate about the impact of legislative recognition upon activist engagement, a feature shared with many other movements. Societal dynamics mean that disability and the associated movements will continue to develop and expand. An example of this can be seen in the efforts of military veterans to gain recognition for the disabling chronic conditions that have followed military campaigns in Iraq and elsewhere.

In the USA, disability rights movements drew on the **Civil Rights Movement** and the **feminist movement** and became increasingly prominent from the 1970s onwards. The campaign for the right to independent living was an early example of the assertion of full human rights for those with disabilities. In 1977 the American Coalition of Citizens with Disabilities organised the occupation of Health Education and Welfare offices in several states to secure legal recognition of rights under legislation. In 1981 the United Nations declared an International Year of Disabled Persons as recognition of this area grew.

The tensions between medical and social models and approaches to disability have been a prominent feature of disability movement development in the United Kingdom (Shakespeare 2006) and elsewhere. These tensions relate to issues of mobilisation and engagement, for example, in relation to the area of mental health (Crossley 2002) and can be extended to the increasing importance attached to identity issues and disability.

The right to a disabled identity is an area which is assuming increasing importance following the mapping of the human genome. The ability to perform prenatal genetic tests for a range of 'disabilities' raises profoundly challenging issues of choice for parents faced by test results. This is particularly intense when results detect a propensity towards a condition rather than a clear-cut diagnostic result. Habermas (2003) has expressed concerns over the prospect of a neoliberal eugenics emerging from the combination of testing and parental choice, resulting in the termination of pregnancies with 'defects'. On the other hand some families with genetic deafness have expressed a preference for children with the condition. This is an area where disability rights activism can be expected to become increasingly prominent.

References and resources

Crossley, N. (2002); Habermas, J. (2003); Fleisher, D. Z. and Zames, F. (2001); McBryde, H. and Johnson H. (2005); Scotch, R. K. (1988 1989 2001). Shakespeare, T. (2006); Shapiro, J. (1993); Umansky, I. and L. (eds. 2001).
Disability rights movement web resources: http://bancroft.berkeley.edu/collections/drilm/

DISOBBEDIENTI (TUTE BIANCHE/WHITE OVERALLS)

The disobbedienti (disobedients) were a **network movement** of radical left and autonomist groups, youth and solidarity organisations that were associated with squatted social centres in Italy in the early 2000s. They were particularly well represented in the Central and Northern towns of Milan, Padua, Bologna, Venice and Rome. The disobbedienti emerged as a development of the Tute Bianche or 'white overall' movement soon after the 2001 protests against the G8 in Genoa, which were among the most violently repressed of all the alter-globalisation movement's 'days of action'. There was little formal organisation in either of these overlapping networks and no primary documents or ideological texts. However, both networks were influenced by, and influential in, the autonomist theories proposed by Hardt and Negri (2000, 2004) and activists routinely appropriated the conceptual discourse that emerged from this interaction including the concepts of **multitude** and **precarity**. The emphasis on multitude as an inclusive class concept representing everyone living under capitalist social relations and not just waged labour, in an era where formal employment is increasingly precarious became prominent features of the disobeddienti's repertoires.

The Tute Bianche (white overalls) first came to prominence in 1997 when a group of young people in Rome began calling themselves 'the invisibles' and took to wearing white overalls as a symbol of visibility/ invisibility and as a play on the end of the blue overall/white collar class distinction. This is a distinction that the Tute Bianche perceive as having broken down in a post-Fordist era where a plurality of socially productive yet precarious class positions have emerged. This use of white overalls also consciously echoed the tactics of social centre activists at the *Leoncavallo* Social Centre in Milan, where in 1994, during one of many evictions, the occupants were described by a local politician as 'ghosts', existing on the margins of society, easy to disperse and soon to disappear. The return of these activists in white overalls and the retaking of *Leoncavallo* provided a powerful narrative and a new symbolic resource for social centre activists. The Tute Bianche were also heavily influenced by the **Zapatista** movement and involved solidarity groups including the 'Ya Basta' association, who came together with youth organisations, social centre activists and intellectuals many of whom also had direct links to the autonomist Marxist groups of the 1970s. Despite their participation in numerous protest events directed at global governance institutions and multinational corporate actors before 2000, it was in September of that year that the Tute Bianche first became widely known and celebrated outside of Italy after they participated in protests in Prague against the IMF and World Bank. Their strategy of 'civil disobedience' included dressing in protective padding, including rubber inner tubes, foam cladding, plastic bottles and various other protective measures, including helmets. They then made disciplined and repeated attempts to breach police lines around the conference centre consciously constructing the situation as a symbolic dual between black-clad riot police and white-clad Tute Bianche activists, thereby subtly invoking a black/white binary opposition between 'good' and 'evil' (Chesters and Welsh 2004).

Such tactical innovation led to the Tute Bianche becoming one of the most influential groups to emerge from the **alternative globalisation movement** and their tactics, protest repertoires and ideology led to the formation of similar groups in the United Kingdom and the USA (Graeber 2009: 1–8). The largest mobilisation of the Tute Bianche was during the Genoa protests against the G8 where thousands of activists attempted to lay siege to the fortified 'red zone' housing the G8 meetings and were met by unparalleled use of police and military force including armoured personnel carriers and live fire, leading to the death of a young protester – Carlo Giuliani. The outcome of these events was profound and led to a reassessment by movement leaders which led to a move from 'civil' to 'social' disobedience, meaning in practice a move from direct mass confrontation with global institutions to a localised and regional engagement with global actors using more specific interventions. This turn towards 'molecular' forms of engagement also involved an attempt to reach social centre activists who had previously been outside the Tute Bianche and gave rise to the regional networks of the disobbedienti. This transition was responded to in some quarters as a threat to the autonomy of social centres, and the increasing involvement of many of the leaders of the disobbedienti with leftist and green political parties, in particular Rifondazione Communista, led to declining participation which was amplified by exhaustion and prolonged disagreements over the tactics employed in Genoa. The disobbedienti gradually faded as a **network movement** as many of its leading activists became absorbed into the Italian anti-war movement, whilst many ex-activists also continue to be influential in the anti-precarity movements associated with euromayday mobilisations.

References and resources

Chesters, G. and Welsh, I. (2004); Graeber, D. (2009); Hardt, M. and Negri, A. (2000, 2004).
Disobbedienti web resources: http://www.nadir.org/nadir/initiativ/agp/free/tute/

EARTH FIRST!

Earth First! emerged in the 1980s as a North American movement prioritising direct action to protect the environment (Foreman 1991; Scarce 1990) as a result of disillusionment with more established approaches, particularly amongst younger activists. The origins and early years of EF! in the USA are complex and contain multiple threads spanning the left–right political spectrum. The backwoods, pioneering tradition based on a return to nature and a simplified way of life, prominent within US conservation and environmental circles, was re-appropriated by an activist caucus including people with military service. The novel *The Monkey Wrench Gang* (Abbey 1975) established the commitment to monkeywrenching or ecotage as the principle mode of engagement adopted by EF!. Monkeywrenching referred to the act of damaging equipment being used to the detriment of nature and was justified as an act of ecotage. Damage or destruction of construction and earth-moving machinery being used in environmentally sensitive developments such as road developments would be an act of ecotage, for example. The use of such tactics to defend nature became highly controversial when the practice of hammering metal spikes into trees in order to break chainsaw belts, potentially endangering the life of the operator, was developed as a means of preserving forests.

Controversy centred around the prioritisation of nature over the life of humans endangered by flailing, snapped chainsaw blades. The sanctity afforded to all life by some EF! members extended controversy when the HIV virus was included and presented as a control on planetary degradation caused by humans. Wall (1999) traces the origins of many of the techniques adopted by EF! USA, including tree spiking, to the International Workers of the World movement operating at the turn of the twentieth century. EF! were also criticised for being eco-warriors advocating macho forms of direct action including the destruction of developers' machinery.

Irrespective of these controversial origins EF! became a significant movement outside the USA with numerous groups becoming active in the United Kingdom during the 1990s. Many of these groups were campus-based including those at Oxford University, Brighton and Glasgow. EF! UK activists were prominent in the consolidation of 'anti-roads' protests, many of which involved local communities threatened by motorway extensions. The crossover membership, typical of network actors, made EF! UK an important influence on **Reclaim The Streets** which went on to be a prominent actor in the **alternative globalisation movement**. By 1999 London RTS members were amongst the activists invited to Seattle to prepare for the protests at the World Trade Organisation. The influences upon the United Kingdom that had originated in the USA thus returned as carnival and the street party became significant repertoires of action once more. The combination of committed forms of direct action with artistic expression originated in the stance of EF! US and became a significant feature of direct action interventions around the world.

EF! can be thought of as one of the early **network movements** that prefigured the consolidation of the **alternative globalisation movement** and re-invigorated environmental **direct action**. EF! contributed to the creation of a radical flank which intensified and extended environmental contestation attracting mounting attention from police and security services.

References and resources

Abbey, E. (1975/1991); Foreman, D. (1991); Foreman, D. and Haywood, B. (1993); Scarce, R. (1990); Wall, D. (1999).

ECOLOGY OF MIND AND ECOLOGY OF ACTION

An ecology of mind is an approach to life – an ontological position – based on the recognition that individual and human well-being are dependent upon a diverse and viable environment. Our work (Chesters and Welsh 2006) argues that this ecology of mind provides a primary sense-making device – a frame – to guide action consistent with this recognition. The ecology of action envisaged is negotiated and refined through a process of reflexive framing involving multiple actors in an iterative process.

Gregory Bateson introduced the term Ecology of Mind (1973/1978) in work which influenced Goffman's *Frame Analysis*. Within social movement studies Bateson is acknowledged as an influence by Melucci and figures prominently in our own work. Bateson graduated in Natural Science and Anthropology and was an early advocate of the idea that the survival of any species, including human kind, depended upon a viable environment. In 2009 this sensibility featured prominently in debates on climate change. An ecology of mind required transcending the key ideas consolidated through the industrial revolution.

Bateson lists seven ideas, or habits of mind, that have dominated progress:

- us against the environment;
- us against other man (*sic*);
- it is the individual, my firm or my country that counts;
- belief in unilateral control over the environment;
- belief in infinitely expanding frontiers;
- the primacy of economic determinism;
- reliance on technological fixes.

Bateson argued for an Ecological Habit of Mind with a default mode which not only rejected these established habits but automatically recognised the inseparable unity of self and environment. He argued that citizens should trust no policy decisions made by anyone who had not developed this ecology of mind but acknowledged that achieving this was a major challenge.

Our 'reflexive framing approach' (Chesters and Welsh 2006: 9–21) develops Bateson's emphasis on framing as a multilayered activity and applies this in an era where digital recording and communication technologies and physical mobility have transformed the framing process. In traditional uses, **frame analysis** was applied to a strip of activity with a short duration resulting in an outcome through the exercise of sense-making judgement. Sense-making and judgement were individual acts. Multiple digital recording, web mounting and distribution technologies make extended, multifaceted and repeated acts of sense-making possible. Reflexive framing thus represents a process rather than an outcome.

We argue that the challenge of achieving the ecology of mind envisaged by Bateson is significantly reduced through the increase in framing resources available facilitating ecologies of action. Ecologies of action formalise forms of collective action consistent with the unity of self and environment prioritised by Bateson and are discernible within the **alternative globalisation movement** which sustains 'plateau events' during which sustained periods of intense reflexive framing occur. Typically plateau events occur within large moblisations involving a diverse range of activists and participants engaged in the negotiation and definition of collective stakes.

Plateau events generate ecologies of action that are iterative and cumulative. Action denotes the capacity to counter the seven detrimental habits of mind identified by Bateson and the beginning of the capacity to constitute the planetary action systems envisaged by Melucci for a viable self and viable environment. These ecologies of action are properties of network actors participating in networks of networks rather than features of established social movement organisations.

References and resources

Bateson, G. (1973); Chesters and Welsh (2006); Goffman, E. (1974/1986).

EMERGENCE

The concept of emergence was introduced and applied to the study of social movements through our own work on the applications of complexity theory to social movements (Chesters and Welsh 2005, 2006). The concept describes the unexpected macro outcomes produced by social movement actors engaged in complex patterns of interaction and exchange, outcomes that are determined by the history and context in which they occur, but which are unknowable in advance. This means that whilst the unexpected 'outcome' – the discrediting of policing strategy perhaps or the collapse of a trade agreement – is a product of systemic interaction over time, it would be impossible to precisely predict this outcome or analytically reveal how it happened through disaggregating the parts of the system. A 'system' here could be a social movement, a **political opportunity structure** or some other field of relations defined by the analyst. In this way, the concept of emergence describes how system outcomes are never reducible to simple aggregates of behaviour but are always more than the sum of their parts. Social movements are networks of individuals, groups and organisations involved in complex interactions in real and virtual spaces representing and embodying a variety of causes, ideological positions and expressions of identity. As such they are non-linear systems and liable to produce emergent outcomes.

We argue that contemporary social movements (see **alternative globalisation movements)** have been able to recognise the emergent properties of acting in a decentralised, participatory and democratic manner. The outcome from such practices we suggest are recognised at a collective level as affording a strength, durability, and interconnectivity that would otherwise be absent and this recognition has promoted positive feedback loops that reinforce these 'horizontal' practices. This feedback is, in turn, able to reaffirm the praxis that gave rise to the emergent properties. Work in the field of complexity theory has demonstrated that emergent properties are ubiquitous in complex systems, although they often go unrecognised (Barabasi and Albert 1999).

What appears to have occurred within some contemporary movements is that their affinity with participatory and democratic means and their adoption of a decentralised praxis has encouraged organisational forms with emergent properties that are politically and culturally efficacious within a network society. Thus, we have seen the emergence of durable networks (see **network movements**) that are highly effective at information management, communications, material and symbolic contestation, and mobilisation at the local and global levels. This has been coupled with recognition amongst certain actors of the primacy of process in catalysing these effects and a prioritisation of process as a means to maximise these emergent outcomes. This leads to an interesting set of research questions that can be applied to any social movement that appears to be engaged in **knowledge-practices** concerning emergent outcomes. For example, how does the recognition of an emergent outcome at the system level get causally attributed within the system and how does this reinforce or change behaviour or activists' sense of agency?

References and resources

Barabasi, A.-L. and Albert, R. (1999); Chesters, G. and Welsh, I. (2005, 2006).

EMOTIONS

Some of the earliest studies of social movements explained them as the outcomes of irrational behaviour driven by emotions and amplified collectively through crowds (Le Bon, 1960). This corresponded with a general denigration of the emotions within social sciences, where they were largely naturalised as embodied sensations over which individuals had little control. One could be 'gripped' or 'seized' by emotions and these feelings were evident physically through a heightened pulse rate, reddened face, shortness of breath etc. In this understanding, emotions were very much of the body and therefore irrational in terms of the classic Cartesian dualism of the mind-body. After the intense cycle of movement mobilisation and protest experienced globally in the late 1960s and early 1970s social movement scholars were very keen to emphasise the rational, political aspect of collective action and to normalise the idea of social movement (see **resource mobilisation theory, political opportunity structure**). This resulted in the effective exclusion of emotions from mainstream social movement studies, as they were considered unhelpful or irrelevant to the conceptual presentation of social movements as rational and purposive collective actors. The role of emotions in the production of moral values and rational action was therefore effectively ignored in the rush to normalise social movements.

A concentration on emotions and their relationship to social movement formation and mobilisation is therefore a comparatively recent innovation in social movement studies and is closely connected to the pioneering work of Jasper (1997, 1998) and particularly his co-edited volume *Passionate Politics* (Jasper *et al.* 2001). Jasper takes a largely 'constructionist' approach to emotions, suggesting they consist of learned behaviour that is culturally variable and context specific. He does, however, differentiate between primary emotions that are associated with particular physiological states, such as fear and anger and which appear to have certain universal physical responses, and more complex secondary emotions, that are socially learned and culturally variable, such as pride and outrage (1997: 110). Jasper argues that for the most part, the display of emotion can be viewed as either appropriate or inappropriate according to the context in which it takes place, and it is amenable to reasoned argumentation concerning that context. For example, it is possible to persuade someone that their anger about a situation is unjustified or to persuade them to empathise with another who is being punished unjustly.

Consequently, emotions are open to cognition and reason and are produced in complex ways derived from one's beliefs about the world and one's moral values. This frequently involves a positive feedback loop where a breach of moral values by an external actor (state/corporation etc.) leads to emotional distress and feelings of anger and resentment. These emotions prompt action, which, in turn, opens the individual actor to a wider or different set of moral values, the incorporation of which facilitates further anger relating to newly identified injustices and therefore further mobilisation.

Jasper (2003) also introduced the concept of emotion management into the social movement literature to describe the work activists do to produce the emotions they believe will be good for their movement (anger, solidarity, hope, outrage, desire) and to reduce emotions they feel will be unhelpful (despair, fear, hopelessness etc.). An interesting list of the emotions he believes are particularly relevant to protest and a summary of their possible effects is contained in his work *The Art of Moral Protest* (1997: 114).

Scholarship on emotions in social movements has since developed in a number of ways. There has been an explicit recognition by scholars within the main traditions of social movement studies that emotions are important at both macro (causal) and micro (collective action dynamics) levels, and are therefore an important part of the study of social movements (Aminzade and McAdam 2002). Calhoun (2001) argues that this has been tempered somewhat by a tendency amongst certain scholars to view emotions as a plug-in, as another rational preference that is instrumental to mobilisation and as another 'resource' to be managed or deployed against adversaries. However, there has also been a considerable growth in work that places emotions at the forefront of explaining social movements and collective action (Flam and King 2005) and that which explores the subtlety of the connections between emotions, embodiment and experience (McDonald 2006).

References and resources

Aminzade, R. and McAdam, D. (2002); Calhoun, C. (2001); Flam, H. and King, D. (eds. 2005); Goodwin, J., Jasper, J., and Polletta, F. (eds. 2001); Jasper, J. (1997, 1998, 2003); Le Bon, G. (1960); McDonald, K. (2006).

ENVIRONMENTAL JUSTICE MOVEMENT

Environmental justice movements pursue environmentally related goals, such as clean air or water, in the context of wider social, economic and political issues related to inequalities. The inequalities in question typically relate to 'race', class and gender but can also include the claims of indigenous peoples. The term is relatively recent having been in use for a little over twenty years.

The term environmental justice movement came to prominence through an American literature which examined the relationship between the location of toxic waste facilities and communities of colour. Bullard's (2005) seminal contribution *Dumping in Dixie* was central in establishing the term and drawing attention to the forms of environmental racism. The pursuit of, and campaigning around, environmental justice issues in the USA drew attention to the vibrancy of community-based activism (Lichterman 1996) at a time when Robert Puttnam's (1995) influential 'bowling alone' thesis was suggesting a significant decline in citizens' engagement with political and public life. Environmental justice became a focus for an extensive body of writing by activists and academic commentators. The North American focus of much of this work and the tendency for writers to be embedded within community actions led to criticisms. These focussed on the predominance of American case studies and the tendency for published accounts to adopt a sympathetic stance towards the goals of engaged communities to the neglect of internal power dynamics.

Bullard (2005) has been amongst those (Agyeman 2005; Pellow and Brulle 2005) to respond to such criticisms through comparative and analytic scholarship aimed at differentiating the dynamics and strategies of environmental justice movements which have achieved increasing prominence in a range of countries. Bullard's book includes case studies from South Africa, Colombia, Nigeria and the Philippines reflecting the increasingly global nature of environmental justice issues, including those associated with toxic waste. Beyond the well-established cases, such as those associated with chemical and nuclear hazards, environmental justice concerns are established around the disposal of electronic equipment, shipbreaking, oil spillages and a wide range of issues relating to the operation of multi and transnational organisations. These include Shell's operations in the Niger Delta and the global distribution and operation of waste smelters.

Environmental justice movements are thus located at the intersection of local and global processes in the context of the particular sets of social, economic, cultural and political processes operating in a place. As such, they are particularly diverse and rich sites for social movement studies containing an equally diverse range of repertoires of action and orientations. The continued engagement with environmental justice movements in countries like South Africa (Cock 2006) suggests that this is an area which will continue to develop. The tensions created through the sheer diversity of cases addressed by the range of environmental justice movements will continue to be an analytical challenge in terms of axes of solidarity (Dobson 1998).

It is an area where recognising the importance of difference and unity in diversity is important.

References and resources

Agyeman, J. (2005); Bullard, R. D. (1990, 2005); Cock, J. (2006); Dobson, A. (1998); Lichterman, P. (1996); Pellow, D. N. and Brulle, R. J. (2005); Puttnam, R. (1995).

ENVIRONMENTAL MOVEMENT

This term is widely used as a collective expression to denote the range of actors campaigning on the environment. In most uses it refers to the post-1970s era of new social movements. It is important to recognise that environmental and animal rights issues have also been a focus for activism in the nineteenth century and earlier periods (Wall 1994).

Environmental movements frequently have their origins in conservation initiatives dedicated to the preservation of particular habitats or species. The rise of environmental movements in the 1970s was an acknowledgement of the need for wider campaigning to gain influence within the public sphere, policy making and political circles. These initiatives were associated with the then fledgling **social movement organisations Friends of the Earth** and **Greenpeace** in Canada, America and Europe.

Given the diverse range of actors engaged within the environmental arena use of the term should always be approached with caution and a questioning attitude. It is commonplace to differentiate between 'shallow' and 'deep' environmentalist approaches. Shallow or light green environmental movement approaches include the advocacy of alternative technology approaches, such as renewable energy rather than nuclear power, for example. Shallow or light green environmental movements do not advocate radical changes to the prevailing political, economic or gender order. Deep or dark green environmental movements are distinguished by their more fundamental questioning of established practices like consumerism and advocate significant social, political, economic and lifestyle changes. The distinction draws on the work of the Norwegian philosopher Arnie Naess (1989).

Environmental movements can be distinguished from **green movements** on a number of grounds relating to the scope and scale of their

74

political engagement. Green movements have typically adopted deep or dark green approaches which have extended to the creation of political parties with electoral programmes. The political mainstreaming of issues initially formalised by environmental movements, such as climate change, has raised some major debates. Rowell (1996) argues that there has been a backlash against the green agenda leading to the subversion of the environmental movement by powerful vested interests capable of sustained lobbying, media campaigns and the capacity for legal sanctions.

The once common association of environmental movements with systemic critiques of liberal democracy and capitalism is widely regarded as having come to an end to the detriment of environmentalism (Wissenberg and Levy 2004). Long-standing environmentalists such as Jonathan Porritt (2005) have embraced capitalism and others now accept nuclear power. Environmental movements are currently operating in the context of mainstreaming, global environmental agenda setting, and the post–2008 crisis of capital. Blühdorn and Welsh (2008) argue that this represents a transition to a politics of unsustainability in which environmental agendas receive increasing attention while the underlying social and economic drivers of environmental degradation continue unabated.

References and resources

Blühdorn, I. and Welsh, I. (2008); Porritt, J. (2005); Rowell, A. (1996); Wall D. (1994); Wissenberg M. and Levy Y. (eds. 2004); Young, J. (1990).

FEMINIST SOCIAL MOVEMENTS

The linguistic root of feminism can be traced back to the nineteenth-century French medical term *féminisme* which was applied to the feminisation of the male body or to women with masculine qualities. Attention to the social, political and economic status of women predates this linguistic root, featuring prominently with the 1789 French Revolution, for example. The subsequent development of multiple feminisms makes a unitary definition almost impossible. However, it is reasonable to begin from the proposition that feminist positions start from the recognition of the systematic subordination and inequality experienced by women because of their biology and a commitment to challenge the associated social relations. The basis of subordination, inequality and oppression are subject to multiple interpretations and strategies of redress.

Approaching feminism as a movement that has occurred in a number of waves has become widely accepted and is the approach adopted here. The predominant focus is on the trajectories of feminism as they have unfolded within Europe and North America and we acknowledge the many other feminisms that have been, and are being, formalised on other continents including Africa and India as well many Arab nations. The classification of feminism in terms of 'waves' raises the question of the relationship between feminism per se and earlier work on the position of women. After noting some of the significant precursors the convention of first, second and third wave feminism will be followed. The entry concludes by speculating on a possible fourth wave imminent within the contemporary network of networks.

Some precursors

The prevalence of patriarchal social relations and their normative status in Western societies made the inequality, subordination or oppression of women effectively invisible. Mary Wollstonecraft's *A Vindication of the Rights of Women* published in 1792 is one clear precursor of feminism. It is also important to recognise that feminism develops in the context of industrial capitalism within the West. Engels' (1884/1972) study of the historical significance of gender in the consolidation of an economic surplus, *The Origins of the Family, Private Property & The State*, represents an important early text within the socialist tradition. Rosa Luxemburg's work on the Woman Question in Socialism is another example. Within the Liberal tradition Mill's consideration of the place of women is another prefigurative text. Perhaps the most important point here is to remember that each of the waves that are written about stand in relation to each other in specific national contexts and each wave can draw on and be influenced by a range of precursors. From this perspective feminism is a social movement that expresses different forms of social force through time and across space. Feminism is a form of movement that is necessarily reconfigured over time as the place of women in societies is subject to changes in terms of the form and types of contradictions confronted and the range of resources available through which to mount critique and social challenge.

First wave feminism

In the USA and the United Kingdom first wave feminism is widely regarded as occurring between roughly 1850 and 1920. This was a key period in which industrial capitalism was consolidated creating a diverse range of social change. Within first wave feminism there were three main areas of engagement which enjoyed differing levels of support. Suffrage, rights-based equality and reproductive rights were all present during this period of mobilisation. The period is one where class differences between feminists represented a significant divide. In the United Kingdom the Suffragists are the best-known example of first wave feminism but there were also forms of evangelical feminism and a minoritarian social feminism which questioned the dominant family form and stood for the collectivisation of childcare and housework (Randall 1982). The ability to control fertility represented another minoritarian theme within first wave feminism in the United Kingdom with Mary Stopes being a prominent pioneer founding the Mary Stopes Clinic.

The UK suffrage movement of 1897, initially formalised through The National Union of Women's Suffrage Societies, represented a predominantly middle class reform movement. Differences over tactics led the Pankhursts to form the Women's Social and Political Union which pursued the use of high profile **direct action**. These included members chaining themselves to railings in public places and the death of Emily Davison who threw herself in front of one of the King's race horses. In Northern England working class women in Lancashire advanced their cause through the guilds and were suspicious of the more individualistic actions taking place in London. Irrespective of these differences it is widely accepted that the focus upon the vote produced at least the appearance of a united movement. The partial extension of the vote to some women in 1918 fractured this apparent unity.

After the First World War the issue of women and work produced an 'anti-feminist' current which argued that women should give up their place in the labour market which had expanded during the war. The National Union of Women's Suffrage Societies became the National Union of Societies for Equal Citizenship. The leader of the new organisation, Eleanor Rathbone (Rathbone 1920), campaigned for a 'radical' variant of 'family allowance' paid to women at a rate that secured their needs independent of male income. This ambition was never realised and marked a shift to the negotiation of rights for women which did not question the prevailing gender order. The more radical equal rights feminists opposed this focus and the passage of protective legislation for women such as maternity leave. Working class feminists supported such legislation, leading to renewed divisions within first wave feminism. The recession of the 1930s was accompanied by an emphasis on the maternal role of women and the importance of social welfare and is widely accepted as the point where first wave feminism reached the limit of its potential.

Second wave feminism

In the late 1960s and early 1970s there was a significant wave of collective political action by feminists in the developed nations in the aftermath of the youth and counter cultural movements. In America and Europe second wave feminism was in part a response to womens' experience of the New Left and counterculture which had pursued forms of liberation which had not questioned the normative gender order (Evans 1978). In America and the United Kingdom small consciousness-raising groups proliferated throughout urban areas in multiple locations spanning workplaces, educational establishments and friendship networks.

Feminism was also located within the wider questioning of the post-Second World War social order based on consumption and the nuclear family as unproblematic social forms. In America (Huber 1976) and the United Kingdom (Oakley 1974) feminists argued that increasing female participation rates in the labour market resulted in a 'double burden' of paid and domestic labour. To this could be added the burden of care for the elderly and sick creating a triple burden. As with first wave feminism, second wave feminism erupted in the face of significant changes in the organisation of industrial capitalism which had established another normative gender order which made notions of oppression, inequality and subordination effectively invisible. Betty Friedan's book *The Feminine Mystique* (2001) was amongst the titles that breached the silence. Second wave feminism had very different mobilising capacities and resources at its disposal and had a major impact upon the prevailing gender order. These impacts included formal legislative programmes on birth control, abortion, equal pay as well as significant cultural and social normative challenge and change.

Analytically, second wave feminism (Nicholson 1997) is often divided into liberal, socialist/Marxist and radical forms reflecting differing primary orientations. Liberal feminism is understood as the pursuit of formal equality between women and men within substantive legislative areas. Socialist/ Marxist feminism was committed to building an inclusive mass movement based on the incorporation of gender within an analysis of capitalist social relations. The reliance on consciousness-raising groups, forms of direct action, street theatre and staged situations – such as the disruption of Miss World competitions – produced a high public profile. Both liberal and socialist/Marxist feminism prioritised a range of women-specific concerns consistent with what Kate Millet (2000) regarded as 'sexual politics'. These included the family, abortion, sexuality, the sexual division of labour, rape, domestic violence and the relationship between capitalism, patriarchy (Walby 1990) and war and exploitation (Enloe 1983, 1990).

Radical feminism prioritised patriarchal relationships in its analysis of gender oppression and subordination emphasising sex and sexuality with significant campaigns against pornography. Violence and subordination were approached as patriarchal attributes linked to heterosexuality. Radical feminism campaigned using forms of direct action including significant 'reclaim the night marches' in the form of torchlight processions through urban areas associated with assaults on women. Other initiatives with which radical feminism was associated included the creation of 'women's refuges' open to the victims of domestic violence. This sort of campaigning is a far more important legacy of radical feminism than the view that it stood for the uncompromising antipathy towards men.

Second wave feminism has had lasting impacts on the societies in which mobilisations occurred but is widely seen as having fallen far short of its potential by protagonists such as Lynne Segal (1987). The attempt to forge an inclusive movement for all created immense pressures as women from different social classes and women of colour debated the relative standing of oppression based on gender, race and class. These internal tensions developed alongside the wider crisis of social democracy and socialism confronted by the rise of Neoliberalism, which in the United Kingdom was driven forward through a female prime minister. Whilst feminism never became moribund in the 1980s and 1990s nor did it regain the popular impact enjoyed during the second wave.

A notable exception in the United Kingdom during the 1980s was the prominence achieved by **Greenham Women** opposed to the stationing of American theatre nuclear weapons on British soil. This radical feminist initiative drew increasing support from an increasingly diverse range of social locations over time and attracted increasingly derogatory attention from sections of the press and political establishment. The practice of maintaining permanent camps at the Greenham base was an innovative return to direct action (Roseneil 1995). The recognition that the type of systemic change sought by feminism could only be realised by changes in the approaches towards masculinity was one important insight formalised during this period (Segal 1987). The inclusion of men and masculinity can be seen as one of the preconditions for the emergence of a third wave of feminism.

Third wave feminism

The apparent decline of feminism and arguments that feminism had become a social movement in abeyance (Bagguley 2002) should be treated with some caution. A third wave of feminism, influenced by post-structuralism which rejects essentialism and approaches the gender order as universally problematic and hybrid, is beginning to be defined. The prominence of the daughters of second wave feminists within this 'wave' raises interesting issues of inter-generational transmission and reinterpretation of feminism. This distinguishes the relationship between second and third waves from those between first and second. There are at least two discernible positions in terms of this relationship: a conservative post-feminism that is a rejection of second wave feminism and a progressive feminism which seeks to reconfigure the second wave for the contemporary milieu (Gillis *et al.* 2004).

Progressive third wave feminism can be seen as a re-engagement with the aim of achieving an open movement by including women of colour and diverse class backgrounds (Zack 2005). Whilst criticising and protesting against beauty competitions, such as Miss London University, the condemnation of cosmetics and glamour per se is not a feature of this movement. Third wave activism includes cultural interventions and performances with Riot Grrrl being a prominent US example. Drawing on 1970s punk, Riot Grrrl spread beyond the music scene to create a wider movement, holding conventions and gatherings reminiscent of consciousness-raising events of the second wave.

Third wave feminism adopts an avowedly global perspective and an engagement with lived experience, extending to the impacts on masculinity of economic restructuring leading to male unemployment. There is a marked generational profile to third wave feminism which contributes to a diverse presence on the internet. Sites such as The F Word (www.thef word.org.uk) contain a wide range of material including engagements with and reinterpretations of the second wave. The third wave is still in a nascent and formative stage where the future lines of fight and flight remain immanent (www.3rdwwwave.com and www.womensstudies. homestead.com).

There are, however, some indications that the openness associated with the third wave is beginning to produce forms of hybrid direct action. In the United Kingdom Climaterush exists as a mixed gender group using direct action to highlight the importance of climate change (www.climaterush.co.uk). Their repertoire of action has included the re-enactment of interventions first made by the Suffragettes. Wearing sashes in the colours of the Suffrage movement, a climaterush group chained themselves to the same statue within the Palace of Westminster, assuming the same poses as the original Suffragettes. This represents an example of the sort of hybridisation of social movement repertoires and symbolic resources available in the contemporary milieu. If third wave feminism pursues this sort of hybrid extension of its engagement with gender then it may become possible to speak of a fourth wave with the potential to deliver the systemic transformations immanent within each wave of feminism.

References and resources

Bagguley, P. (2002); Enloe, C. (1983, 1990); Evans, S. (1978); Freidan, B. (2001);
   Gillis, S. Howie, G. Munford, R. (2004); Haywood, L. and Drake, J. (eds. 1997);
   Huber, J. (1976); Millet, K. (2000); Nicholson, L. (ed. 1997); Oakley, A. (1974);
   Randall, V. (1982); Rathbone, E. (1920); Roseneil, S. (1995); Segal, L. (1987);
   Walby, S. (1990); Zack, N. (2005).

FRAME ANALYSIS

Frame analysis is a concept that originates from the pioneering work of the
American sociologist Erving Goffman (1974) and the British social anthro-
pologist Gregory Bateson (1973). Frame analysis studies the ways in which
meaning is attributed to events through the combination of observational
prompts, established cognitive categories and the lived experience of individuals. A frame is a sense-making device that permits an observer to attri-
bute meaning to social interactions, events and processes. These individual
meanings can then become the subject of discussion and negotiation with
other observers to achieve a collective or shared frame. In Goffman's account
there is thus a social process in which initial frames are renegotiated resulting
in an outcome in the form of a durable agreement on an event or issue.

   Goffman wrote before the widespread availability of digital video capture which, combined with **computer mediated communications**, has
multiplied the framing resources available to citizens and social movement
activists alike. Goffman's insight, that framing activity which challenges
dominant interpretations and accounts of events represents an exercise of
power, underlines the continued importance of this approach within social
movement studies.

   The primary focus of frame analysis in the social movement literature
has been the process through which the interpretative schemata of individuals are translated into collective frames through the work of **social
movement organisations** (SMOs). This approach has generated a
number of useful descriptors for processes through which SMOs establish and progress particular issues within prevailing **political opportunity structures** (POS). However the tendency for these descriptors to
become accepted as analytical categories has sometimes limited frame
analysis to addressing the evolution of comparatively durable movement
agendas (frames), represented by the larger social movement organisations. Another assumption underpinning frame analysis within social
movement studies is that all social movement activity is aligned towards

the prevailing political opportunity structure in an attempt to introduce new grievance foci within existing forms of nationally constituted interest representation.

Frame analysis is well represented in social movement theory and has frequently been used to augment **resource mobilisation theory** (RMT) as a means of paying attention to the ideational resources that a movement generates. In this sense it is seen as part of an emerging tool-kit which can be used to interrogate the previously neglected realm of **culture** (Johnston and Klandermans 1995). The additional analytical benefits of frame analysis can be explained through a comparison between RMT's emphasis upon movement intellectuals and the entrepreneurial aspect of movements, and the work of scholars who have utilised a form of frame analysis, derived from Goffman's micro-action sociology (1974), to explain the links between cognitive schemata, movement discourse and mobilisation (Johnston and Klandermans 1995; Klandermans 1997; Snow and Benford 1988).

Within this second approach, movement intellectuals are viewed as important actors in 'frame alignment', the means of constructing a consensus for mobilisation, based upon a particular interpretative framework that legitimises collective action. This, Snow *et al.* (1986) argue, is characterised by four processes, summarised as:

1   frame bridging – 'the linkage of two or more ideologically congruent but structurally unconnected frames regarding a particular issue or problem' (1986: 467);
2   frame amplification – 'the clarification and invigoration of an interpretative frame which bears on a particular issue, problem or set of events' (1986: 469);
3   frame extension – the expansion of a 'movement's primary framework so as to encompass interests or points of view that are incidental to its primary objectives but of considerable salience to potential adherents' (1986: 472);
4   frame transformation – the redefinition of 'activities, events, and biographies that are already meaningful from the standpoint of some primary framework, such that they are now seen by the participants to be quite something else' (1986: 474).

Consequently, the analysis of frame alignment provides theorists with a means for understanding the cognitive work movements and movement intellectuals do, in elaborating symbolic appeals to mobilise sections of a population through reference to a shared cultural heritage or other commonality. In this sense frame alignment 'presupposes a dynamic relationship between the development of a movement and the cultural heritage of both the country in which it operates, and of its institutions' (della Porta and Diani 1999: 75). Frame analysis is therefore a means of interrogating the processes by which a movement accesses cultural resources and attempts to produce interpretations that resonate with a broader constituency. It is in this turn towards culture, indicated by the analysis of frames as well as other arenas of inquiry (for example **collective identity**, discourse and drama-turgy), that the most rich and textured elaborations of social movement theory have been produced and it is in this sense that frame analysis bridges the European and North American approaches. Zald (1996) has noted that, whilst the analysis of frames is a recent innovation in social movement theory and in comparison to RMT the literature is somewhat amorphous, it is, however, rooted in the same intellectual tradition of symbolic interac-tionism and provides a method of understanding how:

> specific metaphors, symbolic representations, and cognitive cues (are) used to render or cast behaviour and events in an evaluative mode and to suggest alternative modes of action.
>
> (1996: 262).

Frame analysis is a means of elaborating the cultural work movements engage in during the mobilisation of resources, cognitive, material and ideological, highlighted by RMT, which in turn is dependent upon and situated within a **political opportunity structure**.

References and resources

Bateson, G. (1973); della Porta, D. and Diani, M. (1999); Goffman, E. (1974); Johnston, H. and Klandermans, B. (eds. 1995); Klandermans, B. (1997); Snow, D., Rochford, B., Worden, S. and Benford, R. (1986); Snow, D. and Benford, R. (1988); Zald, M. (1996).

FREE RIDER PROBLEM

The free rider problem has been central to rational choice theories and revolves around the question of why an individual should choose to act in a potentially contentious situation when others are already taking action consistent with their interests. The classic text addressing this paradox in rational choice theory is that of Olson (1968). Olson attempted to explain why a rational egoistic person would participate in collective action, when they might benefit from such action irrespective of their participation.

Putting to one side the inherently problematic category of the 'rational', a classic formulation of this problem for rational choice theory is the example of union membership. Why would a rational person entering a workplace join a union when wage increases negotiated by the union would be received by all the workers, unionised or not? Olson responds to this paradox by formulating a 'logic of collective action', which argues that actors engage in collective action when there are selective benefits to be gained from such participation. He uses a classic cost benefit analysis to distinguish between collective and selective benefits, and argues that where a collective actor is sufficiently large that a benefit will accrue to those outside its membership regardless of their actions, the rational individual is unlikely to participate. However, selective benefits that are contingent upon participation would explain processes of mobilisation, because they would allow an individual to rationalise collective action in terms of individual gain. In the example of union membership, such benefits might include acceptance by fellow workers, combined with an acknowledgement of the self-interest in the union's maintaining its bargaining position, or because of certain tangible selective benefits such as those now offered by unions, including legal assistance, discounted insurance schemes etc.

Olson's (1968) work is important because it underpinned the assertion by **resource mobilisation theory** that mobilisation was inherently problematic. If mainstream political actors such as trade unions or other interest groups faced such difficulties, how could social movement mobilisations be explained when they had little in the way of selective benefits to offer? The obvious problem with Olson's thesis is its tendency to express human motivation in purely instrumental terms, and it has frequently been criticised on these grounds. However, for resource mobilisation theorists the utility of Olson's work was that it went some way to explaining why people did not take part in collective action. The challenge for advocates of the RMT approach was therefore to explain the conditions under which they would.

References and resources

Moore, W. (1995); Olson, M. (1968).

FRIENDS OF THE EARTH

Friends of the Earth (FoE) is one of the most important **social movement organisations** in the environmental area to originate in the 1960s,

besides **Greenpeace**. Like Greenpeace, FoE consists of national organisations and FoE International (FoEI).

FoE originated in the USA as one of the 'new' environmental organisations of the era. Its origins lay in the Sierra Club, an established conservation movement. FoE was founded by David Brower when he was forced
to resign as executive director of the Sierra Club. The intention was to
replicate the dynamism of the student protest movement within the environmental movement at a time when it was becoming clear that conser-
vationist approaches were not enough (McCormick 1995). FoE America
operated initially from an office in San Fransisco in 1969. FoE spread
quickly to England, France and Sweden.

In London, the arrival of FoE in 1970 saw the use of media to focus
attention on recycling and the establishment of strong campaigning stances
on nuclear energy. FoE was a major objector at the 1977 Windscale Inquiry
into British Nuclear Fuel's proposal to build a plant to reprocess used
nuclear fuel rods from a number of countries including Japan. Following
the decision to give the go-ahead to the reprocessing plant FoE did not
participate in or endorse direct action taken by other sections of the UK
anti-nuclear movement. This predominantly mainstream stance has
dominated national FoE positions, though FoE members have frequently
participated in other forms of action in an individual capacity.

Friends of the Earth International (FoEI) was established in 1971 by the
FoE organisations from the USA, England, France and Sweden. With an
initial focus on nuclear energy and whaling FoEI had a similar issue focus
to Greenpeace International. Unlike Greenpeace, however, FoEI's agenda
moved towards the intersection of development and justice issues and
evolved a less centralised organisational form. FoEI effectively operates as
a centre of affiliation for relatively autonomous national organisations.
Doherty (2006) notes that in 2005 there were 71 member groups totalling
1.5 million supporters. This federal structure with each affiliate having
equal voting rights irrespective of size has contributed to a more pronounced focus on the 'Global South' irrespective of a predominantly
Northern membership.

Based in the Netherlands, FoEI has a modest annual budget of around
2 million Euro. derived from development organisations, such as Oxfam,
and government agencies such as the Dutch Foreign Ministry and the UK
Department for International Development. FoEI explicitly challenges
neoliberal economic orthodoxy and seeks to build alliances with civil
society actors including **indigenous peoples' movements** and farmers'
movements. This has generated significant tensions within FoEI between
North and South which the organisation has attempted to resolve (Doherty
2006).

FoE at national and international levels represents another example of a social movement organisation that has consolidated to become a durable presence. Whilst adopting an openly critical stance on prevailing political orthodoxy it remains firmly aligned with formal institutional channels.

References and resources

Doherty, B. (2006); McCormick, J. (1995).
Friends of the Earth International: www.FoEI.org

GLOBAL CIVIL SOCIETY

Global civil society (GCS) is both an analytical concept and a normative-ideal. It is used rhetorically by a range of political actors for its capacity to invoke solidarity and to mobilise international non-governmental public action, appealing as it does to the idea of a global community built upon potentially universal values and practices, such as equality, civility, rights and justice. It is also deployed analytically to describe forms of non-governmental co-operation and solidarity that stretch across borders and which are directed towards some vision of the 'good society'; in this sense it has a cosmopolitan aspect to it. It is almost uniformly perceived as progressive and democratising, and its composition varies according to the ideological position of its varying advocates.

Mary Kaldor's (2003) explanatory framework provides a useful orientation here. In what she terms the 'activist' definition of GCS, one which is perhaps closest to that used by social movement activists and scholars, it takes on a utopian quality and is manifest in the interstices between markets and states. In the 'neoliberal' version, it is an essential adjunct to the globalising forces of free trade and privatisation, providing goods and services in the absence of a retreating or restructured state.

Finally, in the normative 'ideal-type' Mary Kaldor and John Keane favour, it is a 'dynamic non-governmental system of interconnected socio-economic institutions' that is capable of pluralising power and problematising violence (Keane 2003: 8). It is also importantly in their understanding of the concept, a sphere which incorporates both global social movements and globally active economic actors including the likes of Sony and News International. Critics, however, suggest that the term is problematic as the concept of civil society is only meaningful in the context of a state and given the absence, and undesirability of a global state, the concept itself is flawed.

Global civil society is therefore a highly contested term and one which is deeply connected to the ideas about a good society offered by many social movement activists and to the intellectual frameworks which seek to explain how those movement activists might catalyse and subsequently constitute that which they desire to bring into being. In short, for many social movements, the definition of GCS is an activist one, and it is conceived as those largely non-economic, autonomous spaces of interaction and exchange between non-governmental public actors seeking to promote transnational co-operation around issues of justice and equality. These spaces and the ways in which they are formed, however, are frequently complex and varied. This is illustrated vividly by John Keane who describes how

> The movements of global civil society comprise a cluster of intersecting forms: face to face encounters, spider-web-like networks, pyramid-shaped organisations, hub-and-spoke structures, bridges and organisational chains, charismatic personalities. Action takes place at multiple levels – from the micro-local through to the macro-global – and sometimes movement organisations create vertical alliances for the purposes of communication and synchronisation

> (2003: 60)

In this sense then, with all its open boundaries and organisational complexity GCS is a particularly slippery concept to grasp and a difficult domain to research. However, this elusiveness is perhaps the quality that encourages so many of those commenting on, or describing, it to make such grand claims for its potential. These include Kaldor's suggestion that through its commitment to multilateral forms of humanitarian governance it is an 'answer to war' and Keane's suggestion that it might be conceived as a 'universal ethical ideal' capable of guaranteeing respect for its participants' moral differences through a commitment to the open acceptance of difference (2003: 202–203). This demonstrates once again how those drawn to such a concept frequently have its political potential at the front of both their description and their analysis and why global civil society continues to provide an absorbing point of discussion for social movement studies.

References and resources

Chesters, G. (2004); Kaldor, M. (2003); Keane, J. (2003).

GLOBAL SOCIAL MOVEMENT (TRANSNATIONALISM)

A global social movement is one that involves conscious co-ordination of action and resources at an international level directed toward shared goals including social and political change (Cohen and Rai 2000; della Porta *et al.* 1999). These movements are also commonly referred to in the literature as transnational social movements (Smith *et al.* 1997; Tarrow 1998), although this difference in terminology also represents a conceptual difference between different 'generations' of activism that is explored below. Global social movements are both a response to and an effect of globalisation processes, including the growth of inexpensive and instantaneous communications, new patterns of mobility and cultural exchange and the emergence of global governance bodies and global corporations. McDonald (2006: 3) describes global movements as 'the emergence of new kinds of networks and flows of communication, action, and experience'.

The growth of interest in global social movements partially corresponds to the development of the **alternative globalisation movement** and the rise of intentionally coordinated actions around issues of global trade, the environment, social justice and the architecture of global governance, including the World Trade Organisation, International Monetary Fund, World Bank and the G8. Commentary on this movement (Chesters and Welsh 2006; McDonald 2006) conceives it as qualitatively different from descriptions of earlier transitional activism based upon Non-Governmental Organisations and advocacy groups working towards specific policy objectives at an international level (Keck and Sikkink, 1998; Smith *et al.* 1997). Instead, it is argued that the conscious articulation of highly differentiated, geographically dispersed movements by network actors such as **Peoples' Global Action** and the **World Social Forum** should be understood as suggestive of a new basis of solidarity and action, which is rooted in relationship building, commitments to participatory democratic processes, and the absence of teleological imperatives. Neither standpoint ignores the specific contexts of the actors involved, including local and national factors; differences between political cultures; symbolic codes; protest repertoires and state and security responses. However, there are important distinctions to be made between what Bennet describes as 'first- and second-generation transnational activism', which is characterised as the difference between 'an NGO-led transnational activist order, and the more recent emergence of direct action social justice networks' (2005: 213).

First generation transnational movements build upon the latent trans-nationalism that is evident in the political practice and theorisation of a number of movements that have articulated universal claims, such as the labour movement, the **feminist movement**, the **peace movement** and the human rights movement. In these instances, local or national interven-tions are inevitably tactical struggles within larger global processes of resist-ing capitalist, patriarchal and other degrading forms of oppression that are experienced everywhere (Cohen and Rai 2000: 9–10). In this manifesta-tion of transnationalism the coordination of issue-specific demands (labour laws, environmental protection, human rights) is conducted by NGOs and campaign groups operating at the national or international levels with specific goals and targets.

This is evidence of what Tarrow (2005) and others within the political process school see as 'scale shift', the shift in focus from local to national to international scales determined by the new **political opportunity struc-tures** that are occasioned by the growth of transnational institutional frameworks. However, this perspective has been criticised for overdeter-mining the analytical focus of global movement studies by concentrating attention on those transnational movements that look most like the national ones with which we are familiar (McDonald 2006: 20). The con-cern is that such a concentration might preclude the idea that global movements that are qualitatively different in form, organisation, commu-nication and effect might emerge. In his description of these 'second gen-eration' transnational (global) movements Bennett (2005: 213) argues that they embed 'established NGO-centred networks in sprawling loosely interconnected network webs populated by organisations and individuals who are more resistant to conventional social movement practices of coali-tion formation, brokerage, framing, and establishing straightforward insti-tutional relationships to influence policy'.

From the perspective of movement theorists who seek to reorient anal-ysis towards an approach based in cultural pragmatics and personal experi-ence, such movements are also more likely to be concerned with 'embodied grammars of subjectivity, intersubjectivity and action' (McDonald 2006: 18) as they are with traditional forms of political persua-sion and lobbying.

In summary, Bennett highlights the distinctiveness of second generation transnationalism by describing what he sees are the crucial distinguishing points of second generation (global) movements: 'less NGO dominance of campaign and policy networks; the evolution of multi-issue organizations; more direct individual involvement setting the agenda from below; and the proliferation of permanent campaigns that are not centrally controlled by NGOs or coalitions of organizations' (2005: 213).

References and resources

Bennett, W. L. (2005); Chesters, G. and Welsh, I. (2006); Cohen, R. and Rai, S. (eds. 2000); della Porta, D., Krien, H. and Rucht, D. (eds. 1999); Keck, M. E. and Sikkink, K. (1998); McDonald, K. (2006); Smith, J., Chatfield, C., Pagnucco, R. (eds. 1997); Tarrow, S. (1998, 2005).

GREEN MOVEMENTS

The environment became one of the prominent sites of social movement activity following the emergence of new social movements of the 1960s and 1970s across the industrialised nations. The consolidation of green movements marked a shift in emphasis from a focus on nature conservation and environmentalism to one focussing upon the relationship between human societies and the organic realm. The work of green movements is diverse and includes economics, political and social relations, culture, gender, science and technology as these impact upon both the organic realm (i.e. 'nature') and social systems. The pursuit of progressive social agendas consistent with sustainable ecological practices through a diverse range of political, social and cultural interventions distinguishes Green movements from environmental movements. Doherty (2002) argues that the UK green movement is a social movement on the grounds that there is an emphasis on action outside formal political institutions, use of protest repertoires including direct action, operating as an informal network and challenging dominant forms of power. In what follows we will remain true to this definition by distinguishing between green movements as social movement actors and the more formalised organisational sections of the green movement milieu such as green political parties and large social movement organisations such as **Greenpeace**. This is consistent with our emphasis on social movement as informal networks which we believe have historically typified these forms of social innovation and transformation.

Green movements have formalised a diverse range of critiques and alternatives since the nineteenth century and earlier (Wall 1994) emphasising, in different ways, the insight formalised by Bateson (1973) that the unit of survival is the organism and the environment. Green formulations based in this approach emphasise the centrality of mutualism and co-operation in human–nature and human–human exchanges and reject ideas such as the domination of nature or other people. Not all forms of green movement are based in this sort of approach and it is important not to lose sight of the strong links between blood and soil and right wing political movements from German National Socialism in the 1930s to the eco-nationalisms that emerged following the collapse of the Soviet Union in 1989, for example. Green movements are clearly phenomena with a long history and a diversity of forms that make a unitary definition problematic. Contemporary green movements operate within an increasingly globalised computer mediated context within which co-operative **capacity building** activities take place. In this entry we will outline the emergence of green movements within the North Atlantic Rim countries, focussing on the USA and Europe; contrast this trajectory to green movement formation in Africa and Latin America; consider the intersection of green movements with feminist and network perspectives and conclude by considering the historical and contemporary significance of green movements. The aim here is to provide a sense of the diversity of the historical and contemporary green social movements that does not reproduce the dominant European and North American account.

An antomy of green movements

Green movements became theoretically important as one of the 'new' collective actors to emerge from the constellation of protest movements of the 1960s and 1970s with theoretical implications for approaches towards transformative social actors. The social dynamics underpinning this transition in the USA and Europe illustrate key features of social movement formation. In the USA, the Sierra Nevada club of environmental conservationists recognised that a focus on political campaigning was needed as conservation efforts alone were insufficient. The creation of **Friends of the Earth** in 1971 created an environmental social movement organisation that rapidly established itself in other countries. **Greenpeace** similarly had its origins as an informal group at this time before expanding rapidly to a place of prominence amongst environmental social movement organisations.

Whilst these membership organisations established themselves rapidly within Europe, the role of informal networking in the creation of social movements engaged with the environment was also prominent. In Germany a wide range of citizens' initiatives aimed at improving the quality of life in predominantly urban areas represented the social roots of both the German anti-nuclear mobilisations and Die Grünen – the German Green Party. This was a process widely replicated in France with a greater emphasis on the migration of urban activists to rural areas. Variants of these trajectories also unfolded within the United Kingdom particularly as anti-nuclear activism grew in the 1970s at a time when UK Friends of the Earth decided not to endorse forms of intervention outside the mainstream such as direct action (Welsh 2000).

Green movements marked a shift to a wider range of interventions including the pursuit of media coverage, often utilising direct action, to heighten the profile of 'green' concerns within the public sphere. Significant cleavages shaping the green movement milieu included debates between those advocating alternative trajectories e.g. alternative technology and those emphasising the need for more fundamental changes in consciousness, values, and the economic order. Gender represented a further significant divide with the eco-feminist movement emphasising the centrality of patriarchal political, economic, scientific and military institutions in subordinating and exploiting both the 'natural' and social order. To many commentators, green movements represented the 'most radical and important political and cultural force since the birth of socialism' (Porritt and Winner 1988: 9). Eco-socialism was theorised by a number of commentators with Bahro (1982) and Gortz (1987) being prominent examples.

Throughout the 1980s the consolidaton of neoliberalism in the United Kingdom and USA coincided with the inclusion of prominent environmental issues, particularly climate change, within the global political arena. Following the collapse of Soviet Communism green movements were identified as the most significant ideological challenger to the resultant neoliberal orthodoxy. The UN-sponsored Rio Earth Summit of 1992 endorsed Sustainable Development, Bio-diversity and Rainforest protocols. The Earth Summit also began the process that yielded the Kyoto Protocol on climate change in 2005. The United Nations continues to orchestrate global climate change negotiations and was responsible for the December 2009 meeting in Copenhagen to pursue a successor treaty to Kyoto.

The environmental social movement organisations of the 1970s, like **Greenpeace** and **Friends of the Earth**, became increasingly engaged within formal political and regulatory initiatives at both national and global levels throughout the 1980s and 1990s. As the green agenda began to be mainstreamed a further wave of 'modern' green social movements lacking formal membership structures became prominent. Some of these emergent actors, such as **Earth First**! (EF!) an American movement emphasising direct action, were explicitly green and spread quickly to other industrialised nations (Wall 1999). The clear green focus of EF! was prominent in anti-roads protests but became hybridised to create a diverse direct action milieu. In the United Kingdom **Reclaim The Streets** (RTS) originated within EF! networks but extended its repertoires to include more culturally orientated campaigns. The new wave of movements has been widely theorised in terms of identity, neo-tribalism, culture and reflexive subjects.

This marked a major shift in the tactics and level of engagement of green movements. Tactically and strategically the adoption of **direct action** repetoires reflected alienation from and scepticism about the integrity of formal politics at a national and international level. Whilst green movements had traditionally contested macro-level issues such as global warming and high prestige modernist technologies, such as nuclear power, attention widened to include mundane features of modernity such as road building, shopping malls and airport locations. The integrity of food became a significant green focus in Europe following attempts to introduce genetically modified crops during the 1990s. Locally focussed activist engagements increased contacts with sections of local communities opposed to contested developments re-emphasising work on community activism and cross-class alliances. These processes operate on both sides of the Atlantic and more widely within countries experiencing the impacts of modernisation. In America the fusion of green campaigns with local communities (Lichterman 1996) formalised the notion of environmental and social justice with Bullard (1990) showing that toxic waste disposal sites in the USA were located adjacent to communities composed of 'people of colour'.

Green movements and modernisation

The 1980s and 1990s diversification of green movements within the developed world coincided with the rise of environmentally engaged **indigenous peoples** and workers movements responding to modernisation agendas pursued under the auspices of the International Monetary Fund (IMF) and World Bank (WB).

Here, rainforest clearance, high impact infrastructure developments, genetically modified seed programmes, the assertion of Trade Related Intellectual Property rights (TRIPs) and the consolidation of free trade zones, notably the North American Free Trade Area (NAFTA) were prominent. As the industrialised and industrialising economies of the world made increasing demands on a wide range of natural resources the populations of the originating countries were simultaneously confronted by economic, social and environmental changes. In effect wage relations, environmental engagement and the process of class formation occurred in parallel. In each country these forces played out in different ways shaped by the specific prevailing circumstances and social forces. Within this process some cases have been well documented.

In Latin America the late Chico Mendes, a Brazilian rubber tapper, simultaneously campaigned for trade union recognition and rainforest protection as rainforest clearance gathered momentum. His writings make clear that support from Northern green movements played a crucial role in consolidating indigenous campaigning activities. In the Niger Delta, Ken Saro Wiwa campaigned to allow indigenous people to secure the protection of their environment from the profits of Shell's operations. Throughout India sustained opposition to the introduction of genetically modified crops persisted prior to the emergence of similar concerns in Europe. The green movements in these countries are best known through the names of key activists but reflect a generic shift in green movement formation which also takes place in the context of a consolidating **global civil society**. In Mexico the **Zapatistas'** resistance to the impact of the North American Free Trade Area, led directly to an engagement with a range of movement actors from around the world. Green movements understood in this way are simultaneously local and global actors (Notes from Nowhere 2003).

Networks of networks and green movements

The intensification of resource exploitation and production in countries of the 'South' has contributed to the emergence of a diverse range of green social movement actors. In many cases 'modernisation' has impacted most intensely upon women and children, leading to feminist and eco-feminist movements (Mies and Shiva 1993). The recognition that environmental degradation and poverty are inextricably linked was one of the reasons behind the massive mobilisations to win an explicit G20 commitment to abolish poverty. The network of networks constituting contemporary green movements can be seen to exert social force through such means. Theoretically, the increasingly networked nature of green movements elevated debates on the importance of civil society and particularly the emergence of a **global civil society** to a position of prominence with Castells (1996) arguing that neoliberalism ascendancy unifies the movement mileu around a common opponent.

Whilst it is clear that green movements have been a particularly potent social movement over the closing decades of the twentieth century there is little agreement about how to evaluate their role or their future significance. These debates have been formalised in a number of ways which can be summarised as three main positions. Following the collapse of the bipolar world order and the 'success' of the 1992 Rio Earth Summit, commentators such as Maten Haajer argued that the green agenda had achieved ascendancy marking a transition to Ecological Modernisation. The greening of the global world order through the success of 'green knowledge' is a position also shared by Andrew Jamison (2001).

Rather than ascendancy Claus Eder argues that there has been a top-down global capture of the green movement which has stripped out the progressive social elements. A key element of this capture arises from the subordination of the Rio measures to the development models of the World Trade Organisation (WTO), World Bank (WB) and International Monetary Fund (IMF). The prominence of global negotiations on climate change has intensified this process with Blühdorn and Welsh (2007) arguing that this denotes the arrival of an era of 'post-ecologist politics'. Giddens's (2009) rejection of green movement approaches such as the precautionary principle and advocacy of nuclear power in responding to climate change is symptomatic of this turn. As much of the agenda forged by green movements is mainstreamed it would appear that the combination of social and environmental justice will remain important as a radical leading edge that combines with the historical emphasis on local initiatives. This will differentiate green movement stances from the predominantly economic focus of political initiatives aimed at establishing a price for CO_2 releases to create a market in offsetting (Welsh 2010). The UN conference at Copenhagen in 2009 did not produce a successor to the Kyoto treaty. Amidst significant divides between: Island States; the developing economies, particularly China, India and Brazil; and the developed economies, particularly the USA, the conference produced an accord. The accord established the aim of limiting global temperature increases to 2 degrees Celsius but contained no binding emissions reduction targets, action programmes or binding commitments on financing. Significant amounts of money were committed to assist developing countries but much was left to future negotiations (Clémençon 2010).

Following Copenhagen the commitment to tackle climate change was questioned in Australia and America as domestic political agendas reasserted themselves. In the United Kingdom the release of climate change scientists' e-mails from the University of East Anglia became dubbed 'Climategate' and was followed by an apparent reduction in public confidence in the importance of anthropogenic climate change. In the light of these events it is clear that climate change will occupy a prominent place within green movements agendas for some time to come. As we have argued elsewhere, the creation of planetary action systems will be a process of conflict and co-operation within which green movements will continue to be key actors (Chesters and Welsh 2006).

References and resources

Bahro, R. (1982); Bateson, G. (1973); Blühdorn, I. and Welsh, I. (2007); Bullard, R. D. (1990); Castells, M. (1996); Clémençon, R. (2010); Doherty, B. (2002); Giddens, A. (2009); Gorz, A. (1987); Jamison, A. (2001); Lichterman, P. (1996); Mies, M. and Shiva, V. (1993); Notes from Nowhere (eds. 2003); Porritt, J. and Winner, D. (1988); Wall, D. (1994, 1999); Welsh, I. (2000, 2010).

GREENHAM WOMEN

In 1981 a group of women marched from Wales to the US Air Force cruise missile base at Greenham Common to establish a peace camp. Greenham Women or Greenham Wimmin was rapidly adopted as the collective term for those involved in the Greenham Common Women's Peace Movement which was a diverse and constantly changing group of women. The idea to march to the base was inspired by a Nordic women's march from Denmark to Paris in 1980. Reading of this march in *Peace News* Ann Pettit announced her intention to march from Cardiff to Greenham and issued an open invitation for others to join her (Pettit 1983). The initiating march included a few men and the initial camp was at first maintained with a male presence until a second march from London was held. The decision to make Greenham a women-only peace camp reflected women's experience of the sexism within other campaigns and a feminist analysis linking patriarchy, militarism, violence and war. Whilst this is a UK example, broadly similar initiatives occurred in other countries around this time. These included Women for Peace in the then West Germany, Women's Pentagon Action in the USA and the Shibakusa in Japan.

Greenham Women exemplify a number of features of social movement mobilisation that have become increasingly prominent. Whilst the term Greenham Women suggests a collective identity there were in practice several different camps at each of the gates into the air field. Participation in a particular camp reflected a personal alignment with the particular interpretation of feminist politics and praxis embodied at that site. Greenham was actively networked within the United Kingdom and beyond through the stance taken against militarism and this contributed directly to its longevity as very few women maintained a constant presence at their camp. Greenham had a fluid composition and enabled a diverse range of women to participate either within one of the camps or through one of the organised mass events. These events included 'Embrace the Base' weekends involving thousands of women who encircled the base with linked arms. Greenham made it possible for women to participate despite the normal constraints of a working life and other commitments. The solidarity and consciousness-raising within this network consolidated a distinct feminist agency that spread to other significant sites in 1980s' Britain including the coal communities involved in the miners' strike.

The mainstream media coverage of Greenham Women created a national profile that persisted throughout the hot-cold war until US cruise missiles were removed from British soil in 1991. Whilst tabloid papers parodied and stereotyped the feminist politics their direct actions created some classic iconic imagery. A picture of women danc-ing on the roof of a blast-hardened cruise missile bunker is amongst the better-known examples. Legal attempts to have the camps removed were unsuccessful and the combination of publicity and support for the camp made it a constant reminder of opposition to the stationing of US nuclear weapons in the United Kingdom. When activists attempted to start a second camp at Upper Heyford decisive force was used immediately to pre-empt another established presence develop-ing. Greenham Common Peace Camp was formally ended in 2000 to make way for a permanent memorial display and site. Trident Ploughshares (see **peace movement**) and a range of feminist initia-tives continued after Greenham which underlined the significance of establishing a long-standing presence for network extension and net-work mobilisations.

References and resources

Harford, B. and Hopkins, S. (eds. 1984); Junor, B. (1995); Kirk, G. (1989); Pettit, A. (1983); Roseneil, S. (1995).
Greenham Women web resources: http://www.greenhamwpc.org.uk/

GREENPEACE

Greenpeace originated in Vancouver in 1971 when a small number of activists took direct action to highlight the risks of the atmospheric testing of atomic weapons by sailing into a test zone. From the start Greenpeace was intended to bridge the environmental and peace movements through the principles of ecology. From these origins Greenpeace developed through the founding of national Greenpeace organisations in the USA and the United Kingdom to its current status. There are now 40 national Greenpeace organisations affiliated to Greenpeace International which is one of the biggest and most important **social movement organisations** (SMOs) in the environmental area (Brown and May 1991).

In 2007 Greenpeace International declared a total income of 49.9 mil-lion Euros, an increase of 17 per cent compared to 2006. National Greenpeace operations generate the majority of the income for Greenpeace International, with the level of contributions being reflected in member-ship of the Board of Directors. (see www.greenpeace.org/international/about). The dominance of the Board of Directors by members from the wealthier nations, such as the Netherlands, Germany, the United Kingdom, USA and Australia, results in an under-representation of members from the Global South. Whilst establishing national organisations in regions such as East and Central Europe (Tickle and Welsh 1998), China and the Pacific Greenpeace has been seen as imposing a 'Western' model of organisation honed in countries such as the USA and the United Kingdom. This underlines the challenge that global social movement dynamics can pose for large SMOs (Rootes 2005).

Whilst Greenpeace is widely known for high profile direct action interventions these are only one part of its activities. As an SMO, Greenpeace engages in a wide range of professional practices. Greenpeace International paid 548,000 Eur. in salaries and 44,000 Eur. in pensions in 2007 to support its activities. These include: lobbying governments, private corporations and global institutions; independent scientific work; commercial collaborations in areas like renewable energy and active market research work. By combining these activities Greenpeace establishes its environmental campaigning agenda at the executive level involving its membership through publicity and fundraising activities. High profile direct actions are the preserve of a cadre of highly trained and well equipped specialists.

Direct action campaigns are informed by careful market research techniques, including focus group work, which give Greenpeace insights into factors such as the campaigning areas and types of images likely to attract public support and media attention. Significant campaigns have included those against seal culling, whaling, sea disposal of nuclear waste, the sea dumping of oil industry installations and genetically modified crops. There is some variation in campaigning emphasis within national Greenpeace operations. Greenpeace UK, for example, have historically prioritised nuclear power particularly sea pollution from Sellafield (aka Windscale), the sea dumping of nuclear waste and genetically modified crops. The capacity of national Greenpeace organisations is mediated by the potential for network partnerships and coalitions. In the United Kingdom instance the involvement of unions was a significant component in ending the sea dumping of nuclear waste. The 'Western' style of campaigning utilising dramatic forms of direct action aimed at high profile media exposure is more difficult to deploy in countries such as China where the public sphere is less well established.

Greenpeace pursued direct action against nuclear weapons testing until the UN adoption of the Comprehensive Nuclear Test Ban Treaty in 1996. In 1985 this led to the sinking of the Greenpeace ship *Rainbow Warrior* by French secret service personnel (DGSE) in New Zealand. Currently Greenpeace International's priorities are directed towards marine operations and climate change with peace and disarmament representing a relatively small part of expenditure in 2007 (Greenpeace International 2009).

Since its inception Greenpeace has pursued effective media strategies as part of a commitment to making its acts of 'bearing witness' public. In cases like the Brent Spar oil platform where the action took place in the middle of the North Sea this gave Greenpeace significant control over the images available to broadcast media outlets. The Brent Spar event occurred in the midst of some of the best-resourced national Greenpeace affiliates and reflected the enhanced capacity the organisation has in the 'North'.

The establishment of national Greenpeace affiliates in the South remains relatively modest. Nations such as Australia, New Zealand, Brazil and Chile have been joined by Papua New Guinea, Solomon Islands, Indonesia and the Philippines. Rising sea levels associated with climate change and Greenpeace's prominence in this area seem likely to see an expansion in the region.

Greenpeace stands as one of the clearest examples of a social movement achieving institutional permanence, influence and impact as a social movement organisation. The relationship between Greenpeace and the emergent 1980s and 1990s movements of the industrialised nations and social justice movements of the South will continue to be dynamic. Whilst it remains to be seen whether the environment will become a site for global activism (see **green movements**) Greenpeace's commitment to climate change and ability to combine scientific work with high profile direct action and targeted campaigning and lobbying suggest it will retain its prominence. In 2009 the first African Director of Greenpeace was appointed and declared his commitment to broadening the elite direct action model to enable mass participation.

References and resources

Brown, M. and May, J. (1991); Greenpeace International (2009); Rootes, C. (2005).

HEALTH SOCIAL MOVEMENTS

Increasing attention to the relationship between human health, economic growth, technological progress, environmental pollution and risk has been accompanied by an increase in the number of citizens in the North and South campaigning on health issues. Brown and Zavestoski (2004: 679) define Health Social Movements (HSM) as 'collective challenges to medical policy, public health policy and politics, belief systems, research and practice which include an array of formal and informal organisations, supporters, networks of cooperation and media'. HSMs are thus combinations of dedicated organisations with specialised knowledge, resources and staff and less formal coalitions of citizens. Whilst many of these organisations and coalitions form around specific medical conditions or issues the focus on HSMs suggests that there are generic issues sufficient to define a field of social movement activity.

Three main axes shape this field and together are regarded as constituting a challenge to political power, professional authority and established approaches to personal and **collective identity**. The first involves issues of access to established health care services and the overall structure of provision. The second relates to the experience of disease and illness, disability and disputed medical conditions such as chronic fatigue syndrome. The third relates to issues of health equality and inequality structured through 'race', ethnicity, gender, class and/or sexuality. Within the sociology of health and illness the three related ideal types of HSMs are *health access movements* (see **Claimant Movement**); *embodied health movements* and *constituency-based health movements* relating broadly to the three axes defining the field (Brown *et al.* 2004).

Politically, HSMs formalise demands for access to resources, such as retroviral drugs to combat HIV, which have implications for big pharmaceutical companies, governments, medical and scientific professionals. Whilst health and safety at work, housing and sanitary reform were key class-based health issues associated with modernity and industrialisation, HSMs extend these important areas to wider domains. The mapping of the human genome and subsequent developments in genetic diagnostic, therapeutic, surveillance and enhancement techniques represent an emergent area where HSMs and broader social movement actors are increasingly engaged (Welsh *et al.* 2007).

The growth of an increasingly diverse range of HSMs can be seen as the emergence of an increasingly systemic engagement with the UN World Health Organisation definition of health as a sense of physical, emotional and psychological well-being. Heightened awareness of environmental impacts reinforces the link between personal and planetary well-being.

References and resources

Brown, P. and Zavestoski, S. (2004); Brown, P., Zavestoski, S., McCormaick, S., Mayer, B., Morello-Frosch, R. and Gaisor, R. (2004); Welsh, I., (2007); Welsh, I., Evans, R. and Plows, A. (2007).

IDENTITY POLITICS

The question of identity is a crucial one for social movement studies. Movements are often described through reference to what is perceived to be the primary and defining characteristic of their participants' identity – including the women's movement, the gay and lesbian movement, the youth movement, the students' movement, the disabled movement, the trade union movement, the civil rights movement, the indigenous movement and so on. In this way movements are conceptualised as the outcome of work by people mobilised around a shared and specific characteristic such as gender, ethnicity, class, sexuality, disability, age, historical location or profession. This characteristic is presumed to be the source of either a grievance with, or a claim against, the political system, which is then vocalised by 'minorities', defined as such because they are repressed, stigmatised or devalued by the structure of domination in a given society. It is worth noting that a 'minority' in this sense might be qualitative rather than quantitative, for example women might constitute over half the population yet remain a 'minority' because of systemic (structural, political and cultural) barriers to power and political representation. In many ways, it was the rise of such movements in the late 1960s that effectively launched the modern sub-disciplinary domain of new social movement studies as a theoretical and empirical endeavour (see Darnovsky *et al.* 1995: section III).

The term 'identity politics' is also used to describe the actions of social actors for whom the distinction between political engagement and identity has been attenuated to the extent that the prioritised identity stakes become the political. This inevitably brings with it the criticism that the privileging of a specific identity invokes an essentialism that is neither ontologically nor empirically justifiable given the complexity of theorising particularistic identities (Appiah 1992; Butler 1990; Haraway 1989; hooks 1981). The social movement theorist Alberto Melucci (1996: 187–188) suggests that this occurs partially because political institutions require a reduction of the multi-dimensionality of the issue at stake. Consequently, what might begin as a complex problem of land rights, environmental protection, access to food or shelter quickly becomes an 'indigenous' issue when translated into political discourse. In this context, differing marginalised and oppressed groups are forced to compete with each other for political mediation and representation by seeking the extension of mechanisms for their integration within institutional politics, in order that their claims can be heard. This degree of competition can undermine attempts at wider movement building and undermine the tactical use of scarce resources across movements. However, it is also worth noting that these identities are seldom constrained by traditional political frameworks and they often find other means of expression through social or cultural activities (Stephens 1998). These forms of action can also be coexistent with and constitutive of social movements.

The important point here is that there is a distinction to be made between the use of a particular characteristic of identity as the basis around which to mobilise, and the work a movement does in constructing a **collective identity**, which involves the ongoing negotiation of being together, the aims, tactics and strategy behind the collective action undertaken etc. This, Melucci (1996: 187–188) argues, is why the concept of collective identity should be separated for analytical purposes from the idea of identity politics, meaning that identity politics can be an integral aspect of the social practice of a movement, without the movement being reducible to it.

Theoretically, then, Melucci (1996) illustrates how 'identity politics' are a form of political practice within social movements that may invest and disturb a variety of different political and social systems, sometimes paradoxically through the development of a mutable or tactical concept of identity. Such practices might cause legislative changes, facilitate cultural experimentation and result in a host of differing outcomes for their participants. However, despite the centrality of such forms of expression to social movement activity, ultimately social movement networks are irreducible to identity politics.

References and resources

Appiah, K. A. (1992); Butler, J. (1990); Darnovsky, M., Epstein, B. L. and Flacks, R. (1995); Haraway, D. (1989); hooks, b. (1981); Melucci, A. (1996); Stephens, J. (1998).

INDIGENOUS PEOPLES' MOVEMENTS

An indigenous peoples' movement promotes and protects the rights and interests of an indigenous population or people. This can take place in the face of the contemporary modernisation process, such as the rights of rainforest tribes in the face of deforestation, for example, or in the light of past appropriations. The place of American Indian peoples is a clear example of this type. Indigenous peoples movements typically assert the right to autonomy and control over resources, established culture and customs and an active role in shaping engagement with agents of modernisation. The contemporary use of the term arises from the increasing contact with indigenous peoples since the 1970s as rainforest exploration and exploitation intensified. Africa and Amazonia are prominent areas. This period is also marked by a re-engagement with the position of indigenous peoples during earlier periods of colonisation and development. Australian Aboriginals, New Zealand Maoris and Native Americans are prominent examples here.

In the 1970s Native Americans established an International Indian Treaty Council (IITC) to consolidate the position of indigenous peoples within the United Nations. Together with the World Council of Indigenous Peoples (WCIP) the IITC became the first indigenous non-governmental organisation (NGO) to gain UN recognition. The UN Working Group on Indigenous Populations (WGIP) continues to be at the forefront of formal incorporation and representation within the UN processes (Feldman 2000).

As deforestation became accompanied by the search for plant species of potential use to bio-technology companies during the late 1980s and 1990s the pursuit of rights for indigenous peoples intensified (Purdue 2000, Varese 1996). Bio-prospecting by pharmaceutical companies combined with developments in human genomics intensified UN activity leading to the establishment of the UN Universal Declaration on the Human Genome and Human Rights. This was accompanied by calls for deeper inclusion of NGOs and social movements (Rothman 2000) and the relationship between genomics and indigenous peoples has been a feature of the **World Social Forum** movement (Welsh et al. 2007).

Indigenous peoples movements raise some profoundly difficult methodological issues (Smith 1999) including questions of autonomy and the right to avoid inclusion within the modernisation process. The exercise of autonomy led the Goshute tribe of Utah to accept the deep disposal of radioactive waste under their homelands in return for significant payment to secure the needs of their community. The Goshute's decision to exercise their land rights in this way conflicted with the policy of the local authorities and underlines the complexity associated with acts of autonomy like this.

Indigenous peoples movements will continue to grow in prominence within social movement studies as the process of modernisation continues to meet the challenges associated with economic growth. The pursuit of a carbon-free economy and green transport options, for example, have resulted in the creation of a market in lithium batteries. The largest reserves of lithium lie in salt flats in the mountains of Bolivia and the interests of the local population currently lie in the midst of negotiations between the Bolivian government and multinational companies. Climate change is also raising issues of indigenous peoples' rights particularly in the Pacific where many small island states are threatened by rising sea levels. The search for host recipient states in the advent of inundation is one response. This raises issues of the contribution of major CO_2 emitter states to displaced population re-settlement agreements (Welsh 2010).

References and resources

Cohen, R. and Rai, S. (eds. 2000); Feldman, A. (2002); Purdue, D. A. (2000); Rothman, H. (2000); Smith, L. T. (1999); Varese, S. (1996); Welsh, I. (2010); Welsh, I., Evans, J. and Plows, A. (2007).
Survival International *The movement for tribal people*: http://www.survivalinternational. org/info

INDYMEDIA

The collective title for a web-mounted independent open publishing project that aims to be participatory, interactive and dialogical. Indymedia was initiated within the **global social movement** milieu, achieving prominence through the Independent Media Centre (IMC) that was founded and operated successfully during protests against the World Trade Organisation (WTO) meetings in Seattle in 1999. In this context, alternative media (Atton 2001) activists came together and combined their expertise in audio, video and print production with the capacities of new internet communication and distribution platforms to produce a web resource – Indymedia.org. This website managed to log one and half million hits in the week of the WTO protests – more than established news outlets such as the CNN website, whilst the IMC also produced daily video reports that were made available for satellite broadcast (Notes from Nowhere 2003: 238). Indymedia.org has subsequently become a portal site for a decentralised and autonomous network involving in excess of one hundred other Indymedia sites on every continent, making it the largest open publishing project for social movements in the world. One commentator described its rise to prominence as follows:

> Indymedia has become the fastest growing, international, alternative media network in the world, mushrooming into dozens of physical and virtual sites that span six continents and work in a globally collaborative spirit which is a model to all.
>
> (Nogueira 2002: 294)

Indymedia is 'open' in a number of key ways including its source code, contributions, management processes, access and usage. An 'open' posting policy – subject to evolving ethical and political criteria – attenuates the producer/consumer dichotomy associated with mainstream media product. It therefore represents one of the first and most advanced examples of many-to-many media, as opposed to the traditional one-to-many model employed by most corporate media. Indymedia plays important roles as an information source for mainstream media; a means of movement network communication; debate and agenda formation and has been increasingly targeted by state security services.

Indymedia is also important as one of the first collaborative and co-operative manifestations of what is referred to as Web 2.0, exemplified by social networking sites, wiki-based collaborations (wikipedia) and blogging. Although the proliferation of these platforms has subsequently reduced the recognition of Indymedia as a prominent example of a platform for user-generated content, it continues to be a novel instantiation of the political potentials of Web 2.0 having been developed through the application of free software. This distinguishes it from the proprietary systems built and owned by corporations that form the basis of many Web 2.0 platforms.

References and resources

Atton, C. (2001); Nogueira, A. (2002); Notes from Nowhere (eds. 2003); Pickerill, J. (2003, 2006).

KNOWLEDGE-PRACTICES

The term 'knowledge-practice' and the closely allied concept cognitive-practice (Eyerman and Jamison 1991) reflect theorisations of social movements as knowledge producers, rather than merely as objects of knowledge for social movement scholars. The use of the compound term 'knowledge-practice' (Casas-Cortés *et al.* 2008) is used to indicate where activism is understood as productive of critical subjectivities whose situated and contextual knowledge is prioritised in its own right.

Social movements have long been bearers of knowledge about forms of oppression and injustice, expressing political claims, identifying social and economic grievances and bringing new or neglected issues to public prominence. They have been in the forefront of debates about how social divisions including gender, race, sexuality, age and religion structure society and reproduce power structures including prevailing norms and values. They have also been prominent in highlighting the social and environmental implications of the application of new sciences and technologies from manufacturing processes to nuclear fission, genetically modified organisms to cloning and nanotechnology. Social movements produce knowledge that is often challenging to those in power or which might be difficult for a society to confront – levels of sexual abuse, the treatment of the mentally ill, the stigmatisation of those with HIV/AIDS etc. However, rarely are social movements explicitly recognised as producers of knowledge, despite their influence in shaping various academic disciplines including womens' studies, peace studies, adult and popular education, black and post-colonial studies, queer studies etc. These disciplines have been richly innovative in both their approaches to, and work with, movements, and yet for the most part social movements are still considered as objects of knowledge for researchers and academics, rather than as knowledge producers in their own right.

This began to change during the last decade of the twentieth and the first decade of the twenty-first century, during a wave of social movement mobilisation focussed on resistance to the globalisation of neoliberal capitalism and the promotion of 'social justice'. It can be argued that these movements were prescient in identifying issues that would subsequently move to the centre of mainstream political debate and were amongst the first to offer a cogent critique of the inequity and structural limitations of the global financial system that had been emerging from the late 1980s. It has also been argued that the reflexive practices of social movement activism during this period, from the Zapatista-inspired (see **Zapatismo**) encuentros (encounters), to the dialogical and deliberative spaces of the **World Social Forum** also represented a qualitative shift in the methodology of **global social movements**, which emphasised meaning making and knowledge production as key activities (Cox and Fominaya 2009).

This wave of mobilisation produced a generation of activist-researchers who sought to challenge the epistemological premises of orthodox social movement studies. This included theoretically and methodologically operationalising long-established critiques of positivist and Cartesian epistemologies (natural science influenced theories of knowledge based upon rational observation), by blurring the boundaries between the subject and object of knowledge and pursuing practices of co-producing knowledge with, rather than on, movements (Casas-Cortés *et al.* 2008; Conway 2004; Cox and Faminaya 2009). This milieu also includes some interesting work on the specificities of local and indigenous knowledges and their implications for understanding the 'global' (Escobar 1998, 2009), as well as a variety of attempts to develop 'knowledge-practices' (Casas-Cortés *et al.* 2008) that bridge academic and movement domains (Graeber and Shukaitis 2007; Notes from Nowhere 2003, Sen *et al.* (2004)).

References and resources

Casas-Cortés, M., Osterweil, M. and Powell, D. E. (2008); Conway, J. (2004); Cox, L. and Fominaya, C. F. (2009); Escobar, A. (1998, 2009); Eyerman, R. and Jamison, A. (1991); Graeber, D. and Shukaitis, S. (eds. 2007); Notes from Nowhere (eds. 2003); Sen, J., Anand, A., Escobar, E. and Waterman, P. (eds. 2004).

LATENCY PERIOD

Taken literally this is a period of time in which observable social movement activity by established actors declines and loses prominence within the public sphere and becomes latent. Alberto Melucci's discussion of visibility and latency (Melucci 1989: Chp. 3) developed themes which are increasingly important given the development of network society arguments. Melucci differentiates between the political significance of social movements which tend to be assessed through the study of visible interventions and the social and cultural significance of movements that are latent activities. The latent portion of movement activity takes place at the 'molecular' level of day to day social relations and is central in constituting collective identities capable of resistance and conflict. For Melucci 'the latency of a movement is its effective strength' (1989: 71). The notion of latency has important methodological implications for the study of social movements. Approaches based on the observation of visible, for example, mainstream media accounts do not engage with the latent activities of the movement milieu. Consideration of the latent work of movements requires qualitative engagement and longitudinal approaches.

Whilst latent work is a continual process, a latency period denotes a time when the dynamics of contention in a society or social formation are changing in ways that make established movement frames (see **frame analysis** and **repertoire of action** inadequate or inappropriate. Established forms of visible intervention disappear from prominence. At such times the movement milieu is confronted by new challenges and engages in an internal dialogue between established and emergent movement actors. Examples of latency periods in Europe include that confronted by anti-nuclear and environmental campaigners as a resurgent CND opposed the deployment of new US nuclear weapons in Europe at the end of the 1970s.

This particular transition was one facet of the systemic challenge posed by the ascendancy of neoliberalism embodied in the political administrations of

Margaret Thatcher in the United Kingdom and Ronald Regan in the USA. In countries with established welfare states, associated with commitments to full employment and collective provision to meet social needs through State-run agencies, neoliberalism represented a particularly acute and systemic challenge to all forms of social movement 'old' and 'new'. The common challenge of neoliberalism was experienced within movement milieu in both the Northern and Southern hemispheres heralding the start of a latency period lasting several years.

In this latency period the work of (re)defining the collective stakes for society associated with the neoliberal project occurred within the movement milieu. To Melucci latency periods are part of the process through which movements 'join past and future' by reconfiguring the demands and concerns of past movements and situating them in the present. This is a process of negotiation and conflict through which individuals and groups construct, adjust and express the multiple forces that constitute a contemporary field of collective action through reflection upon and engagement with the past (Melucci 1996a: 351–355). Advances in **computer mediated communications** increased the connectivity between a diverse range of movement actors that identified neoliberalism as a 'common enemy' (Castells 1997) and consolidated into the anti or **alternative globalisation movement** (Chesters and Welsh 2006; Tormey 2004) during this period.

Latency periods are a necessary part of the process through which social movements act as agents of social innovation in Touraine's terms. The increasing use of a diverse range of direct action tactics throughout the 1980s and 1990s was a prominent feature of this process. In Northern countries these included direct action in defence of the environment by groups such as **Earth First!,** resistance to road building programmes and cultural actions to reclaim the right to carnival (McKay 1996). In Southern countries direct action surfaced in the rejection of GM crops in India and elsewhere.

The crisis of accumulation arising from neoliberal deregulation and profit maximisation in 2007–2008 is likely to mark the onset of another latency period as past and future are renegotiated in the context of the debt mountains with implications that will play out for some decades to come.

References and resources

Castells, M. (1997); Chesters, G. and Welsh, I. (2006); McKay, G. (1996); Melucci, A. (1989, 1996, 1996a); Tormey, S. (2004).

LEADERSHIP

The role of leadership in new social movements has received surprisingly little attention in the academic literature (Barker *et al.* 2001), although it remains a central issue for debate amongst social movement activists. In social movement studies attention to theories of leadership has been problematised by the theoretical concentration on movement irrationalism in **collective behaviour** approaches, the bias towards structuralist explanations within **resource mobilisation theory (RMT)** and **political opportunity structure** approaches, and the narrative of spontaneity that persists in some accounts of the new social movements. Taken together with the desire of many social movement scholars to escape the 'great man' theories of historical development and their reluctance to give credence to conservative arguments about militant agitators whipping up otherwise peaceful citizens, this has meant that leadership has remained a minority interest despite being a crucial element of building and sustaining movements.

Social movement mobilisations are a result of the sustained work of capacity building amongst social movement organisations that occurs in the 'subterranean networks' (Melucci 1989) beneath the view of most academic and media commentary. A key part of this 'hidden' work is that carried out by those individuals or organisations that undertake leadership roles: promoting interaction; catalysing meetings and events; building networks; producing literature and commentaries etc. Within the RMT literature this work has been characterised as conducted by 'movement professionals' or movement 'entrepreneurs' (McCarthy and Zald 1987). These are terms that reflect the influences of economic theory in RMT where movements are sometimes discussed as phenomena that are comparable or congruent with the economic or business sector. However, they also indicate the role such individuals play in securing and manipulating cognitive, symbolic or material resources. The centrality of such individuals to movement outcomes is also widely acknowledged in the social-psychological literature on social movements, where typologies of 'movement intellectuals' have been developed (Eyerman and Jamison 1991) that emphasise the role of intellectual leadership and **knowledge-practices**. Often the role of these individuals is akin to the Gramscian notion of the 'organic intellectual' – someone closely associated with their community and its struggles, Foucault's 'specific intellectual' – someone who is concerned with how 'truth' can support power, or what Crook *et al.* (1992: 153) have called 'exemplary figures' – those whose militancy and activism makes them a beacon for social struggle. Unfortunately, as

Klandermans has pointed out 'systematic studies of the way in which movement leaders function are scarce' (1997: 333).

In the absence of empirical research on contemporary social movement leadership, Barker *et al.*'s edited collection on leadership and social movements (2001) is a useful resource for conceptual tools to study the *specificity* of the leadership of social movements. These include understanding leadership as a dialogical relationship, a discussion of the personal and structural resources of leadership, a focus upon the relationship between leadership and followership skills, the structural contexts of leadership, inclusive and exclusivist leadership forms, the authoritative and the authoritarian, and the possibility of 'democratic leadership'.

The role of leadership continues to be a contested and vital topic for social movements themselves, with a renewed impetus due to the decline of traditional movement organisations with clearly differentiated leadership roles – shop steward, treasurer etc. and the rise of **identity politics** and **network movements**. Much of this debate concerns the efficacy of informal structures or processes that aim to be democratic and transparent but which might be open to informal hierarchies and subtle manipulation. The most often cited and foundational source for this debate is Jo Freeman's (1973) essay on the 'Tyranny of Structurelessness' derived from her experience within the women's liberation movement. Freeman's argument, which concerns the role of informality in structuring interactions and disguising the operation of power within movements, has received renewed attention because of the popularity of informal and 'horizontal' organising amongst **global social movements**.

References and resources

Barker, C., Johnson, A. and Lavalette, M. (2001); Crook, S., Pakulski, J. and Waters, M. (1992); Eyerman, R. and Jamison, A. (1991); Freeman, J. (1973); Klandermans, B. (1997); McCarthy, J. D. and Zald, M. N. (1987); Melucci, A. (1989).

LESBIAN, GAY, BISEXUAL AND TRANSGENDER (LGBT) MOVEMENTS

Social movements campaigning for the social acceptance of gender and sexual minorities are commonly identified by the acronym LGBT. These movements are often classified as part of the wave of collective action associated with the **new social movements** of the 1960s and 1970s, which privileged particular identities that were considered marginal and oppressed (see also **Black Power Movement**). However there are many antecedents for these movements including historical examples of groups organising to campaign for social and legal reform around LGBT issues that are less well known outside the LGBT community (Miller 2006). They are also closely associated with the concept of **identity politics**. The focus of LGBT movements is varied and ranges from militant assertions of difference and arguments for separation through to queer activism which suggests the need to destabilise overdetermined concepts of sexuality or gender that might otherwise reinforce heternormativity. However, many LGBT movements have been centrally concerned with the promotion of equalities and rights issues and they have used a range of collective action repertoires to achieve these aims in different contexts, although it should be remembered that in many parts of the world LGBT groups still face severe sanctions and are continuously under threat from either the state, religious groups or others.

Although there are many examples of individuals and groups campaigning for LGBT rights before the late 1960s, a founding moment for the emergent Gay Liberation movement was the Stonewall riots of 1969, when a group of LGBT patrons of a New York bar forcibly resisted a police raid (Duberman 1993). This event is commemorated in carnivalesque street parades known as Gay Pride marches that take place annually in a number of cities globally and which act as both a celebration of LGBT culture and people whilst also drawing attention to contemporary issues, or grievances affecting LGBT communities. The UK LGBT rights organisation Stonewall (http://www.stonewall.org.uk/) also took its name from the Stonewall Inn. The emergence of a new collective radicalism and the appropriation of the term gay to describe non-normative sexualities followed the Stonewall riots and is exemplified by the Gay Liberation Front (Power 1995) which published the Gay Manifesto. Gay Liberation was a prominent part of the late 1960s and early 1970s **counterculture**, and Gay Lib groups also campaigned around issues such as militarism, sexism and racism and used a range of tactics including **direct action** in their attempts to promote sexual liberation. By the late 1970s this countercultural orientation was largely replaced by a concern with more reform-oriented and single-issue-based politics that became known as the Gay Rights movement, using a rights based discourse to assert the minority status of LGBT communities and to appeal for equivalence for LGBT people in terms of marriage or civil partnership, rights to adopt children, to be recognised for service in the armed forces etc. The return to more militant repertoires of collective action was subsequently resumed with the arrival of HIV/AIDS in the mid 1980s and direct action groups such as

ACT UP (Aids coalition to unleash power) who used **direct action** to campaign around the public health implications of the disease as well as to oppose the social and political context that enabled and encouraged homophobic responses to the crisis. ACT UP were organised along anarchistic (see **anarchism**) principles of organisation with responsibilities split between differing committees and affinity networks, they were also influential in the founding of Queer Nation and the Lesbian Avengers.

Whilst the term LGBT remains contested and is considered problematic by some activists who argue that this term conflates identities and issues and has historically privileged certain groups or struggles at the expense of others. Lesbian Gay, Bisexual, and Transgender, as well as Intersex and Queer groups have worked in various combinations as well as in solidarity networks with each other on a range of common issues.

References and resources

Armstrong, E. (2002); Cruikshank, M. (1992); Duberman, M. (1993); Miller, N. (2006); Power, L. (1995).

LIFEWORLD

Jurgen Habermas introduced the concept of the lifeworld into social movement studies in the early 1980s (Habermas 1981) within his larger project addressing communicative action (Habermas 1987). Within social movement studies the lifeworld refers to the intersection of lived experience, the social and cultural resources available through which to interpret and understand this experience and the social and cultural forces shaping resistance.

Habermas situates the phenomenological roots of this term in the context of late modernity where science, technology and bureaucracy increasingly shape lived experience. The associated processes of rationalisation and colonisation of the 'lifeworld' become social and cultural forces which social movements respond to as *defensive* and *offensive* **social movements**.

Habermas's notion of the lifeworld and the place of cultural practices in interpreting lived experiences and the forces which structure it are closely aligned with Pierre Bourdieu's notion of habitus. Both authors also share an interest in acts of spoken communication as expressions of power. Whilst communicative action has been a major focus of his work Habermas also argues that the citizen's right to civil disobedience is a defining feature of democratic states (Habermas 1985). Civil disobedience is legitimate when communicative action has been circumscribed in an unacceptable manner. Habermas identifies a number of processes likely to breach the limits of communicative action.

In particular he identifies the 'horror of a new category of literally invisible risks' which not only 'intrude into the life-world' but 'explode the dimensions of the life-world' (Habermas 1981: 35). These developments raise far-reaching moral stakes because, whilst moral responsibility can be attributed to those who 'set them in motion both technically and politically', the consequence of the techniques have an 'uncontrollable magnitude' (ibid.). These concerns prefigure Ulrich Beck's (1992) work on risk where radiation is taken as an examplar for invisible risks with inter-generational implications.

Advances in genetic sciences associated with the mapping of the human genome have made a range of diagnostic and therapeutic techniques possible. These techniques can be used to detect genetic defects or weakness in a foetus and to determine or enhance particular genetic characteristics. Genetic enhancement has been included in Habermas's work since at least 1971 and now raises stakes which explode the dimensions of the lifeworld. His recent work addresses these concerns in terms of inter-generational moral responsibility and argues for inclusive deliberation on the kinds of genetic techniques which are socially and culturally acceptable rather than technically possible, warning that individual market choices in this area would lead to a form of 'no-liberal eugenics' (Habermas 2003).

References and resources

Habermas, J. (1971, 1981, 1985, 2003).

MARXISM

The importance of Marx and Engels' work for social movement studies lies in the way that they theorised the capacity for self-organisation by workers movements as logical responses to systemic relations of exploitation rather than deviant or pathological behaviour (Ruggiero and Montagna 2008). Their political writing (Marx and Engels 1848; Marx 1852, 1859), and engagement through the First International (an international gathering of left wing groups), represented the pursuit of political agency by a global working class in and for itself. The primacy afforded to waged labour in the definition of class detracted from their commitment to an open movement and was one area of significant debate and dissent within the First International which contributed to its dissolution. Another significant area in this respect was the prioritisation of capturing the apparatus of the state to achieve this end prior to the 'withering away of the state'. In a European context where capitalism developed various forms of welfare state through a process of social and political interest representation involving classes and social movement actors Marxist approaches have been prominent within social movement studies.

The work of Marx and Engels laid the foundation for a range of neo-Marxist traditions at least two of which have been influential within social movement studies. The Frankfurt School, which sought to combine Marxism and psychoanalytic traditions, and emphasised the importance of marginal social actors as agents of progressive social change, represents one significant strand. The other strand draws on the work of the Italian theorist Antonio Gramsci emphasising the importance of social movements in contesting the prevailing hegemony (the matrix of power) of capitalist social, economic and ideological relations. Italian autonomism also represents an influential contemporary form of Marxism (see **multitude**, **precarity**). The Frankfurt School were prominent in theorising the rise of the **new social movements** during the 1960s and 1970s with Gramscian approaches gaining prominence in the 1980s and 1990s as neoliberalism became ascendant.

The rise of the **new social movements** of the 1960s and 1970s gave rise to an emphasis on the 'New Left' in both Europe and America (Williams 1989). The centrality of wage labour as the seat of revolutionary or systemic social and political change was re-theorised by members of the Frankfurt School. Consumerism and the development of modern media of mass communication had been theorised in terms of 'repressive desublimation' by Herbert Marcuse. In *One-Dimensional Man* (1964) Marcuse argued that the process of capitalist commodification had pervaded political life pre-empting radicalism by permitting its expression in commodified forms. This theory suggests that people are controlled through a system where one is allowed to express a little of one's instinctual energy as long as that desire is channelled towards consumer goods. However, events in Paris and elsewhere in 1968 reinforced Marcuse's re-evaluation of the repressive desublimation theory. In Frankfurt, students occupied the university confronting members of the Frankfurt School with the practical issue of whether they should support their eviction by the police.

Marcuse's 1969 *Essay on Liberation* argued that in contemporary capitalism significant agents of social change were to be found in marginal social locations such as ghetto populations and the student and militant intelligentsia. Marcuse dedicated the Essay to the young militants of 1968 who represented a 'turning point' by declaring a 'permanent challenge' based in the prioritisation of 'the life of human beings which has become a plaything in the hands of politicians, managers and generals' (Marcuse 1969: 11). Habermas (1971) drew on Marcuse's work in his analysis of scientific and technological relations as ideological components of capitalism. The implications of techno-scientific rationality to all areas of life became an important focus for his work on forms of action (see entries on **defensive** and **offensive social movement**). The development of social movements throughout the 1970s and 1980s became increasingly analysed in the context of the postulated transition from modernity to post-modernity which became increasingly influential within social theory. Latter day descendants of the Frankfurt School, such as Claus Offe (1985), argued that the new social movements represented a social and political force committed to the selective modernisation of modernity through the reassertion of the political will of citizens. This is also a prominent feature in the work of Ulrich Beck who allocates social movements an important role as agents of reflexive modernisation through their work in making invisible risks tangible (1992). The descendants of the Frankfurt School can be seen as having embraced the shift towards debates on governance that have increased in prominence in the current century.

The relevance of Gramsci for the analysis of the consolidation and rise of free market neoliberalism in Europe and America throughout the 1980s and 1990s was advanced by a range of thinkers (Boggs 1986). Stuart Hall's work at the Centre for Contemporary Cultural Studies (CCCS 1982; Chen and Morley 1996) in Birmingham placed the cultural contestation of capitalist hegemony at the heart of an intellectual project which sought to reposition Marxism in a post-colonial, neoliberal era. Themes of 'race', racism, migration, immigration and political identity featured prominently in an approach that related multiple social movements in the context of shifts in capitalist social and economic relations. This work was important in consolidating the significance of 'race' and class within social movement studies (Gilroy 1987). Gilroy's emphasis on culture distinguishes it from other approaches in this area such as that of Weiviorka (1995). Weiviorka emphasises the importance of strong trade unions as a prerequisite of social movement mobilisation around areas like 'race'. The importance of class and strong union forces ensures the maintenance of a public sphere within which it is possible to mobilise.

The influence of Marx and Marxism within social movement studies has been a persistent feature of the area and continues to develop (see entries on **disobbedienti, multitude, social movement unionism**). We are broadly sympathetic to Bensaid's (2002) argument that the end of

Soviet Communism, far from ending Marxism, made a reinvigoration and reformulation of Marxism possible. He argues that the success of this resurgent project depends upon 'establishing an organic relationship with the revived practice of social movements', particularly 'the resistance to imperialist globalization' (Bensaid 2002: xv). The 2008–09 crisis of capitalism, the subsequent recession and tightening of credit throughout the world has witnessed the re-emergence of the State in the face of systemic market failure. The long-term dynamics of recovery will lend renewed relevance to a wide range of established and emergent Marxist categories spanning the spheres of production, consumption and circulation. Nilsen (2009) is amongst those returning to the area of social movement studies from a Marxist position emphasising the significance of political praxis and attention to movements from above and movements from below.

References and resources

Beck, U. (1992); Bensaid, D. (2002); Boggs, C. (1986); CCCS (1982); Gilroy, P. (1987); Habermas, J. (1971); Marx, K. (1852/1977; 1859/1970); Marx, K. and Engels, F. (1848/2002); Marcuse, H. (1964, 1969); Nilsen, A. G. (2009); Offe, C. (1985); Ruggiero, V. and Montagna N. (eds. 2008: Part One); Weiviorka, M. (1995); Williams, R. (1989).

MORAL ACTION

Moral action is a concept that describes freely directed behaviour that seeks to achieve a moral outcome irrespective of whether that action involves self-interest. Some social theorists argue that a primary purpose of social movements is to perform actions that are directed at communicating, articulating or recovering a moral agenda in secular societies, thereby giving 'moral voice' to neglected minorities and highlighting previously hidden dilemmas (Jasper 1997; Szerszynski 1999). As these actions are often performed in comparatively marginal spaces on the periphery of societies they have also been likened to other forms of moral action, such as the acts of pilgrimage that occur in religious rights of passage through 'liminal' spaces – spaces of individual change and social transgression (Hetherington 1998). This has led some culturally oriented theorists (Goodwin *et al.* 2001; Hetherington 1998; Jasper 1997; Maffesoli 1995) to emphasise the ethical, performative and expressive aspects of identity formation over the political claims or grievances that were more typically considered to be constitutive of **collective identity** formation in social movements.

Primarily, the concept of moral action reveals an assumption that is implicit in most collective action, the presumption of a common moral purpose that is recognised by the actors and is therefore essential for the formation and maintenance of a **collective identity**. In a good deal of social movement discourse, including internal discussion documents and external propaganda an implied moral hierarchy is in evidence. This frequently requires affirmation and recognition at the level of cultural practice and lifestyle, and through performances of collective action, that signify moral intent.

However, whilst moral appeals are useful in building a shared identity and in bridging the frames of movement activists and a wider public, in the context of a sustained struggle the 'performance' of moral voice can sometimes promote significant tensions, which can, if not addressed, subsequently re-emerge to potentially damage the maintenance of **collective identity**. The interpersonal dynamics of a fluid and open community engaged in resistance are often volatile (see Katsiaficas 1997; Roseneil 1995; Stephens 1998). So whilst appeals to a common moral framework are often sufficient in terms of mobilisation, and for purposes of tactical confrontation, the negotiation of individual relationships, responsibilities and reciprocal obligations is difficult in a highly moralised setting populated by what is often a community of otherwise diverse social actors. Thus, issues such as the supply and use of resources, divisions of labour, food, accommodation, sexual relationships, drug-use etc. often combine with differing emphases, occasionally disrupting and sometimes affirming the identity gained in the performance of moral voice.

References and resources

Goodwin, J., Jasper, J. and Polletta, F. (eds. 2001); Hetherington, K. (1998); Jasper, J. M. (1997); Katsiaficas, G. (1997); Maffesoli, M. (1995); Roseneil, S. (1995); Stephens, J. (1998); Szerszynski, B. (1999).

MOVEMENT AS MEDIA

Alberto Melucci (1996) argues that in contemporary, complex societies with multiple and instantaneous means of communication movement actors become media channels in their own right. Movements' actions as media are regarded as a key means through which dominant discourses and ideologies are simultaneously revealed to society and challenged through the declaration of symbolic stakes.

The argument advanced here draws on the notion that there is no such thing as an untouched witness to an event. Movement as media thus includes: the day to day practices of movements such as dress codes, music and performance; movements' strategic use of established media forms such as newspapers, radio and television; and movements' independently produced media including print and internet forms.

The notion of movements as media thus extends beyond the notion of movements as users of media. For Melucci 'it is ... at the level of codes that movements distance themselves most radically from the prevailing norms'. (1996: 359) and offer a radical alternative to society. Whilst Melucci recognised the potential for movements as media to be 'incorporated into the market', he also recognised that 'new forms tend to appear elsewhere with other actors involved' (1996: 350).

Since Melucci wrote, technological advances have multiplied the number of channels of communication available, adding to the importance of this insight. Mainstream media images of direct action campaigners in underground tunnels heightened public debate on UK road-building programmes during the 1990s. Atton (2002) is amongst those commenting upon the importance of autonomous movement media forms including both print and electronic forms. His work begins to redress the neglect of 'alternative and radical media . . . in the dominant traditions of media research' (2002: 7). Atton emphasises the ways in which movements as media both impact upon mainstream media forms and forge independent circuits of communication that constitute collective actors.

The universal download potential of electronic forms links the local and the global multiplying the range of symbolic codes and challenges available. This contributes to the development of global movements within which the Zapatistas feature as a prominent example. The development of **Indymedia** underlines the increasing importance of **computer mediated communications** in this context.

References and resources

Atton, C. (2002); Melucci, A. (1996, 1996a).

MULTITUDE

The concept of the multitude originates in the writings of the Italian political philosopher Niccolo Machiavelli but finds its fullest expression in the later work of the Dutch philosopher Baruch Spinoza. It has been popularised as a concept relevant to social movement studies by Michael Hardt and Antonio Negri in their books *Empire* (2000), *Multitude* (2004) and *Commonwealth* (2009), as well as in the lesser-known work of Paolo Virno (2004) and in activist/academic publications such as the French magazine *Multitudes*. Multitude is a complex concept with a long history that has been deployed and interpreted in a variety of ways. However, for the purposes of understanding its relation to the study of social movements we will concentrate here on its contemporary use by Hardt and Negri, who define it by comparison to the common political concept of 'the people'. The people they argue, is a unified identity, which acquires sovereign power when constituted as a foundational part of the nation-state. This is a reciprocal and mutually constituting relationship, whereby the State requires a 'people' on behalf of whom it can act, and the people are designated as sovereign because the State acts on their behalf.

In opposition to this undifferentiated unity and its role in constituting the power of the State, Hardt and Negri propose the multitude as 'a set of singularities ... a social subject which cannot be reduced to sameness, a difference that remains different' (2004: 99). Although abstract, this is a crucial distinction as they suggest that in political philosophy 'only the one can rule, be it the monarch, the party, the people, or the individual' (2004: 100). Therefore, the concept of the multitude, as an active social subject that remains differentiated but is able to act on the basis of what it has in common, poses a challenge to the tradition of sovereignty. It also follows that the multitude is neither inside, nor outside, the State, but instead challenges the premises of the sovereignty of the State and its foundational construct – the people. As Paolo Virno points out, this opposition between people and multitude is one of the reasons it was 'detested' by seventeenth-century philosophers of the State such as Thomas Hobbes, who see it as contradicting 'the state monopoly of political decision-making' and as a resurgence of the '"state of nature" in civil society' (Virno 2004: 22). Thought of in this way the multitude resembles a self-organising assemblage of groups and individuals, working inside and outside state boundaries, that comes together democratically to co-operate around common issues and in opposition to abuses of power. Therefore the concept comes very close, and has been attributed to describing, the emergence of transnational or **global social movements**.

A further argument for the importance of the concept is derived from two related claims that are a direct development of the autonomist-Marxist tradition represented by Virno, Hardt and Negri (see **autonomy**). The first is the claim that capitalist globalisation creates the conditions for the return of the multitude to political significance by undermining the role of the nation-state and accelerating methods of interaction and communication that allow for new patterns of self-organisation and co-operation between movements. The second claim is that the multitude, as articulated in social movements of the 1960s and 1970s, is also the source of this capitalist innovation. This it is argued is evidenced by the post-Fordist reorganisation of the workplace in order to co-opt workers' desires for communication, affectivity and interaction and to meet the demands for more differentiated products and services associated with the performance of identity. In this way, the multitude is defined as both the sustaining and productive force of Empire *and* the source of its ultimate demise. This leads to criticism that the concept is being used by Hardt and Negri to re-pose the idea of a bi-polar struggle between opposing actors, albeit one in which their 'new proletariat' is somewhat more inclusive than the industrial working class (Lotringer 2004).

References and resources

Hardt, M. and Negri, A. (2000, 2004, 2009); Lotringer, S. (2004); Virno, P. (2004). Multitudes web resources: http://multitudes.samizdat.net/

NETWORK MOVEMENTS

Social movements are networks of individuals, groups and organisations involved in complex interactions in real and virtual spaces representing and embodying a variety of causes, ideological positions and expressions of identity. This network aspect of a social movement is relatively uncontested and a feature of many attempts at defining the term. However, the rise of **computer mediated communication** (CMC) and the opportunities for new configurations of existing networks and the formation of new movement networks, has given an impetus to the application of network theories to social movement studies. Consequently, networks and network theory are prominent elements of contemporary work on the social movement milieu (Diani 2000; Diani and McAdam 2003).

It has also given rise to the concept of network movements, which can be understood in at least two ways. Specifically, it can refer to movements that are partially, or completely catalysed by the availability of CMC and which are often concerned with the use and appropriation of that information architecture – the free software, or open source movement, for example (Stallman 1999). In its broadest sense this concept also refers to the entirety of the social and communicative networks that constitute a social movement. These networks consist of at least three elements, which are present to varying degrees in different instances. These three elements are the *virtual*, including electronic mailing lists, websites, chat rooms, bulletin boards etc. These are places of information exchange, coordination, deliberation and debate; they are also crucial to maintaining a sense of identity and connectedness within transnational and **global social movements**. The *situated*, these are the spaces and places of physical co-presence, such as protest sites, 'encounters' (see **Zapatismo**), social forums (see **World Social Forum**) and festival gatherings, all of which involve considerable 'facework' – close interaction, trust-building etc. Finally, network movements are still partially constituted by the *textual*, both in combination with the virtual, as electronically circulated documents, but also in terms of flyers, newsletters, 'zines, journals, books etc. Movements are producers of information and knowledge about themselves and their issues of concern (see **knowledge-practices**) and whilst the virtual domain provides good opportunities for circulation of texts, there remains within many movements an affinity with the circulation of well produced culturally resonant paper publications (See Notes from Nowhere 2003).

The concept network movement also opens up a number of related concepts including network actor; network density – a term with a technical meaning within the network literature (Emirbayer and Goodwin 1994) network extension and network node. A network actor may be an individual or group that is particularly adept at utilising the communications opportunities of a network to popularise a particular cause or issue, or to facilitate mobilisation of those who might otherwise be socially disconnected. The emphasis here is upon the role of the network as a multiplier of the agency of the network actor, and the potential positive feedback if the network actor is able to recognise and become skilled at using the network in this way. Network density is used to refer to the thickness of meaning that is socially embodied within a particular network. The denser a network the greater its solidarity and capacity for certain forms of mobilisation e.g. direct action. Network nodes denote a particular 'place' – virtual, situated or textual – that performs particularly intense communicative work for a movement. Certain free festivals, protests, gatherings, websites and bulletin boards would be examples of network nodes (Purdue *et al.* 1997). Network extension refers to the process of developing links between social movement networks, integrating interest networks and building upon the weak links that allow networks to access new information and resources (Granovetter 1973).

References and resources

Diani, M. (2000); Diani, M. and McAdam, D. (2003); Emirbayer, M. and Goodwin, J. (1994); Granovetter, M. S. (1973); Purdue, D., Dürrschmidt, J., Jowers, P. and O'Doherty, R. (1997); Stallman, R. (1999).

NEW SOCIAL MOVEMENTS

The resurgence of social movements in the 1960s and 1970s prompted renewed theoretical reflection upon structural change and collective action, and a school of thought evolved amongst European scholars which is often referred to as the 'new social movements' approach (Melucci 1980, 1981). This approach stemmed from a critique of the **Marxist** paradigm's inability to explain emerging collective phenomena (Touraine 1977). Instead of the working class, uniquely positioned at the heart of the structural contradictions of capital, there emerged a raft of opposing and seemingly paradoxical assertions given voice by those who had previously been conceived as marginal actors in the drama of social struggle: women, students, black and ethnic minorities, young people, lesbians, gays and bisexuals, the unemployed.

Melucci as the originator of the phrase was keen to point out that the concept of 'newness' at an analytical level is relative (1995), and that if the term were used conceptually it could lead to a misunderstanding of collective actors as 'unified empirical objects', meaning it could encourage scholars and activists to think of social movements almost as persons, actors on a political stage, a way of thinking which would neglect the complexity of how these movements are formed, their historical antecedents, and the process of how they construct a **collective identity**.

However, there is little doubt that many of the movements that emerged in the 1960s were 'new' in the sense that they raised different possibilities for collective action around issues that had previously been marginalised – identity, gender, sexuality, race and ethnicity, age, the environment, health and so on. The conditions under which they mobilised were also new in that the Western European society that was the concern of social theorists was becoming highly differentiated and informationalised (Melucci 1995: 113).

In the tradition of European social science, a number of macro-theoretical approaches had evolved to account for and document this structural re-ordering, and a proliferation of terms were used to describe and analyse the emerging society. Originally these included 'post-industrial' (Bell 1973), 'technocratic' or 'programmed' (Touraine 1971) and latterly 'post-Fordist' (Murray 1989) and 'postmodern' (Lyotard 1984), all of which were contested and some of which, particularly 'postmodern', have been subsequently stretched to the point at which their utility as explanatory terms is questionable. However, they all chart similar territory in their exposition of a more differentiated, complex, technologically advanced, aestheticised and pluralistic society: a society where the new movements are conceived both as symptoms of change and as increasingly important actors, in upholding, defending, contesting or withdrawing from those forces, frictions and fissures which are uncovered by structural change (Castells 1997; Chesters and Welsh 2006; Urry 2003).

Habermas (1976, 1987) evokes the image of a colonisation of lifeworlds, where the bureaucratic logic of state and market and their intrusion and penetration of social life are countered by the opening of autonomous spaces of communication fostered by new movements. Similarly, Offe (1985) describes the decentralised and participatory methods of organisation the new movements use to oppose the normative arrangements of institutional politics as indicative of the disembedding of collective action from an industrial context. Alternatively, Touraine (1981) posits the new movements as the central focus of sociological study, as 'the banner of the entire sociology of action, which heads all other sociologies' (1981: 30); that is, they lie at the very heart of the action system through which society reproduces itself by conflictual praxis.

In turn, these claims have been criticised as seeking to substitute a theory of social movements for social theory itself (Rucht 1991). Both Melucci (1996: 45) and Castells (1997) have drawn extensively upon what they see as Touraine's preservation of a metaphysics of conflict. This conflict arises from the ongoing socio-cultural conflict between those who produce and define the dominant rules, and those who resist and redefine them through their assertion of resistant identities. Transformative conflict thus becomes wider than that commonly associated with industrial capitalism with its two diametrically opposed classes. From this snapshot, it should be evident that for social theorists, social movements are a major source of evidence for macro-social change, and as such, are constantly used as barometers of structural, institutional and cultural innovation.

Klandermans et al. (1988) identify four characteristics that are held to be indicative of 'new social movements' as expressed by the authors they surveyed. They argue that these are anti-modernism, small-scale participatory action forms, a new middle class displaying post-material values, and the satisfaction of needs that have been endangered. Fleshing these points out, they indicate two distinct population groups, which they argue are particularly inclined towards participation in social movement activity. The first is those who have been marginalised by the pace or particularities of societal development; this group is not easily represented in orthodox class terms, but it can be argued that those most likely to feel the fallout of structural transition are those who are closely bound to industrial society, usually the working class (Gorz 1982), although it is acknowledged that the change associated with such transition encourages and reveals greater social differentiation than that encapsulated in class terms. The second group identified as being well represented in social movements is the 'new' middle class who derive their prestige and position from their work as producers of knowledge. This class is often associated with the growth of welfarism and the increasingly important part played by teachers, social workers, health care professionals and others in the regulation of social behaviour (Castells 1996: 208-220). It is argued that the growth of these professions and congruently the values and needs embedded within them encourages an increased sensitivity towards what are termed 'post-material' values (Inglehart 1990).

The role of the 'new middle class' and post-material values has received a lot of attention in the literature on the 'new social movements', and remains highly contested (Maheu 1995). Post-material values are perceived as originating in structural changes and as such are distinct from either the process of framing grievances (symbolic manipulation, cognitive cues and metaphors) conducted by movements, or the concept of a movement ideology. They are instead, it is claimed (Inglehart 1977, 1990), the result of enculturation processes in affective environments determined by the growth of welfare services, increased access to education, and economic prosperity (Rootes 1995).

Whilst there is considerable evidence of the growth of post-materialist values (Inglehart 1997), it has proven difficult to substantiate a causal chain between a new middle class, post-material values and participation in social movements (Bagguley 1992; Middendorp 1992). Although it can be argued that those who exhibit such values are more likely to be well disposed to social movement activism, there is no reason to impute from this a causal link between the existence of such values and new forms of collective action. There are many people who ascribe to what can be termed post-materialist values but do not participate in any form of social movement activity. The existence of such values, whilst no doubt contributory, does not explain mobilisation, or indeed, why such differing movements emerge at the same time in different countries despite the similarity of their value systems. This is akin to the point made by resource mobilisation theorists (see pages 147–149) when confronted with theories that understand collective action as a response to a breakdown in society's ability to mitigate grievances; grievances are ubiquitous in all societies, they do not explain why a social movement coalesces at a particular time around a particular issue. There are also reservations expressed in the literature (Brookes and Manza 1994) about the criteria for assessing values as expressed in Inglehart's work (1990, 1997), which is heavily reliant upon codifying responses to questions based upon perceptions of economic indicators.

Explanations of collective action, involving new class constituencies and value systems, are symptomatic of the European approach, in their attribution of increased and differentiated social movement activity to major structural change, involving new political cleavages and culturally received repetoires of protest. However, such analyses often overlook the micro and mezzo levels of analysis typified by the North American approach, which have attempted, often with a great deal of success, to explain why particular movements emerge to prominence at particular times, through reference to the availability of resources, and the opportunities for action offered by a political structure.

References and resources

Bagguley, P. (1992); Bell, D. (1973); Brookes, C. and Manza, J. (1994); Castells, M. (1996, 1997); Chesters, G. and Welsh, I. (2006); Gorz, A. (1982); Habermas, J. (1976, 1987); Inglehart, R. (1990, 1997); Klandermans, B., Kriesi, H. and Tarrow, S. (eds. 1988); Lyotard, J.-F. (1984); Maheu, L. (ed. 1995); Melucci, A. (1980, 1981, 1995, 1996); Middendorp, C. (1992); Murray, R. (1989); Offe, C. (1985); Rootes, C. (1995); Rucht, D. (1991); Touraine, A. (1971, 1997, 1981).

OFFENSIVE SOCIAL MOVEMENT

Habermas introduced this term to differentiate emancipatory potential from the potential for resistance and retreat within the social movement milieu at the start of the 1980s. An offensive social movement is therefore one that has radical transformatory agency and emancipatory potential. Looking back at the 1960s and 1970s from this vantage point Habermas concluded that the only movement following the tradition of bourgeois-socialist liberation movements was feminism. This was a significant shift from earlier work which had identified student movements as radical subjects (Habermas 1971) and serves to underline the importance of particular historic junctures or time frames in the framing of analytic approaches.

Habermas argued for feminism as an offensive movement with emancipatory potential on a number of grounds: the struggle of feminism against patriarchal oppression *sui generis*; a universalist moral foundation to feminist claims; and a universalist legal basis for feminist claims. Combined, these grounds add up to more than formal equality and the elimination of male prejudices. If realised, the feminist agenda would result in 'the toppling of concrete life styles determined by male monopolies' (Habermas 1981: 35). This would constitute a systemic transformation of the lifeworld rather than a particularistic defense.

There are two elements embedded in Habermas's condensed argument here. First, the history of women's subordination within the bourgeois nuclear family and second, the 'virtues' that arise from this in terms of a distinct 'set of values that are both in contrast and complementary to the male world and at odds with the one-sided rationalized praxis of everyday life' (ibid.). Whilst Habermas does not cite Engels' work on the family, which argues that the rise of the bourgeois nuclear family was central to the transmission of capital through a male line (Engels 1884/1972), he is clearly arguing that the realisation of a feminist agenda would be a systemic transformation.

Whilst the notion of an offensive social movement contains echoes of the prioritisation of class over all other dimensions of social conflict (see **old social movement**) the prioritisation of feminism rooted in a critique of patriarchal social order arguably prefigured more contemporary work (see **feminist social movements**). Alan Touraine continues to argue that feminism alone has the potential for systemic change.

References and resources

Engels, F. (1884/1972); Habermas J. (1981); Ruggiero, V. and Montagna, N. (eds. 2008: 201–205).

OLD SOCIAL MOVEMENT

This term is used predominantly within the European literature and derives from a Marxist theoretical tradition which identifies social movements as the origins of the process of class formation. Old social movements are analytically linked to the rise of industrial capitalism, the modern capitalist nation state and the associated institutions, apparatus and techniques of class domination. Old social movements originating within the production process become central agents of class struggle with the potential to achieve systemic social change. Understood in this way social movements give rise to historic agents of change through class struggle.

The relationship between predominantly male organisations and the place of women in this process represents one of the longest-standing tensions within this approach. The rise of **new social movements** in the late 1960s and 1970s intensified debates about the relative standing of different social movements to effect change (Scott 1990). The relationship between class, second wave feminism, ecological and environmental movements are prominent examples where intense debates develop. Marxist stances argued that feminism and ecologism represented diversions from the class struggle.

Such tensions resulted in variants of feminist and ecological movements. Marxist Feminists prioritised workplace and wages for domestic labour issues whilst writers such as Gorz (1982) and Bahro (1982) argued it was necessary to combine socialist and green critiques (see **green movements**).

The relationship between social movements originating within the productive sphere and those originating within wider civil society remains an area of intense debate. Within European writing on social movement major figures have adopted a range of positions on this. Melucci, who was amongst the first to apply the term 'new' to such movements, argues that contemporary movements are not new or old in themselves but reflect different orientations expressing different historical layers within a given society (Melucci 1996: 79). Alan Touraine emphasises that he has always 'spoken of social actors' replacing the idea of 'social class' with 'social movement' and addressing 'the labour movement as a social movement' (Touraine 1995: 209, 240).

Both writers are arguing that the sociologists task is to identify transformative collective actors within a prevailing set of relations typified by globalisation and complexity. The debate between old and new social movement reflects a trajectory of societies which industrialised in the nineteenth century prior to the development of twentieth century new social movements. The relationship between labour-based social movements, feminist, environmental and ecological movements within contemporary societies undergoing rapid developments means that labour organisation and ecological mobilisations are simultaneous processes (Welsh 2000). The increasing prominence of collective stakes associated with global production and consumption patterns is reconfiguring thinking on the relationship between labour movements and traditional conceptions of trade unionism (see **social movement unionism**).

References and resources

Gorz, A. (1982); Melucci A. (1996); Scott. A, (1990, 1992); Touraine, A. (1995).

PEACE MOVEMENT

Peace movements reject the use of violence and the recourse to war as an extension of the political process by nation states. Peace movements are not 'anti' movements and have proactive stances emphasising the importance of dialogue and mediation as means of conflict resolution. Peace movements frequently distinguish between structural and physical violence. Structural violence can include systemic material deprivation and exploitation based on gender, race or ethnic status. Over time, issues such as these have increased in importance alongside the long-standing engagement with issues of war and the use of violence. Activism in peace movements embodies principles of non-violence and has given rise to wide range of **repertoires of action**.

Passive resistance and civil disobedience are two widely used forms of action. Court cases resulting from such actions can test and establish legal precedents. A prominent UK example was the dismissal of a case of criminal damage brought against Trident Ploughshares (www.tridentploughshares.org) activists who damaged a Hawk jet aircraft destined for Indonesia. A jury accepted that the women acted on the basis of a lawful excuse to prevent British Aerospace and the British Government from aiding and abetting genocide. The example underlines the way in which peace movements are engaged in campaigns which constantly contest and redefine the legal use of violence with the ultimate aim of making war illegal.

Peace movements stand in a long historical tradition and are included within Smelser's (1962) category of general social movement. Smelser traces their origins to England at the time of the Napoleonic Wars and notes the existence of specific forms of peace movement associated with international arbitration, codification of international law, disarmament and the cessation of nuclear testing (Smelser 1962). In the twentieth century, peace movement activity was established in the nations of the North Atlantic Rim in the run up to and aftermath of the First World War. These included America, Canada, the United Kingdom, the countries of mainland Europe as well as Southern Nations including Australia and New Zealand (Young 2010).

In terms of social movement studies, peace movements became increasingly significant after the Second World War, which ended following the use of nuclear weapons on the Japanese cities of Hiroshima and Nagasaki. The division of Germany between the Soviet Union and the Western Allies was one feature of a bi-polar world order in which capitalist and communist states developed large inventories of nuclear weapons. The doctrines of use associated with these weapons initially revolved around Mutually Assured Destruction (MAD) and were accompanied by a nuclear arms race.

Peace movement mobilisations against nuclear weapons became prominent in the West. In the United Kingdom CND was formed in 1958 (http://www.cnduk.org/) and established an annual march to Aldermaston where work on nuclear weapons was conducted. In 1961 4,000 people took part in a sit-down protest at the Ministry of Defence in London. Police arrested 1,300 people including the philosopher Bertrand Russell. The sit-down protests had been organised by the Committee of 100 but marked the start of the widespread use of non-violent **direct action** by CND and the wider peace movement. Whilst sociological studies of CND (Parkin 1968) suggested that it was a predominantly middle class movement there was significant support amongst Trade Unionists, the Labour Party, and Quakers. Members of the Communist Party, anarchists and a range of left wing political groups also played a prominent part in CND. Extensive support also existed across a range of academic disciplines spanning the natural and social sciences. Peace movements are typically diverse coalitions which vary over time.

The overlapping membership of academic and peace movement circles was central in establishing the specialism of Peace Studies, usually located within the disciplines of Politics and International Relations. The formation of the International Peace Research Association (IPRA) in 1964 played an important role in advancing this academic area. IPRA contributes to United Nations work on peace and disarmament and represents an important element in the attempt to render war an illegal act.

Opposition to nuclear weapons in America was formalised through The National Committee for a Sane Nuclear Policy (SANE) founded in 1957. It was opposition to the Vietnam War that brought the peace movement to prominence in the USA during the 1960s. The 1960s US peace movement was part of the 'new left' and the mobilising capacity drew on civil rights activists and **Students for a Democratic Society**. Between 1963 and 1969 opposition to the Vietnam War grew steadily as local peace group initiatives became co-ordinated at a national level. Mass mobilisations occurred regularly and grew in size as working class and black Americans joined in opposition to a war where the majority of casualties were from poorer backgrounds.

In November 1969 somewhere between 500,000–750,000 people demonstrated against the Vietnam War in Washington DC. College campuses, draft offices and recruitment centres were occupied and subject to disruption through acts of civil disobedience and draft cards were burned in public across America. In 1970, amidst intensifying campus occupations, Ohio National Guardsmen opened fire on student demonstrators at Kent State University killing four and wounding sixteen. Public campaigning broadened as details of massacres and battlefield atrocities were reported and prospects of a military victory receded. Protests against American involvement spread to other countries as pressure mounted for an end to military engagement. The Vietnam War ended in 1975 when Saigon was captured by North Vietnamese forces.

The end of the war marked a decline in mass mobilisations by peace movements with core campaigning groups continuing to press for the reduction and elimination of nuclear weapons. In the 1980s the American decision to modernise its theatre nuclear forces in Europe and to develop a strategic missile defence system as part of a strategy to undermine the USSR led to a renewed wave of activism. The stationing of Cruise and Pershing missiles in Europe resulted in a resurgence of national campaigning groups like CND alongside pan-European initiatives, notably the European Nuclear Disarmament movement (END).

In the United Kingdom citizens formed convoys to follow mobile cruise missile launchers as they left military bases. Following a march originating in Wales the peace camps at Greenham Common were established, becoming a focus for feminist peace movement activists. Feminist scholarship emphasised the militarisation of society and the social dominance of patriarchal structures in the organisation of war and domestic violence (Alonso 1993; Cohn 1987; Enloe 1983, 1990). The peace camps and mass mobilisations at Greenham drew on extensive support networks across the United Kingdom, including the child care performed by fathers to enable women to participate in weekend events. This underlines the way that multiple actors constitute networks supporting particular mobilisations. Media coverage of Greenham produced symbolically potent images of women bodily bearing witness and physically transgressing a nuclear base.

Peace movements and network extension

The 1980s mobilisations rendered visible and amplified aspects of peace movements' activities which have been central to such movements throughout their existence. These include the emphasis on direct civil society-to-civil society contact as a way of promoting mutual understanding and trust between people independent of the positioning of political elites. In terms of the cases discussed here **Greenham Women** established network links with women opposing US military installations around the world as the capacity for networking increased with the beginnings of **computer mediated communications** and enhanced mobility. The subsequent activities of groups like Trident Ploughshares, mentioned above (see page 128), are part of the ongoing initiatives dating from this era.

Another feature of the European peace movement of the 1980s was networking which spanned East and West in a Europe divided by the 'iron curtain'. Peace movement civil society-to-civil society initiatives, as well as network links around environmental concerns, played an important part in constituting nascent civil societies in Eastern European countries where they were widely assumed to be absent (Tickle and Welsh 1998). In countries where these network exchanges were particularly dense, such as the then Czechoslovakia and East Germany, the transitions following the collapse of Soviet influence were markedly peaceful. The street vigils which accompanied these transitions drew upon the repertoires of the peace movements and were shaped by activists drawn from this milieu.

Networked movements of movements have continued to be prominent in mobilisations resonating with peace movement orientations. The simultaneous protests against the military intervention in Iraq in 2003 were possibly the biggest single protest event ever staged.

References and resources

Alonso, H. (1993); Carter, A. (1992); Cohn, C. (1987); Enloe, C. (1983, 1990); Parkin, F. (1968); Rochon, T. R. (1988, 1998); Roseneil, S. (1995); Smelser, N. (1962); Taylor, R. (1988); Tickle, A. and Welsh, I. (eds. 1998); Young, N. (ed. 2010).
Adams, D. *The American Peace Movements* available at http://www.culture-of-peace. info/apm/title-page.html
Barringer M. *The Anti War Movement in the United States* available at http://www. english.illinois.edu/maps/vietnam/antiwar.html

PEOPLES' GLOBAL ACTION (PGA)

Peoples' Global Action (PGA) is a global **social movement network** that helped facilitate the growth of what is variously termed the anti-capitalist (see **anticapitalism, alternative globalisation movement** (AGM) or global social justice movement). It was perhaps the first example of a self-organised globally co-ordinated social movement network to achieve global reach and to be capable of significant global impact without membership or funding. PGA was enabled by the increased mobility of protesters and the rise in **computer mediated communication** that enabled continuous interaction and co-ordination. PGA was instrumental in calling for a number of 'global days of action' against international finance institutions including protests against the World Trade Organisation (WTO), G8, International Monetary Fund (IMF) and the World Bank.

PGA grew out of an international network of solidarity for the Zapatista (see entry on **Zapatismo**) struggle and was proposed at the second Zapatista encuentro (encounter), a meeting of civil society and social movements in Spain in 1997. In February 1998, the founding conference of Peoples' Global Action took place in Geneva. It was attended by more than 300 delegates from approximately 71 countries, many of whom were attracted by the five PGA hallmarks drafted and circulated by Professor Nanjundaswamy, leader of the Karnataka State Farmers' Association, one of the largest farmers' movements in India, and a key advocate for PGA. The hallmarks expressed 'a very clear rejection of the WTO and other trade liberalisation agreements', but this was subsequently amended at the Third International Conference of PGA in Cochabamba, Bolivia to reflect the broader concerns of the PGA network:

1   A very clear rejection of capitalism, imperialism and feudalism; all trade agreements, institutions and governments that promote destructive globalization.
2   We reject all forms and systems of domination and discrimination including, but not limited to, patriarchy, racism and religious fundamentalism of all creeds. We embrace the full dignity of all human beings.
3   A confrontational attitude, since we do not think that lobbying can have a major impact in such biased and undemocratic organisations, in which transnational capital is the only real policy-maker.
4   A call to direct action and civil disobedience, support for social movements' struggles, advocating forms of resistance which maximise respect for life and oppressed peoples' rights, as well as the construction of local alternatives to global capitalism.
5   An organisational philosophy based on decentralisation and autonomy.

These hallmarks became the basis for co-operation between a variety of autonomous groups and movements and they have since been adopted as a common platform by a diverse range of social movements worldwide. Some indication of their widespread appeal can be drawn from the range of groups attending the founding conference of PGA in Geneva, which included striking teachers from Argentina, Canadian postal workers, women campaigning against the labour conditions of the Mexican 'Maquillas' factories, farmers' movements from India, Honduras, Nicaragua, Senegal, Togo, Peru, Brazil and many other countries and indigenous peoples including the Ogoni, Maori, Maya, Aymara, U'wa and others struggling for political recognition and personal and cultural survival. Also present were striking workers from the Ukraine, anti-free trade activists from the USA, environmentalists, peace activists, anti-racists, animal rights advocates and others associated with issues of equality, diversity and **autonomy**.

Despite the 'traditional' model of a manifesto and 'mission statement', there was little attempt at defining an organisational identity for PGA, instead the organisational principles appeared to be paradoxical. For example, the 'PGA is an instrument for coordination, not an organisation' the 'PGA has no membership', 'no organisation or person represents the PGA, nor does the PGA represent any organisation or person' and 'the PGA will not have any resources' (see PGA website: http://www.agp.org). These principles are the antithesis of organisation as usually understood and emerge from a desire to emphasise encounter around mutually agreed terms – the PGA hallmarks – from which the expectation is that solidarity bonds established by physical proximity and face-work will enable effective coordination of the network based upon trust, reciprocity and confidence that can be further maintained and elaborated through computer mediated communications.

The explosion of internationally co-ordinated protest against global governance and finance structures that was initiated by PGA in Geneva grew exponentially through protest events that have since become synonymous with the cities in which they took place. This historiography varies according to the involvement and preferences of those documenting the growth of the **alternative globalisation movements** (AGM), but most would agree the key locations include London (City institutions/ G8), Seattle (WTO), Washington (IMF/World Bank), Prague (IMF/World Bank), Melbourne (World Economic Forum), Quebec (Free Trade of the Americas Act), Genoa (G8) and Gleneagles (G8).

This period of growth and action by the AGM precipitated regional PGA networks as personal enthusiasms, connections and affinities grew; this included the adoption of the PGA hallmarks as a statement of intent and a condition of participation in organising certain protest events. During this period, PGA-inspired groups and movements established regional networks in Latin America, Asia, North America and Europe. The aim was that the convenorship for each regional network would rotate between movements and those convenors would form a Convenors' Committee that would organise conferences of the network. This was entirely fitting with the PGA's organisational principles of decentralisation and autonomy and it was also anticipated that the Convenors' Committee would be enabled to manage flows of information and advise on technical issues of resourcing, organisation and communication between regions.

In practice, this proved extremely difficult due to the inability of convenors to fully assume their roles because of existing commitments to local movement activities. This was further complicated by the problems of working at a distance, including cultural and language barriers and differentials between Northern and Southern movements with regard to resources, including Internet access and travel. These difficulties tended to encourage the rise to prominence of bilingual or multilingual Europeans with mobility and internet access in the facilitation of the network, with additional support coming from those inspired to promote the network in the other PGA regions. Whilst these individuals performed an increasingly difficult task out of necessity, internal debate on PGA e-mail lists and during conferences focussed on the need for transparency and accountability, and the susceptibility of the network, in security and leadership terms, to the exigencies of an informal and mostly unknown group of individuals, the so-called 'tyranny of structurelessness' familiar to generations of activists (Freeman 1973). These criticisms led to attempts to make participation transparent and to encourage broader involvement by movement actors – groups or individuals who had recently engaged for the first time with the network. This initiative involved additional 'communication tools' including e-mail lists dedicated to 'process', 'strategy', 'resistance' and 'discussion' and the development of local 'info-points'-awareness-raising groups who could act to promote the scaling up of PGA-inspired activity.

Although PGA has been cited as an important actor within global civil society (Keane 2003: 61), excepting work by Chesters and Welsh (2006) and Routledge (2004), little attempt has been made to either describe or analyse its form and structure. This is because understanding PGA's role and influence within the **alternative globalisation movement** is difficult due to the self-organising traits it manifests, including its capacity to rapidly adapt its internal structure in order to cope with and manipulate its environment. As a network it puts out 'calls' for action yet is frequently invisible within those actions, its constituent actors forming new links and co-creating time-or place-specific initiatives. This fluidity is accentuated by its reluctance to be named or represented and its emphasis upon a process of evolution through encounter rather than the espousal of a political cause or goal against which its 'successes' could be measured.

References and resources

Chesters, G. and Welsh, I. (2006); Freeman, J. (1973); Keane, J. (2003); Routledge, P. (2004).

POLITICAL MOVEMENT

This is Alberto Melucci's (1996) term for a movement pursuing a conflict via collective action intended to break the limits of the established political system. Political Movements typically campaign:

1   to extend the criteria for inclusion within decision making;
2   to reveal and fight against bias that privileges certain interests over others within the political system;
3   to gain access to and influence within existing decision-making processes;
4   to open up new channels for the expression of previously excluded demands.

Political movements push participation beyond the initial limits set by a prevailing political system (Melucci 1996: 35).

The political system is regarded as the area of a social structure where normative decisions are made governing exchanges between specific groups or interests. These exchanges take place under specific rules and procedures through which the political system 'produces decisions' which 'guarantee' the maintenance and adaptation of the mode of production and the distribution of social resources (Melucci 1996: 229).

Following the onset of the economic crisis of 2008–2009 States took decisions to underwrite the banking system, as guarantors of last resort, to maintain the existing mode of production. Calls to underwrite sectors of the economy, like car production, resulted in significant political debate over the contribution to climate change from the internal combustion engine. These examples serve to illustrate why political movements are seen as important by Melucci.

He writes that within existing political systems there is a vast area of non-demand or excluded interests that are repressed or marginalised, depriving them of access. These unexpressed interests exist alongside and can overlap with demands that concern society as a whole but can only become manifest through the action of social movements (ibid.: 235). Political movement is the level of collective action necessary to declare the stakes to society by rendering these unexpressed interests as 'problems' or 'issues' which can become sufficiently defined to become the subject of political decisions. Decisions are ways of reducing uncertainty but always contain an element of risk which the decision seeks to minimise.

Green movements have been particularly prominent in articulating a number of environmental and social risks within complex societies. These include the risk of climate change and illustrate the ways in which political movement is an important level of collective action (Welsh 2010). Political movement can only be effective if the political system is sufficiently open to listen and engage with social movement actors. Social movement actors declaring such stakes can also become subject to aggressive policing strategies (see **protest and disorder**) (Chesters and Welsh 2006; Welsh 2007).

References and resources

Chesters, C. and Welsh, J. (2006); Melucci, A. (1996); Welsh, I. (2007, 2010).

POLITICAL OPPORTUNITY STRUCTURE

Political opportunity structure (POS) describes the political and institutional opportunities and constraints that either inhibit or facilitate collective action. For example, an important criterion of difference is seen to be that between federal and centralised political constitutional forms. In this analysis countries with federal constitutions (USA, Germany) that grant local decision-making rights to regional assemblies are seen as more open to certain forms of social movement intervention than countries like the United Kingdom (until 2001) and France where the central state dominates. POS approaches are closely aligned with rational choice theories and complementary to **resource mobilisation theory**.

The person most closely associated with the Political Opportunity Structure approach is Sydney Tarrow (1989, 1998), who also developed the influential theory of protest cycles. Tarrow claims that 'contention increases when people gain the external resources to escape their compliance and find opportunities in which to use them' (1998: 71). Tarrow concurs with resource mobilisation theory that grievances are ubiquitous in society and they will always provide an impetus to some form of collective action. He argues that the likelihood of collective action and its success or failure is largely dependent upon the context of the political system and its openness to change at the time when the action takes place.

> When institutional access opens, rifts appear within elites, allies become available, and state capacity for repression declines, challengers find opportunities to advance their claims. When combined with high levels of perceived costs for inaction, opportunities produce episodes of contentious politics.
>
> (Tarrow 1998: 71)

POS therefore offers an analytical means of distinguishing between the success and failure of different movements in differing historical and geographical contexts. This analysis of comparative degrees of access to institutional mechanisms and procedures, across countries, within historical periods and political cultures led to the development of a series of variables through which the openness or closure of a political system might be evaluated (Kitschelt 1986). One of the most important variables arising from this analysis is state repression most notably through protest policing (della Porta 1996, 1998; Lipsky, 1970).

Despite attempts to pin it down the concept of POS remains a fluid one, and has been stretched to accommodate increasingly diverse factors. This has led Gamson and Meyer (1996: 275) to claim that 'the concept of political opportunity structure is in trouble, in danger of becoming a sponge that soaks up virtually every aspect of the social movement environment – political institutions and culture, crises of various sorts, political alliances and policy shifts'.

These concerns encouraged attempts to describe a definitive conceptual model of the POS. Notable amongst these were the large scale comparative study conducted by Kriesi et al. (1995), which sought to elaborate a comprehensive model of POS based upon four components: national cleavage structures, institutional structures, prevailing strategies and alliance structures (1995: 13–14). Taking these in order gives some indication of the ambitious scope of POS and its potential for framing empirical research.

- National cleavage structures are the established country-specific political cleavages that facilitate or impede the opportunities for movement mobilisation.
- Institutional structures are the framework for the articulation and management of competing political demands.
- Informal strategies are the techniques that are adopted for dealing with collective action outside of institutional frameworks.
- Alliance structures are the opportunities for collective action revealed by a wealth of potentially destabilising factors, which might be continuously present, or emerge as a result of unexpected cleavages between political or institutional elites or during the formation of new political or institutional coalitions.

In this typology alliance structures are the less institutional spaces of opportunity where social movement actors can coalesce during shifts in the configuration of power within a political system (Kriesi et al. 1995: 14). These spaces tend by definition to be contingent, however, and unstable over time and it is therefore somewhat confusing to refer to these as structures. This definition of the POS provided by Kriesi et al. also provides support for the idea of protest cycles utilised by Tarrow (1998) where social movement mobilisation appears to rise and fall according to the opportunities available for collective action. Tarrow asserts the 'strongest argument' is that:

> changes in political opportunities and constraints create the most important incentives for initiating new phases of contention. These actions in turn create new opportunities for latecomers and eventually

for opponents and power holders. The cycles of contention – and in rare cases, the revolutions – that ensue are based on the externalities that these actors gain and create.

(Tarrow 1998: 7)

POS approaches, in a similar way to **resource mobilisation theory**, helped to shift the analysis of social movements away from the perception of collective action as a response to systemic dysfunction – the position prior to the 1960s – and helped replace the 'traditional' collective behaviour paradigm with a rational choice model. In doing so its practitioners have sought to develop analysis of the differing resources, opportunities and constraints upon social movements at the personal, organisational and institutional levels. Hence, the POS approach along with RMT was responsible for the focus of academic inquiry in the USA moving away from consideration of the structural conditions responsible for the production of grievances, the 'why' questions, to consideration instead of the patterns of mobilisation within particular political systems, the 'how' questions.

References and Resources

della Porta, D. (1996); dellaporta, D. and Reites, H. (eds. 1998); Gamson, W. A. and Meyer, D. S. (1996); Kitschelt, H. (1986); Kriesi, H., Koopmans, R., Duyvendak, J.-W. and Giugni, M. (1995); Lipsky, M. (ed. 1970); Moaddel, M. (1992a); Tarrow, S. (1989, 1998).

POOR PEOPLES' MOVEMENTS

Poor Peoples' Movement is a term advanced by the American writers Francis Fox-Piven and Richard A. Cloward (1977) to focus attention explicitly upon movements formalising the lifeworld interests of poor people distinct from work and labour-related concerns. Piven's original work has to be understood against a period in America typified by recurrent urban fiscal crises which eventually resulted in major cities such as New York becoming bankrupt. This intensified a range of long-running urban issues including segregation, housing, educational provision, fuel poverty and wider community provison in a developed nation without a welfare state.

Fox-Piven and Cloward's focus on Poor Peoples' Movements starts from the premise that protest is rarely initiated by the most impoverished sectors of a society and that it is only under exceptional conditions that the 'lower' classes sieze the initiative to press for their own class interests. Parallels are drawn between the Recession of the 1930s, affecting the entire working population of America, and the position of black Americans in the South during the 1960s. These are periods when the deprivation and disorganisation experienced in daily life become perceived as wrong and requiring redress, leading to movement formation. At such times of rapid institutional change dominant class interests are typically divided as an established normative social order is questioned and challenged. Piven and Cloward argue that when the grievances of the poor are declared to be just by members of a political elite then the hopes of the lower classes are nourished whilst the legitimacy of the institutions oppressing them is reduced.

Fox-Piven and Cloward thus offer a structural account of protest cycles linked to fundamental institutional change and their approach to political process emphasises the intersection of political opportunity structures and the social location of poor people in shaping forms of intervention. They thus distance themselves from functionalist, **collective behaviour** and mass society approaches which depict movement activity as irrational (Parsons 1969), primitive (Smelser 1962), extremist and undemocratic (Kornhauser 1959). The social location and resources available to poor peoples' movements lead to acts that are forms of intelligent political behaviour. These behaviours include strategic swings in electoral allegiance, withdrawal of labour, public demonstrations, riots and machine wrecking.

Poor peoples' movements are seen to arise directly out of the day to day experiences, constraints and resources of those involved and are systemic attempts by the least privileged to wrest concessions from their rulers. They note that poor people frequently target the immediate source of their oppression (slum landlords) rather than the deeper sources of their poverty (bank interest rates) but that this is an inescapable feature of the political process overlooked by pluralist interest representation models. Whilst these interventions can lead to violence they note that private and public armies have been responsible for the majority of violence on the streets.

The election of Barack Obama as US President in face of the most serious recession since the 1930s in 2008 is redolent of many of the processes analysed by Fox-Piven and Cloward. The restructuring of the US economy over the coming years is likely to evoke a number of poor peoples' movements as issues of social and environmental justice entwine in a period of institutional restructuring.

References and resources

Fox-Piven, F. and Cloward R. A. (1977); Ruggiero, V. and Montagna, N. (eds. 2008: 170–176).

POWER

Social movements have power, they have the capacity to mobilise people and achieve change, and they have the power to affect the social, cultural and political realms. This is commonly known as 'power to'. Social movements are also produced by power relations (see **political opportunity structure**, **identity politics**) and they are often both opposed, and subject to, the exercise of power by political elites, state institutions and policing agencies, those who have 'power over'. The distinction between 'power to' and 'power over' is an important one, because as Tarrow (1998: 23) points out 'a good part of the power of movements comes from the fact that they activate people over whom they have no control'. This autonomy of movement actors is both a strength and a weakness. It allows movements to avoid centralisation and bureaucratisation, but it can also diffuse the power of a movement and provoke factionalisation and internal competition. Social movements are therefore unlikely to have 'power over', yet their analysis of the prevailing matrix of social and political power relations is often crucial to the identification of an adversary, and the strategic and tactical repertoires of collective action through which that adversary is engaged. Indeed Melucci argues that 'Whether wittingly or not, the debate on the significance of collective action always embraces the issue of power relationships, and on closer examination derives its energy from either defending or contesting a specific position or form of dominance' (1996: 3).

Thinking about power in this way helps us to see that it is complex and relational and social movements may be engaged in contesting or defending its use in specific situations. It also helps us clarify that social movement struggles are not constructed in opposition to power *per se*, but rather against an agent or institution whose power is partially constructed by those who oppose it. This field of relations provides the framework for the contested demands and discourses which produce and refine the individual subject and the collective actor: a subject at once capable of undergoing and articulating power, a subject who in interacting with others is actually partaking of, and reproducing, a discursive set of power and knowledge relations. Power is therefore neither wholly negative, nor *must* it oppress, but in its circulation, it reveals interstices: gaps and crevices in the construction of normative frameworks, spaces that might allow for potentially new situations to emerge.

Some of the most influential work on power is to be found in Michel Foucault's genealogies of disciplinary control (1975, 1977, 1979). In his 'histories of the present', he describes a system of power, beginning in the eighteenth century, that becomes ever more complete through the extension of disciplinary institutions and discursive, linguistic and symbolic formations that regulate and order life. Gilles Deleuze (1992) takes this further in his 'postscript on societies of control' arguing that the pervasive character of technology and disciplinary logic in late modernity allows for the dispersal of control mechanisms throughout society, so that we are now subject to continuous monitoring through the modulation and extension of formerly spatially bounded institutional logics. In Deleuze's account, the institutional discipline present in schools, factories, hospitals and prisons is extended by technologically mediated and 'virtual' means to regulate the entirety of life, introducing a constant sense of anxiety, surveillance and discipline. Examples might include 'life-long' learning, community health regimes, risk assessment, 'performance' management and the 'invisible', immaterial prisons constructed by CCTV, electronic tagging, biometric identity cards and control orders. These forms of control find local and global expressions and have developed in parallel to the extension of systems of governance to the global level, the integration of financial systems and the liberalisation of capital flows to form what Hardt and Negri (2000) describe as 'Empire'.

In this context, it is suggested that a primary role of social movements is to 'make power visible in systems where power becomes increasingly anonymous and neutral, where it is incorporated in formal procedures' (Melucci 1985: 792). One way of doing this is to recognise the ambiguity of power in a society where the production and circulation of information is central to its functioning (Castells 1996; Melucci 1996). Because, despite the diffusion of control it is also argued that power 'has today decisively exposed itself to its own weakness: where symbols enter the constitution of the field, they render it open to multiple interpretations and into something that is never under full control' (Melucci 1996: 176). So as Hetherington (1998) argues, the spaces to escape domination, therefore, may be as symbolic as they are physical, and the very desire to inhabit them a form of resistance.

References and resources

Castells, M. (1996); Deleuze, G. (1992); Deleuze, G. and Parnet, C. (2002); Foucault, M. (1975, 1979, 1997); Hardt, M. and Negri, A. (2000); Hetherington, K. (1998); Melucci, A. (1985, 1996); Tarrow, S. (1998).

PRECARITY

Precarity emerged at the turn of the twenty-first century as a concept describing the condition of precariousness associated with short-term, insecure, flexible and often highly exploited forms of labour. It is a concept that was originally developed by social movements in Italy and Spain who were keen to promote awareness building and unionisation amongst workers involved in precarious forms of employment. It is also closely associated with Italian autonomist Marxist theory and the work of Hardt and Negri (2000) and Virno (2004) on 'immaterial labour theory', a body of work that has generated significant debate and critique in social movement networks (Federici 2010).

The concept was popularised by Chainworkers, a Milan-based 'media and mall activism' group. They argued that the concept of precarity emphasised the need to attend to a new dynamic in the process of class composition – the dynamic field of relations between capital and labour – which changes according to the balance of struggle and the technological, analytical and psycho-social resources available to either side (Shukaitis 2007). They also sought to 'socialise' the concept and to demonstrate how precarity as the prevailing experience of the mode of production was becoming a generalised experience for those subjected to the marketisation of public and private life. For example, whilst precarity can be understood as describing a set of working conditions it also describes how, under conditions of neoliberal restructuring, opportunities for work provided by inward investment in situations of regional competition are uncertain and temporary. Such investment is often premised on large direct and indirect business subsidies, the imposition of planning regimes driven by economic regeneration and processes of social segregation and gentrification that subsequently erode informal solidarities, which might otherwise provide a sense of security and identity.

Those activists and associated academics working with this concept argue that as the process of production becomes distributed across larger geographic scales, and devolved through chains of subsidiary and contracted producers, large-scale, centrally located and corporately owned production facilities such as factories are reduced in importance as sites of resistance. Instead, in a post-Fordist economy other locations and forms of labour become equally, if not more, valuable to capital, including services, marketing and 'affective' and 'emotional' forms of labour. This leads to a recognition that cultural production is as important as material production to the success of capitalist enterprise. It is no longer sufficient to manufacture the latest 4x4 vehicle, one also needs to bond the consumer to the brand, and instil a sense of potential to the purchase that helps build or reaffirm the consumer's sense of their projected identity.

The precarious nature of work within globalised production chains, the promotion and marketing of products and the reliance upon 'soft' or 'affective' skills such as communication and emotionality carried out by workers who are often distant from each other highlights the difficulties involved in organising effective opposition to these processes. The concept of precarity is a shorthand means of raising these issues, whilst retaining a focus upon the traditional capital/labour dynamic and referring to processes which include both 'white' and 'blue' collar workers.

References and resources

Hardt, M. and Negri, A. (2000, 2004); Ross, A. (2009); Shukaitis, S. (2007); Virno, P. (2004).

Carlsson, C. and Foti, A. (2006) *Understanding Precarity: Chris Carlsson interviews Alex Foti*. Available at: http://precariousunderstanding.blogsome.com/2006/07/27/ chris-carlsson-interviews-alex-foti/ Chainworkers: http://www.ecn.org/chainworkers

EuroMayDay: http://www.euromayday.org

Federici, S. (2006) *Precarious Labour: A Feminist Viewpoint*, A lecture given at Bluestockings Bookstore on October, 28th. Available at: http://inthemiddleofthewhirlwind.wordpress.com/precarious-labor-a-feminist-viewpoint/

Mute Magazine's *Precarious Reader*. Available at: http://www.metamute.org/en/ Precarious-Reader

PROTEST AND DISORDER

Theories of social movement protest and social disorder share a common history. They were both originally theorised as examples of societal breakdown caused by irrational responses to crises provoked by periods of accelerated social or economic change. In this context, it was argued, societies' mechanisms for social integration might fail, leading to collective and individual grievances and/or social alienation that would find expression in some form of social movement protest or community disorder (Smelser 1962).

Subsequently, **resource mobilisation theory (RMT)** was able to demonstrate that social movements were in fact a ubiquitous and therefore 'normal' part of the functioning of developed societies and the emphasis within social movement studies moved away from analysing protest events as an outcome of crises and as symptomatic of disorder and towards a concept of protest as routine and rational. Similarly, criminological accounts of 'protest events' tended to reduce a protest to its visible manifestation, with its success measured against a set of political objectives conflated from banners, speeches and other texts and documents. Broader questions concerning the composition of the movement behind a protest, the level of challenge to the normative order – the 'peace' – that the police are charged with upholding, and the impact of particular protest policing strategies upon social movement composition were largely left out of the analysis.

Therefore, social movement protests in both RMT and criminological accounts tend to be conceived similarly. Protest is regarded as an empirical category comprising issue-oriented purposive behaviour, which despite its potential for disruption or violence is essentially an appropriate exercise of dissent in a liberal democracy. Beyond this logic is public disorder, which may or may not carry demands, but which nonetheless omits to engage with the protocols of protest.

Public disorder as an analytical category is frequently defined by description of what it is not – that is, protest. As such, it is distinguished by a lack of an easily accessible and relatively uncontested *raison d'être* for collective action involving violence and disruption. Such disorder can involve events such as localised clashes with police in everyday contexts, such as the housing estates and shopping malls of the inner city (Waddington *et al.* 1989) or in industrial disputes, but it might also involve clashes between football supporters (Dunning *et al.* 1988; Marsh 1979). However, some commentators argue these forms of disorder might also be considered as protests (Benyon and Solomos 1987; Hall *et al.* 1978) which raises further questions about how to distinguish meaningfully between a) protests; b) anomic forms of disorder; and c) instrumental or expressive social movement activity.

The shift in focus from explaining the 'why' of a movement to explaining the 'how' of a movement undertaken by RMT theorists, meant that analysis of the common factor in both protest and disorder – policing – became a minority interest within social movement studies and largely became the preserve of criminology. However, as della Porta (1996) notes, the management and policing of protests is an important indication of the receptivity of the State and the public to the issues raised by movements and is therefore central to analysing the **political opportunity structure** at a given moment. della Porta's (1995, 1998) work is therefore an important bridge between social movement theory and more orthodox criminological accounts of protest.

In summary, 'protest' is normally considered to be an unproblematic expression of particular (rational) interests, not requiring further explanation, whilst 'disorder' is seen as pathological, abnormal and irrational, requiring sociological explanation. The one factor common to both forms of collective action, protest and disorder is policing and an important attempt to reintroduce the policing of protest as a core concern for social movement theorists is the work of della Porta (1995, 1998).

References and resources

Benyon, J. and Solomos, J. (eds. 1987); della Porta, D. (1995, 1996); della Porta, D. and Reiter, H. (eds. 1998); Dunning, E., Murphy, P. and Williams, J. (1988); Hall, S., Chricher, C., Jefferson, T., Clarke, J. and Roberts, B. (1978); Marsh, P. (1979); Smelser, N. (1962); Waddington, D. *et al.* (1989).

RECLAIM THE STREETS

Reclaim The Streets (RTS) was a **network movement** that emerged in the early1990s in Britain, before quickly spreading across the world. It brought together ecological, anticapitalist and social justice themes through carnivalesque parties that blocked roads, transformed public spaces and challenged state and capitalist institutions. Its culmination was a 'Carnival Against Capitalism' in the City of London on 18 June 1999, the second of many 'Global Days of Action' catalysed by the **alternative globalisation movement** and chosen to coincide with the meetings of the G8 on the same day in Cologne, Germany.

In its first incarnation RTS emerged as the idea of a small number of London-based activists who got together in 1991, to campaign: 'FOR walking, cycling and cheap, or free, public transport, and AGAINST cars, roads and the system that pushes them'. RTS was later absorbed into a determined and highly imaginative anti-roads campaign against the M11 motorway through east London (McLeish and Welsh 1996). However, there were significant continuities between the RTS of 1991 and its re-emergence in early 1995, soon after the British Goverment had brought in criminal justice legislation aimed at a variety of countercultural and protest activity (Criminal Justice and Public Order Act, 1994).

The idea behind RTS was to recreate the autonomous, carnivalesque space of the protest against the M11 on major thoroughfares, thereby stopping traffic and transforming spaces previously enclosed by the movement of vehicles. Utilising surprise, and the creative ingenuity acquired by resisting the M11, a form of spatial guerrilla warfare was enacted. A prominent activist John Jordan (1998: 141) suggested that: 'Once again we were introducing play into politics, challenging official culture's claims to authority, stability, sobriety, immutability and immortality by cheekily taking over a main traffic artery.'

After their first party in Camden, word spread quickly through environmental activist networks and amongst those organising free parties or resisting the Criminal Justice and Public Order Act. Over the next six months RTS-type actions took place in Birmingham, Manchester, Bristol and Leeds, and within 12 months of the second party (in London) RTS took over a major motorway (M41) and held it with 8,000–10,000 people, who played and partied whilst activists drilled holes in the motorway and planted trees reclaimed from the route of the M11. Activists from RTS subsequently played a major role in the foundation of **Peoples' Global Action** and the promotion of globally co-ordinated protests including the 'Global Street Party' against the G8 in Birmingham in 1998 and protests against the WTO in Geneva days later.

The audacity of RTS was made apparent on 18 June 1999 in the Carnival Against Capitalism in the City of London, when they managed to close the trading floor of the London International Financial Futures and Options Exchange having built a wall across the entrance doorway and emblazoned it with the slogan 'There's no future in Futures'. On the same day they also produced and distributed a spoof of the London evening paper the *Evening Standard*, entitled 'Evading Standards'; its headline read 'Global Market meltdown' (a somewhat portentous insight into events that were to occur a decade later) and included detailed analysis of the problems associated with and caused by neoliberal capitalism.

References and resources

Jordan, J. (1998); McLeish, P. and Welsh, I. (1996).
June 18th, 1999 – Carnival Against Capitalism: http://www.nadir.org/nadir/initiativ/agp/free/global/j18london/index.htm

REPERTOIRE OF ACTION

Term used to denote a particular form of action developed and deployed by a social movement actor. A repertoire develops in a particular place and is shaped by the prevailing sense of justice to which it must appeal and the type of society within which it is to be used. The disciplined street march is a prominent example of a classic social movement repertoire. The act of sitting down en-mass in a public space and refusing to move is a classic non-violent repertoire of action used in acts of civil disobedience. This was widely used in the US **Civil Rights Movement** during the 1960s and was adopted by a number of other movements. In pluralist interest representation models the establishment of a campaigning organisation would be a repertoire of action. The term can be applied to a diverse range of activities.

Whilst generic repertoires of action can have historically durable forms, such as the withdrawal of labour through strike action, they are also subject to innovation and hybridisation. The combination of strike action combined with the occupation of a factory melds two forms of action. Withdrawal of sexual services, political participation via elections and withdrawal of trust have all become features of movement campaigns. The term thus makes it possible to trace, construct and analyse shifts in the tactical means of social movement interventions and to study how repertoires of action are transferred between movements (Tilly 2004).

The effectiveness of repertoires of action in different places and countries can be the subject of comparative studies. The relative impact of anti-nuclear (Flam 1994) and environmental movements (Dryzek *et al.* 2003) in different countries are examples of such work. This sort of analytical work assesses the extent to which a movement achieves its declaratory posture. The 1990s was a period of particularly rapid innovation in repertoires of action in Europe and America as a diverse range of political and cultural movements consolidated. These combined elements of established repertoires of action such as occupation with elements of the musical and performing arts and guerrilla insurgency techniques such as tunnelling. **Reclaim The Streets** was a prominent example of this movement tendency. Enhanced physical mobility and increasingly widespread video-streaming capabilities increased the spread of particular repertoires of action during this period.

References and resources

Dryzek, J. S., Downes, D., Hunold, C., Scholsberg, D., with Hans-Kristian Hernes (2003); Flam, H. (1994); Tilly, C. (2004).

RESOURCE MOBILISATION THEORY

In the 1970s a number of US sociologists began working on the concept of resource mobilisation as a means of explaining the social movement activity that had become an intrinsic part of North American society. Their starting position was to depart from **collective behaviour** theory to argue that grievances of one form or another are a common feature in all societies, and the existence of such grievances is insufficient on its own to explain the rise of social movements.

Resource mobilisation theorists (McCarthy and Zald 1977, 1987; Oberschall 1973; Tilly 1978) argue that instead of trying to discover *what* grievance gave rise to *which* movement, the focus of theorists' attention should be upon how social movements mobilise successfully. In addressing this question, they assert the primary importance of the resources (money, people, technologies, skills) available to social movement actors in the process of mobilisation. This approach was strongly influenced by rational choice theory and in particular Mancur Olson's (1968) work *The Logic of Collective Action*.

In moving the emphasis from 'why' movements mobilise, to 'how' they mobilise, resource mobilisation theorists shifted the emphasis of movement analysis away from structural factors and towards organisational questions. This work has been attributed, in part, as a response to the growing importance of economics within the US academy at the time (Tarrow 1998).

Resource mobilisation theory (RMT) has had a large impact upon social movement theory, and many familiar terms and concepts originate in this body of literature. Reflecting the influence of economic theory McCarthy and Zald (1977, 1987) introduced the idea of 'movement organisations', 'entrepreneurs' and 'industries', a conceptual language, which as Tarrow remarked (1998: 16), tended to leave cold those who had direct involvement with social movements, but which has nonetheless provided significant analytical insights. These concepts opened the door for an extensive research programme and were important in the rapid growth of RMT as the paradigm for social movement analysis in the USA.

Although the concept of a 'resource' has been stretched by contemporary cultural interpretations of social movement activity to include abstract resources such as ideology (Moaddel 1992), those who have done the most to develop the theory argue that RMT analysts utilise the concept at two levels:

1   First at a mezzo level, or in entrepreneurial mode, 'the analysis emphasizes how social movement organisations and cadre combine money, materials, people and technology into strategic and tactical action' (McCarthy and Zald 1987: 45).

2   Second at a macro level, the level of 'infrastructure', RMT theorists analyse 'the set of roles and facilities that are generally available to people in a society or social segment' (ibid. 1987: 45).

This second level positions social movements within a 'sector' comprised of competing social movement organisations subject to the competition between various sectors of society for generalised institutional and societal resources. Consequently, this second level analysis, manifestly influenced by the pluralist system of political expression in the USA, contains the implicit understanding that the goals of social movements are the articulation of a particular claim on societal resources and, as such, are in competition with various other sectors (business, commerce etc.) for the allocation of these limited resources. This has led to a variety of criticisms, particularly from **new social movement** theorists, who have suggested that RMT is 'indifferent to the political or ideological content of a movement' and is 'applied in an almost mechanistic way to organisations of widely different political and ideological scope, without incorporating these factors within the workings of the model' (Dalton *et al.* 1990: 10). The first 'entrepreneurial' level of analysis, however, has received less overt criticism, due to the wealth of empirically rich research it has produced at the micro and mezzo levels of mobilisation, and because of its salience to the development of other theoretical perspectives, such as **frame analysis**.

Important within RMT (McCarthy and Zald 1987) is the concept of the 'movement professional' or 'entrepreneur' which describes those individuals who play significant roles in securing either cognitive or material resources. This has a certain resonance with the Gramscian notion of the 'organic intellectual', or Foucault's 'specific intellectual'. Subsequently, social movement theorists such as Eyerman and Jamison (1991: 94–119) have developed the concept of the 'movement intellectual' within a broader framework of **cognitive praxis**, which they perceive as the 'core identity' or 'deep structure' (ibid. 1991: 44) of a movement, and which is shaped by the ability of social movement intellectuals to frame conflicts in terms of knowledge and information, and to produce and manipulate ideas and symbols within that context.

References and resources

Eyerman, R. and Jamison, A. (1991); McCarthy, J. D. and Zald, M. N. (1977, 1987); Moaddel, M. (1992); Oberschall, A. (1973); Olson, M. (1968); Tarrow, S. (1998); Tilly, C. (1978).

SCIENTIFIC SOCIAL MOVEMENT

Yearley (1988) argued that science represents a historically significant social movement seeking to harness public opinion behind a utopian vision of progress driven by an uncomplicated scientific rationality. Scientific social movements are thus engaged in a struggle to win social and political acceptance of the overall superiority of scientific method over other forms of knowledge and rationality.

The historic pursuit of scientific interest representation remains important in the contemporary milieu as debates about creationism, for example, continue to be prominent. The relationship between political, social, economic and scientific rationalities within decision-making processes have increased in prominence over time. The Welsh Assembly Government in the United Kingdom describes its stance on scientific advice as ensuring that 'science is on tap not on top' underlining a commitment to prioritise social and political judgements. Debates over the appropriate place for, and weighting attached to, scientific advice clearly continue to be important. Whilst science is often approached in this overarching manner there are also specific sciences and this gives rise to scientific social movements seeking to advance particular scientific or techno-scientific projects.

One example can be seen in *Technocracy Inc* which was a popular social movement with a mass membership comprised of scientists and engineers in 1930s' America. *Technocracy Inc* advocated the resolution of all social and political problems by expert means and convened mass rallies where members, with their distinctive dress codes, would assemble (Ross 1991). In the United Kingdom the Association of Scientific Workers argued that the pursuit of science was central to democracy and that science proved its worth through the defeat of fascism in the Second World War. During the post-war period the relationship between science and democracy in the pursuit of a public good developed as nuclear power held out the prospect of limitless energy (Welsh 2000).

Scientific social movements advocating particular techno-sciences are typically composed of sections of a scientific labour force, sponsoring bodies and parts of the political and administrative elements of a society. The use of public museums and display spaces to mount exhibitions is one example of how these various elements combine. The development of scientific discovery centres, exploratory and technology parks represent contemporary examples of the pursuit of public support for the sciences. The prominence of genetic and genomic installations in these sites reflects the intensity of public responses to products such as genetically modified food in Europe. Within the industrialised nations the prominence given to knowledge economies continues to make the public support for the sciences a prominent theme within scientific governance initiatives.

Movements for social responsibility in the development, utilisation and implementation of techno-sciences represent a third type of scientific social movement. Following the development of the atomic bomb eminent physicists played a prominent role in the creation of PUGWASH, a movement of intellectuals and opinion formers dedicated to opposing nuclear weapons (http://www.pugwash.org/). The organisation was named after the location of its initial meeting in 1957 in response to the 1955 manifesto against weapons of mass destruction issued by Albert Einstein and Bertrand Russell. One of the founders, Joseph Rotblat, was influential in broadening the scope of this movement organisation to address issues of science and world affairs (Rotblat 1997). Rotblat sought to unite the scientific community's heightened awareness of the global interdependence of all nations and citizens behind a campaign for political and scientific responsibility. INES, The International Network of Engineers and Scientists for Global Responsibility, is another example of this kind of scientific social movement organisation (http://www.ines-global.com).

References and resources

Hess, D., Breyman, S., Campell, N. and Martin, B. (2008); Ross, A. (1991); Rotblat, J. (ed. 1997); Welsh, I. (2000); Yearley, S. (1988).

SITUATIONIST INTERNATIONAL

The Situationist International (SI) is known primarily for its role in helping inspire the May uprising in Paris during 1968 and for the publication of two revolutionary texts – *Society of the Spectacle* by Guy Debord (1967) and *The Revolution of Everyday Life* by Raoul Vaneigem (1967). The SI was an experiment in returning the idea of revolution to avant-garde movements and was founded in the Italian village of Cosio d'Arroscia on 28 July 1957 by participants from eight countries (Jappe 1999). Its praxis entailed a total rejection of existing social and political institutions, all of which were representative of what the SI called the 'spectacle' – mediated consumer capitalism and its penetration of every aspect of social, political and cultural life. The spectacle they suggest integrates the economy and the State and produces alienated and passive consumers who spend their time contemplating images chosen for them by others, rather than gaining direct experience of self-determination. If the spectacle is to be resisted its opponents are required to plan and construct situations that radically disrupt and disturb the normative frameworks upon which the spectacle is reliant. To this end, the SI outlined, advanced and practised, a number of forms of intervention and activism that were designed to undermine the spectacle. These included détournement – the practice of re-ordering existing cultural materials to reveal something new or shocking (e.g. cartoons or advertising hoardings subtly changed to articulate critiques of anything from capitalism to militarism and patriarchy, see also **subvertising**) and the dérive – the attempt to analyse the totality of the everyday by drifting through spaces and allowing oneself to be drawn by the attractions of the terrain, the vagaries of mood and ambience, and the encounters that might be forthcoming. The aim was to unsettle the familiarity of a landscape determined by set patterns of work or leisure and a famous example involved navigating one city (Paris) by use of the map of another city (Berlin).

Sadie Plant (1992) has argued persuasively that the influence of the Situationist International can be detected in many of the socio-cultural and political movements that have emerged during the last thirty years, and she contends that social theoretical developments encapsulated in debates about postmodernism and post-structuralism contain within them a stylistic and substantive resonance of situationist debates. A resonance, however, which is often devoid of the revolutionary intent of situationist analyses 'Postmodernity comes equipped with a refusal to countenance the possibilities of social transformation' (Plant 1992: 195). Plant argues that whilst the situationists argued against a 'world view populated by a teleological understanding of history, essentialist conceptions of the subject, and illegitimate references to something better, more real, more true, and more desired than the present' (Plant 1992: 186), they retained a belief in the possibility of constructing collective action that might evade 'recuperation' by 'spectacular society'. This would be achieved through the reflexive capacities of movements who would become attuned to the vagaries in the operation and circulation of power, where power 'is quite different from and more complicated, dense and pervasive than a set of laws or state apparatus' (Foucault 1986: 158, cited in Plant 1992: 117).

The Situationist International have had a remarkably low profile in academic discourse despite their centrality to the 1968 events, and it has been persuasively argued that this is a direct result of their not having renounced the possibility of revolutionary social change, a charge made against other intellectuals of that period (Plant 1992; Shukaitis and Graeber 2007: 18–25). However, they remain a popular source of ideas and inspiration for many contemporary radical movements, particularly in Europe and the USA, and there exists a large and growing set of web resources provided by socio-cultural historians and movement archivists.

References and resources

Debord, G. (1967/1983); Jappe, A. (1999); Plant, S. (1992); Shukaitis, S. and Graeber, D. (eds. 2007); Vaneigem, R. (1967/1994).

SOCIAL MOVEMENT ORGANISATION

This concept was introduced into the literature by resource mobilisation theorists (McCarthy and Zald 1977, 1987; Zald and Ash 1966) and forms part of a series of linked concepts that reflects the influence of economic theory in thinking about social movements, which perceived them as akin to 'businesses' composing a 'sector' within a society. Whilst the use of concepts such as social movement 'entrepreneurs' and 'businesses' has faded, the idea of social movement organisations (SMOs) has maintained a presence within social movement studies. In part, this is due to its straightforward descriptive utility, an SMO is a formally organised component of a broader social movement within which there is likely to be a number of SMOs. Classic examples of SMOs would be the Student Non-violent Coordinating Committee (SNCC) and the Congress of Racial Equality (CORE) in the American **Civil Rights Movement, Friends of the Earth** and **Greenpeace International** within the **environmental movement**.

In their account of what constitutes an SMO, McCarthy and Zald (1977) focus upon a number of what they argue are common characteristics. They suggest that an SMO will identify with the broad aims or preferences of a social movement but will also define specific goals to achieve. It will have resources of some form including specialist skills, facilities, equipment, labour, money or legitimacy to call upon and the amount of effort directed towards goal accomplishment is a function of the resources available to the organisation (ibid. 1977: 1221). When consolidating resources an SMO might also engage in competitive struggle with other SMOs within the same social movement. Although this will be dependent upon the flow of resources available to the 'social movement sector', McCarthy and Zald postulate the idea that 'the greater the absolute amount of resources available to the SMS the greater the likelihood that new SMIs (Social Movement Industries) and SMOs will develop to compete for these resources' (1977: 1225). This can lead to intra-movement conflict that can be further exacerbated by regulatory or legal requirements governing the involvement of members and the acquisition of resources. These regulatory frameworks for the management of formal organisations can impede the use of antagonistic or confrontational protest repertoires, leading to concerns that SMOs might act as a brake upon radical movements. This is a point made by Zald and Ash (1966: 327) in the paper that originally introduced the concept to social movement studies, who suggest that a 'movement organization will become more conservative and that its goals will be displaced in favour of organizational maintenance'.

There have been a number of criticisms made of **resource mobilisation theory** (RMT) that include consideration of its use of SMO as a key concept, and these criticisms focus upon what are considered to be its overly economistic, rational and functional accounts of complex behaviours (see **Resource Mobilisation Theory**). However, other criticisms of this approach also highlight that the concept of the SMO as used by McCarthy and Zald fails to distinguish sufficiently between SMOs and formal interest groups, up to and including political parties, for which they suggest comparisons are applicable. It is also argued that their emphasis upon professional movement organisations detracts from consideration of the many informal grassroots organisations that are essential to movement building (Tarrow 1998: 16).

References and resources

McCarthy, J. D. and Zald, M. N. (1977, 1987); Tarrow, S. (1998); Zald, M. N. and Ash, R. (1966).

SOCIAL MOVEMENT SOCIETY

This is a macro-analytical concept that gained prominence in the mid-1990s through the work of social movement scholars from the resource mobilisation (see **resource mobilisation theory**) and political process (see **political opportunity structure**) schools. It contends that advanced industrial democracies have institutionalised social movement forms of representing claims to such an extent that they have become a conventional part of the accepted mechanisms for democratic participation (Meyer and Tarrow 1998: 4) – therefore it follows that we are living in a social movement society. This argument rests upon three hypotheses:

1   Social protest has become ubiquitous in modern life. It has gone from being a familiar but sporadic form of raising grievances to being a perpetual feature of social and political engagement.
2   Protest is more widely used by all constituencies and in relation to a larger number of issues than was previously the case.
3   Professionalisation and institutionalisation has the effect of bringing social movement behaviour within the practice and discourse of conventional politics.

Essential to this argument is a range of survey research and other quantitative methods utilised to compare protest activity in the USA and a number of European countries (Dalton 1996; Kriesi, *et al.* 1995). This suggested a growing involvement in 'contentious politics' by a wide range of social actors, albeit with distinctive national characteristics including base levels of protest activity and variations in the reported rates of increased participation. After reviewing this work Meyer and Tarrow argue that 'the last thirty years have seen a generalization of the repertoire of contention across age groups, from men to women, from left to right, and from workers and students to other social groupings' (1998: 11). However, they also argue that greater participation in contentious politics does not lead to increased contention more generally, so that whilst people protest more, the repertoires they engage in are more likely to be institutionalised. They suggest that this institutionalisation takes place through processes of routinisation, inclusion and maginalisation, and co-optation. Routinisation involves the recognition by movement actors and their adversaries of a common and acceptable script for action. Inclusion and marginalisation involves institutional recognition of those willing to abide by these routines coupled with exclusion from the political exchange process for those who are not. Co-optation involves the alteration of demands or tactics to forms of activity amenable to the continuation of normal politics.

The macro-theoretical claims of this concept provide an interesting framework for social movement theory and research. The concept provokes historical questions about the nature and form of the challenge movements pose to political structures and processes, as well as methodological and definitional questions about the relationships between movements, interest groups, non-governmental organisations and governance processes. Can movements be sustained without professionalising or becoming institutionalised and what forms of movement are best able to achieve this? Can we determine the point at which a movement becomes something different, what forms of organisation can constitute a movement and do similar actions conducted by different actors mean the same thing? Meyer and Tarrow argue that the processes of institutionalisation and professionalisation that occur at the end of a protest cycle frequently result in the radicalisation of movements who refuse to be co-opted, or for whom the issue at stake is irresolvable within the given political system of interest representation. The explosion of collective action around issues of neoliberal globalisation, corporate power and climate change at the end of the 1990s might serve as support for this hypothesis.

References and resources

Dalton, R. (1996); Kriesi, H., Koopmans, R., Duyvendak, J.-W. and Giugni, M. (1995); Meyer, D. and Tarrow, S. (eds. 1998).

SOCIAL MOVEMENT UNIONISM

'Social movement unionism' is a term applied to the radicalisation of established unions within the advanced industrial societies from the 1990s onwards. A definition of this emergent term is developed in this entry but this requires some historical and spatial contextualisation.

In the nations that underwent industrialisation from the eighteenth century to the start of the twentieth century the right to collective representation for workers in the pursuit of negotiated pay and working conditions arose through social movement activity. In countries such as the United Kingdom the resultant Labour movement led to the formation of a political party, the Labour Party, to advance these rights through legislative programmes. Within the industrialised nations of Europe and North America, trade unions became increasingly bureaucratic organisations aligned with prevailing political opportunity structures. Union politics were dominated by exerting influence on political parties and the use of workplace sanctions such as working to rule or ultimately the withdrawal of labour. In the developed economies of America, the United Kingdom and mainland Europe, trade unions were widely recognised as securing key rights of assembly and free speech which created vital preconditions for the emergence of the **new social movements** of the 1960s and 1970s. The **old social movements** were also seen as separate from, or even antithetical to, areas like the environment. The tensions created via the 'old' and 'new' underline the importance of the 'long duree' or extended timeline approach to social movement studies we advocate in our own work. The concept of social movement unionism, we believe, underpins this insight.

Social movement unionism refers to the re-emergence of locally based union organising aimed at reaching sectors of the workforce not usually represented within the collective bargaining process. The extension of traditional workplace rights approaches include broader agendas of social justice, civil rights, immigrant rights and economic justice for un-unionised workers. Campaigning towards these ends has entailed the adopting of repertoires of action not normally associated with formal trade union activity. These include forms of **direct action**, targeting particular corporations (e.g. Nike, Coca Cola), mounting media campaigns, forging alliances within affected communities, emphasising issues of dignity and fairness within the workplace and participating within broader movement networks such as the social forum process. Justice for Janitors is one of the better-known examples where unions have broadened their traditional repertoires of action to engage within the wider public sphere in the pursuit of members' interests.

Voss and Sherman (2000) argue that the transformation of trade unions from oligarchic institutions to reinvigorated social movement unionism comes about due to a 'negative environmental shift' combined with the emergence of new actors offering novel goals and aims which can be achieved via new strategies. The global ascendancy of neoliberalism has been identified by a range of writers as the systemic shock confronting all forms of social movement (Bourdieu 1998; Castells 1996; Clawson 2008) with trade unions being no exception. Voss and Sherman suggest that in the US case the shift to social movement unionism involved three major factors:

1   an internal political crisis within unions resulting in new leadership through either international union measures or local elections;
2   experience of other social movements amongst the new leadership, resulting in new organisational approaches;
3   a commitment to these innovations at the level of international unions.

It is important to remember that Voss and Sherman's work reflects the structure of union organisation within the USA but parallels in other advanced industrial nations are clearly discernable particularly within public sector unions such as UNISON which have been prominent within the European Social Forum process. The US Justice for Janitors initiative has been adapted and used within the United Kingdom and the intersection of Union campaigning with wider civil rights, social justice concerns and dignity and respect issues in the workplace is also widespread. All these factors suggest that social movement unionism is a contemporary phenomenon. Critically, however, this depends upon the conceptualisation of Unions as something other than social movement actors. Alan Touraine, for example, would argue that workers movements and unions are analytically social movements (see **old social movement**). The analytic stakes addressed by social movement unionism revolve around the question of organisational forms which permit effective action in pursuit of negotiated aims and objectives, whilst remaining sufficiently open to the agency of new entrants to avoid ossification and oligarchic tendencies. This makes it a key concept in the current conjuncture.

References and resources

Clawson, D. (2008); Fairbrother, P. (2008); Hurd, R., Milkman, R. and Turner, L. (2003); Schenk, C. in Fairbrother, P. and Yates C. (eds. 2003: 244–262); Voss. K. and Sherman, R. (2000).

STUDENTS FOR A DEMOCRATIC SOCIETY

This campus–based American student organisation was formally launched in 1962 at a conference coinciding with the publication in New York of the *Port Huron Statement of the Students for a Democratic Society,* (available at http://coursesa.matrix.edu/~hst306/documents/huron.html). In this lengthy document Students for a Democratic Society (SDS) self defined as a social movement presenting an agenda for a particular generation schooled in traditional American values underpinning the global advance of Western influence. SDS found the American traditions of individual freedom and equality, expressed through government of, by and for the people, fine in principle but wanting in practice. The SDS identified an urgent need for further democratisation. An important part of the SDS agenda was aimed at realising the potential of the university campus to generate the critical insights seen as central to realising the ideals of American democracy in the late twentieth century.

The SDS agenda addressed both domestic and foreign policy domains, representing a critique of racism, inequality and poverty at home and military interventionism abroad. The two were fused through an analytical focus upon the reflex to violence and the links between the military and industry structured through the Federal State's permanent war economy. The continuing 'war' against communism was identified as key in under-pinning the need for unquestioning social conformity reproduced through institutions, including the university. The US practice of intervening to destabilise unacceptable foreign governments, or regimes, was presented as 'an objectively justifiable phenomenon' resulting in 'Worldwide amuse-ment, cynicism and hatred towards the United States' (ibid.: 31).

SDS set out to forge links with community activists, the US labour movement, liberal and socialist intellectuals and activists. The aim was to place the campus at the heart of a co-operative effort to reformulate dem-ocratic goals and objectives to meet distinctly modern challenges. Amongst these the nuclear arms race and the accompanying prospect of the anihila-tion of human civilisation represented an important context. The norma-tive recourse to the threat or use of violence within both international relations and domestic politics effectively became a hinge linking the per-sonal and the big 'P' political.

The SDS agenda formalised important concerns which resonated with the **Civil Rights Movement** and anti-Vietnam war movement amongst others. SDS members both formalised and participated in these move-ments. Gitlin (1980), for example, regards the SDS march on Washington on 17 April 1965 as an event which placed both the student anti-war movement and SDS firmly on the wider public agenda. SDS members were also prominent participants within the Freedom Summer event which sought to enfranchise people of colour (routinely referred to as Negros within SDS literature). These national interventions aside, it is also important to recognise the campus-based activities of SDS.

Paper copies of The Port Huron Statement passed from student to student at hundreds of campuses throughout America but a mass membership was not consolidated until 1964. The Statement defined campus life as a key means of social reproduction, being 'a place of systematic study schedules, two nights each week for beer, a girl or two, and early marriage'. In a decade where advances in birth control and sexual liberation were co-causative in changing moral codes the actions of college authorities as parental surrogates enforcing single sex dormitories and limited visiting times were linked to wider political activism. In 1964 mass protests at Berkeley were triggered when students were stopped from displaying 'political' literature on the Bancroft walkway on the basis that it was university property. The ensuing occupation of student halls and mass demonstrations became entrenched and confrontational and eventually saw the President of Berkeley removed from office. Campus protests continued to be important across America until 1970 when a 'threatened' US National Guard unit 'lawfully killed' five students and wounded eight during demonstrations at Kent State University. Of those shot dead the closest was 260 feet away from the Guard's skirmish line.

Increasingly frustrated by the failure of a co-operative mass movement to cohere beyond campus and under different influences following the founding leaderships' graduation, the SDS adopted increasingly militant stances and forms. The Weathermen and Weather Undergound were prominent examples (Gilbert 2002) and featured in the lyrics of Bob Dylan and Jimmy Hendrix. The pre-feminist anatomy of the SDS was another factor in its decline. The SDS in effect lasted for just under a decade but has to be recognised as a key social movement in the formalisation of a 'new left' (US House of Representatives, 2005) in America and an important contributory source of subsequent movements. The campus occupation and opposition to the war in Vietnam and military interventionism more generally was an influential link with student movements in Europe leading to correspondence between Adorno in Germany and Marcuse in America (Leslie 1999). The differences and similarities in the trajectories of these movements on either side of the Atlantic can be easily missed and play an important part in understanding American and European approaches to new social movements.

In 2006 SDS was relaunched via the web and in 2007 launched Movement for a Democratic Society (MDS) (see www.movementforade mocraticsociety.org) as a forum for post-graduate professionals, fulfilling one of the goals of the original SDS. MDS is an education and social action organisation dedicated to increasing democracy in all phases of our common life. It seeks to promote the active participation of ordinary people in the formation of a movement to build a society free from poverty, ignorance, war, exploitation, racism and sexism.

References and resources

Gilbert, D. (2002); Gitlin, T. (1980); Leslie, E. (1999); US House of Representatives (2005).

SUBVERTISING

Subvertising is a form of symbolic protest using interventions that are designed to playfully disrupt the normative meanings of a particular message or space in ways that invoke a critique of the norms involved. The practice of subvertising involves changing the meaning of commercial logos, advertisements or political messages through cut and paste techniques that mirror the form and design of the original whilst reappropriating its message, a primary purpose being to disrupt the perpetuation of corporate and elitist values in public spaces. As a practice, it is also associated with 'ad busting' or 'culture jamming' (see http://www.adbusters.org; Lassn 1999), the latter including performative and artistic interventions to critique dominant social and political discourses. Well-known culture jammers include RTMark (http://www.rtmark.com/) and the Yes Men (http://www.theyesmen.org/). Subvertising also includes some forms of graffiti art, notable examples being the work of the pseudonymous artist banksy (http://www.banksy.co.uk/) whose themes are invariably concerned with social and political change.

Subvertising has its origins in the practice of détournement, a French term originally used by the **Situationist International (SI)** to describe the distortion, misuse or reappropriation of popular cultural forms to challenge and reveal the hidden assumptions, inequalities and forms of structural oppression represented within these forms. The SI (see Debord and Wolman 1956) were very keen to emphasise that this practice is not merely about provoking a scandal along the lines of Marcel Duchamp's drawing of a moustache on the Mona Lisa, but is instead about how such interventions can be used to educate people about the ideological formations behind prevailing cultural codes.

Subvertising pokes fun at the powerful and has been theorised as indicative of a renewed emphasis upon the importance of 'fun' in protest, which is also evidenced by the rise of clowning and other novel repertoires of protest action (see http://www.clownarmy.org/). However, Wettergren (2009) argues that there is an important distinction to be made here between the fake fun of the consumerist ready-made (the promise of products created for the consumers' fun) that asserts 'the replaceability of the consumer', and the authentic fun created by subvertisers and culture jammers, a difference Wettergren describes as that between 'buying pleasure and creating pleasure' (2009: 5).

References and resources

Debord, G. and Wolman, G. J. (1956); Lassn, K. (1999); Wettergren, A. (2009).

URBAN SOCIAL MOVEMENT

The Spanish theorist Manuel Castells (1983) developed this term in the context of a particularly intense period of urban renewal associated with wider economic restructuring. The term was applied to grass roots movements whose aims included a systemic change in 'urban meaning' or the prevailing political and economic status quo. Urban social movements transformed 'urban meaning' by appropriating a significant degree of control over urban processes through negotiated goals of collective consumption (e.g. housing provision; service provision), community culture (e.g. resisting unwanted re-development; inward migration) and political self-management (e.g. participation and influence over planning decisions, tenants' control over public housing). Urban social movements were conceived as agents of systemic transformation distinct from preservation societies and community associations, for example. However, mobilisations seeking to preserve community culture by resisting 'undesirable incomers' illustrate how urban social movements are not *necessarily* radical or emancipatory.

Maintaining the analytical distinction of urban social movements as agents of systemic change, contesting the prevailing political and economic status quo immediately became a challenge. This was further complicated by the range of empirical examples of urban activism in Western societies between the mid-1970s and 1980s. This resulted in significant debates about whether any one of these exhibited all three definitional dimensions. Examples ranged across Spain, Italy, the Netherlands, West Germany,

Britain, Australia, the USA and beyond. The associated practices included squatting and radical community initiatives resisting property developers, tenants' action grounds and urban riots often associated with poverty and ethnic tensions. During these debates even Castells wavered on the issue of whether urban social movements existed or not.

Regardless of these definitional difficulties the notion of urban social movements remains important within Geography, Urban Planning and Development Studies. The concept remains useful precisely because the number of emancipatory struggles pursued by informal social organisations using forms of collective action in urban locations is on the increase in *both* the North and the South.

This resurgence in urban activism reflects two linked phenomena associated with the contemporary wave of global restructuring and deregulation. In Western societies the current wave of urban regeneration initiatives are transforming the urban fabric of major cities, raising significant issues of urban meaning, power and control. Regeneration is one response to the transition to a knowledge economy within which cultural activity, service sector and immaterial labour replace manufacturing activity in the context of heightened migration rates. Urban communities are thus confronted with significant new challenges to established meanings and patterns of life.

The corollary of this is an accelerating rate of urbanisation in the developing nations, predominantly in the Southern hemisphere. As manufacturing, and, increasingly, elements of tele-working, computing and design work are established in the South urban growth rates, often associated with shanty town developments, have accelerated rapidly. Southern urban social movements have become numerous and diverse in Latin America, South Africa, India and elsewhere. These movements typically embody the primary characteristics of Western urban social movements, being grass roots associations pursuing self-help strategies via direct action and the pursuit of political influence, if not control (Appadurai 2001).

References and resources

Appadurai, A. (2001); Castells, M. (1983); Mayer, M. (1999); Patel, S., Burra, S. and D'Cruz, C. (2001); Pickvance, C. (2003); Schuurman, F. and van Naerssen, T. (1989).

WORLD SOCIAL FORUM

The World Social Forum (WSF) is the largest 'open meeting place' of **global civil society** and provides a discursive arena where movements come to communicate their struggles, to deliberate around possible strategies and alternatives and to network with similarly inclined movements and individuals globally (Sen *et al*. 2004).

The intellectual origins of the WSF are traceable to 1996, when intellectuals and activists associated with the Tricontinental Centre (Belgium) proposed a counter-summit to the World Economic Forum, the 'informal' gathering of political and business leaders hosted yearly in Davos, Switzerland. Subsequently, participants in this 'other Davos', buoyed by the success of their meeting, and emphasising the importance of continuity of action, proposed a series of events that would 'feed into the accumulation of knowledge, experience and analysis, becoming part of a long term dynamic' (Houtart and Polet 2001: 115). This proposal was framed by leading activists from France and Brazil as a 'World Social Forum' that would occur in the Southern hemisphere at the same time as the World Economic Forum was being held in the North, an objective finally realised in Porto Alegre, Brazil in 2001, where the efforts of a number of organisations came to fruition. These included the Brazilian Justice and Peace Commission (CBJP), the Brazilian Association of Non-Governmental Organisations (ABONG), the Social Network for Justice and Human Rights and **ATTAC** (France).

The forum was conceived as a participatory, dialogical, and pedagogical space that would be non-directed and non-representative and therefore unique as a self-organised space of encounter between civil society actors including social movements, NGOs, trade unions and engaged activists/ intellectuals. The conditions of participation and engagement with the WSF process are set out in its Charter of Principles formulated by the Organising Committee (now the International Secretariat). Politically, the Charter represents a clear statement of intent, by identifying and declaring the WSF's opposition to 'neoliberalism and to domination of the world by capital and any form of imperialism' (Fisher and Ponniah 2003: 354). The Charter also emphasises interrelations of knowledge exchange and linking of movements and points towards a 'global agenda' based upon the concept of 'planetary citizenship' (ibid. 357).

From the very beginning the WSF has been overwhelmingly successful, according to some of its critics too successful, attracting huge numbers of activists to discuss and debate and to otherwise participate in a vast array of workshops, seminars and plenary events, allowing for a cross-fertilisation of ideas and experiences previously unimagined. The appeal of the 'forum' model has also grown exponentially since the original Porto Alegre meeting, leading to the establishment of regional social fora in Europe, the Mediterranean, Asia, Africa and the Americas, as well as the proliferation of autonomously initiated local and city fora.

However, this rapid expansion has presented a number of practical diffi-culties and organisational problems, which have attracted praise and criticism in equal measure. Movement intellectuals, such as Andre Grubacic (2003) have suggested that radical activism is in danger of becoming 'a permanent conference' whilst Naomi Klein (2003) has expressed concerns about it being 'hijacked' by the 'big men' of Latin American politics – Hugo Chavez and Lula de Silva. Despite such fears and its self-declared status as an 'open meeting place', the WSF has retained its capacity to exclude particular groups through its Charter of Principles, point nine of which reads: 'Neither party representations nor military organizations shall participate in the Forum. Government leaders and members of legislatures who accept the commit-ments of this Charter may be invited to participate in a personal capacity.'

This clause has proven unpopular with leftist political parties, and it is the reason why the **Zapatistas** (an armed organisation) have stayed away from the forum. It has been much debated, particularly in India where it became a source of division during the organisation of the 2004 WSF in Mumbai. Amongst the Charter's other ambiguities are its emphasis upon non-violent struggle without specifically defining or ruling out violence *per se*. This appears to be a way of the WSF avoiding having to criticise self-defensive actions, or the censure of protests that may lead to property damage or other forms of collective action normatively constructed as violent.

However, as the sociologist Bouaventura De Sousa Santos (2003) points out, the minimalist character of the Charter of Principles means that, despite principled opposition by some to the under-enforced exclusion of political parties, or the failure to engage armed groups, in practice, it is difficult for those who would willingly exclude themselves to define what they are excluding themselves from. This applies to both the political parties them-selves, who frequently utilise front groups to attend, and those who wish to curtail participation by these parties. This, he suggests, is the 'WSF's power of attraction' and is the reason why the WSF has grown so quickly; the minimalist criteria for participation acts as an incentive for participation. The emphasis that the WSF has placed upon process and flexibility and its declared intention to defy temporal or geographical boundaries also strengthens this inclusive trajectory as is argued in its Charter:

> The World Social Forum at Porto Alegre was an event localized in time and place. From now on, in the certainty proclaimed at Porto Alegre that 'another world is possible', it becomes a permanent pro-cess of seeking and building alternatives, which cannot be reduced to the events supporting it.

> (Point 2 WSF Charter of Principles)

Peter Waterman (2003), the international labour movement activist, has described this as akin to discovering the 'secret of fire', a secret which he describes as the capacity to 'keep moving', to constantly challenge any process of capture or stratification. The idea of the WSF as process rather than event keeps open an almost continuous and reflexive critique, which when iterated via **computer mediated communications** results in a situation Waterman describes as 'around the world in 80 seconds'.

In these ways, the form and composition of WSF develops through the dynamic interactions between its constitutive parts and its external environment, which is always changing. The WSF and its corollaries such as the European Social Forum are different in each location and with every manifestation new links are forged between actors and participants who reconfigure it once again, meaning it is – as its Charter proclaims – always in process. This is perceived to be problematic by some more orthodox political actors who wish to actualise the social and political force that is immanent to the forum, either by means of a manifesto or through aggregation to form a party or campaigning organisation. However, these attempts come up against the problem of steering a process whose very dynamics are resistant to such control.

References and resources

De Sousa Santos, B. (2003); Fisher, W. F. and Ponniah, T. (eds. 2003); Grubacic, A. (2003); Houtart, F. and Polet, F. (eds. 2001); Klein, N. (2003); Sen, J., Anand, A., Escobar, E. and Waterman, P. (eds. 2004); Waterman, P. (2003).

ZAPATISMO (ZAPATISTAS)

'Zapatismo' is a concept that describes the mix of political, organisational and revolutionary theory that has emerged from the struggles of The Zapatista National Liberation Army (Ejército Zapatista de Liberación Nacional – EZLN) in Chiapas, South East Mexico and which is crafted by their charismatic leader Subcommandante Marcos (see Marcos 2001). Theoretically and in practice, Zapatismo has been influential for activists within a number of movements and has been particularly celebrated within the **alternative globalisation movement**.

The Zapatistas are a hybrid of originally Maoist intellectuals, indigenous peoples' movements and civil society supporters, who have now successfully created an autonomous zone of self-government in the Chiapas region of Southeast Mexico (Holloway and Pelaez 1998). This was achieved

through limited military means and multiplied by their capacity to produce an 'electronic fabric of struggle' (Cleaver 1998), utilising a web-based
network of observers and solidarity campaigners to insure the Zapatistas
against a military onslaught from the Mexican state.

The Zapatistas first came to the world's attention on 1 January 1994, the
day that the North American Free Trade Agreement (NAFTA) came into
force. In an armed uprising, 3,000 Zapatistas briefly occupied seven towns
in the state of Chiapas declaring 'Ya basta!' (Enough is enough!). This was
to be the beginning of the 'war against oblivion' (Ross 2000), an uprising
against the poverty, disease, and environmental desecration that is a common feature of life for indigenous peoples in the region. This was a process
that the Zapatistas argued NAFTA would accelerate, as its interpretation
of Free Trade meant the reform of Article 27 of the Mexican Constitution.
This had been one of the outcomes of the Mexican revolution, the catalyst
for 75 years of agrarian reform and a foundation stone of the *ejido* system
of communal land ownership. With this legal 'barrier' to trade removed,
the way was open for transnational agro-industries to purchase what had
previously been communally held lands. As the Zapatistas' first declaration
makes clear, one of the reasons they rose up was to 'suspend the robbery
of our natural resources' (Marcos 2001: 15).

The significance of the Zapatistas for social movements globally has
been their emphasis upon the encounter (*encuentro*) as a mechanism for
building resistance to neoliberalism and their sophisticated critique of the
operation of power in contemporary societies. In 1996 they invited their
eclectic group of supporters in **global civil society** to *La Realidad* in
Chiapas the Zapatista 'reality' where they held the 'First Intercontinental
Encuentro for Humanity and Against Neoliberalism'. In this context activists from around the world: trade unionists; environmentalists; campaigners
from various non-governmental organisations; sympathetic writers and
intellectuals, gathered to hear of and respond to the particular situation the
Zapatistas had helped create. In the words of their charismatic leader
Subcommandante Marcos:

> Some of the best rebels from the five continents arrived in the moun-
> tains of the Mexican Southeast. All of them brought their ideas, their
> hearts, their worlds. They came to La Realidad to find themselves in
> others' ideas, in others' reasons, in others' worlds.
>
> (2001: 121)

This was crucial in the spread of Zapatismo and emblematic of the
Zapatistas' strategy subsequently, which has been characterised by placing
the local and global in dialogue, defending a place-based model of the

cultural and natural, whilst expressing that defence as a contributory action to a network of global resistance. Zapatismo therefore represents a struggle to actualise a networked, self-organised and reflexive project of interlinked experiments in autonomy and co-operation. A project to affirm the possibility of 'dignity' that 'already exists in the form of being denied' (Holloway 2002: 213) where repression is negated by the diffusion of power and movements strive for the dissolution rather than capture of state apparatus. The struggle of the Zapatistas therefore counterpoises means against ends, advocating a form of a radically democratic praxis towards the emergence of a public sphere, constituted by and from struggle.

References and resources

Holloway, J. (2002); Holloway, J. and Pelaez, E. (eds. 1998); Marcos, Subcomandante. (2001); Ross, J. (2000).

BIBLIOGRAPHY

Abbey, E. (1975/1991) *The Monkey Wrench Gang*, London: Robin Clark.

Adorno, T. and Horkheimer, M. (1976) *Dialectic of Enlightenment*, London: Continuum.

Agyeman, J. (2005) *Sustainable Communities and the Challenge of Environmental Justice*, New York: New York University Press.

Alonso, H. (1993) *Peace as a Women's Issue: A History of the U.S. Movement for World Peace*, Syracuse, NY: Syracuse University Press.

Alvarez, S. E., Dagnino, E. and Escobar, A. (eds.) (1998) *Cultures of Politics, Politics of Cultures: Re-Visioning Latin American Social Movements*, Boulder, CO: Westview Press.

Aminzade, R. and McAdam, D. (2002) 'Emotions and Contentious Politics', *Mobilization*, 7, 2: 107–109.

Anderson, B. (2005) *Under Three Flags: Anarchism and the Anti-Colonial Imagination*, London: Verso.

Appadurai, A. (2001) 'Deep Democracy', *Environment and Urbanisation*, 13, 2: 23–43.

Appiah, K. A. (1992) *In My Father's House*, Oxford: Oxford University Press.

Archer, M. (1995) *Culture and Agency: The Place of Culture in Social Theory*, Cambridge: Cambridge University Press.

Arendt, H. (1958) *The Human Condition*, Chicago: University of Chicago Press.

Armstrong, E. (2002) *Forging Gay Identities: Organizing Sexuality in San Francisco, 1950–1994*, Chicago: University of Chicago Press.

Atton, C. (2002) *Alternative Media*, London: Sage.

Babin, R. (1985) *The Nuclear Power Game*, Montreal: Black Rose.

Badiou, A. (2005) *Metapolitics*, London: Verso.

Bagguley, P. (1992) 'Social Change, the Middle Class and the Emergence of New Social Movements: A Critical Analysis', *Sociological Review*, 40: 26–48.

Bagguley, P. (2002) 'Contemporary British Feminism: A Social Movement in Abeyance?', *Social Movement Studies*, 1, 2: 169–185.

Bahro, R. (1982) *Socialism & Survival*, London: Heretic Books.

Barabasi, A.-L. and Albert, R. (1999) 'Emergence of Scaling in Random Networks', *Science*, 286: 509–512.

Barker, C., Johnson, A. and Lavalette, M. (eds.) (2001) *Leadership and Social Movements*, Manchester: Manchester University Press.

Bateson, G. (1973) *Steps to an Ecology of Mind*, London: Paladin.

Beck, U. (1992) *Risk Society: Towards a New Modernity*, London: Sage.

Bell, D. (1973) *The Coming of Post-Industrial Society*, New York: Basic Books.

Bennett, W. L. (2005) 'Social Movements Beyond Borders: Understanding Two Eras of Transnational Activism', in D. della Porta and S. Tarrow (eds.) *Transnational Protest and Global Activism: People, Passions and Power*, Oxford: Rowman & Littlefield.

Bensaid, D. (2002) *Marx for our Times: Adventures and Misadventures of a Critique*, London: Verso.

Benyon, J. and Solomos, J. (eds.) (1987) *The Roots of Urban Unrest*, Oxford: Pergamon.

Blühdorn, I. and Welsh, I. (2007) 'Eco-politics Beyond the Paradigm of Sustainability: A Conceptual Framework and Research Agenda', *Environmental Politics*, 16, 2: 185–205.

Blühdorn, I. and Welsh, I. (2008) *The Politics of Unsustainability: Eco-Politics in the Post-Ecologist Era*, London: Routledge.

Blumer, H. (1946) 'The Mass, the Public and Public Opinion', in A. M. Lee (ed.) *New Outline of the Principles of Sociology*, New York: Barnes & Noble.

Blumer, H. (1951) 'Collective Behavior', in A. M. Lee (ed.) (1951) *Principles of Sociology*, New York: Barnes & Noble.

Boggs, C. (1986) *Social Movements and Political Power: Emerging Forms of Radicalism in the West*, Philadelphia: Temple University Press.

Bookchin, M. (1974) *Post-Scarcity Anarchism*, London: Wildwood House.

Bookchin, M. (1982/2005) *The Ecology of Freedom: The Emergence and Dissolution of Hierarchy*, Edinburgh: AK Press.

Bookchin, M. (1986/1993) *The Modern Crisis*, 2nd Ed., Montreal and New York: Black Rose Books.

Bookchin, M. and Foreman, D. (1991) *Defending the Earth*, Montreal and New York: Black Rose Books.

Bourdieu, P. (1998/2004) *Acts of Resistance: Against the New Myths of Our Time*, Oxford: Blackwell.

Brookes, C and Manza, J. (1994) 'Do Changing Values Explain the New Politics? A Critical Assessment of the Postmaterialist Thesis', *Sociological Quarterly*, 35: 541–570.

Brown, M. and May, J. (1991) *The Greenpeace Story*, 2nd Ed., London: Dorling Kindersley.

Brown, P. and Zavestoski, S. (2004) 'Social Movements in Health: An Introduction', *Sociology of Health and Illness*, 26, 6: 679–694.

Brown, P. and Zavestoski, S., McCormaick, S., Mayer, B., Morello-Frosch, R. and Gaisor, R. (2004) 'Embodied Health Movements: Uncharted Territory in Social Movement Research', *Sociology of Health and Illness*, 26, 1: 1–31.

Bullard, R. D. (1990/2005) *Dumping in Dixie: Race Class and Environmental Quality*, Boulder, CO: Westview Press.

Bullard, R. D. (2005) *The Quest for Environmental Justice: Human Rights and the Politics of Pollution*, San Francisco: Sierra Club Books.

Burawoy, M. (ed.) (2000) *Global Ethnography: Forces, Connections and Imaginations in a Postmodern World*, Berkeley, CA: University of California Press.

Butler, J. (1990) *Gender Trouble: Feminism and the Subversion of Identity*, New York: Routledge.

Calhoun, C. (2001) 'Putting Emotions in their Place', in J. Goodwin, J. Jasper and F. Polletta (eds.) *Passionate Politics*, Chicago: University of Chicago Press.

Call, L. (2002) *Postmodern Anarchism*, New York: Lexington Books.

Carmichael, S. and Hamilton, C. V. (1967) *Black Power: The Politics of Liberation in America*, New York: Vintage Books.

Carter, A. (1992) *Peace Movements: International Protest and World Politics since 1945*, New York: Longman.

Carter, A. (2005) *Direct Action and Democracy Today*, Cambridge: Polity Press.

Casas-Cortes, M., Osterweil, M. and Powell, D. E. (2008) 'Blurring Boundaries: Recognizing Knowledge-Practices in the Study of Social Movements', *Anthropological Quarterly*, 81, 1: 17–58.

Cassen, B. (2003) 'On the Attack', *New Left Review*, 19: 14–60.

Cassen, B. (2005) 'ATTAC Against the Treaty', *New Left Review*, 33: 27–31.

Castells, M. (1983) *The City and the Grassroots: A Cross Cultural Theory of Urban Social Movements*, London: Edward Arnold.

Castells, M. (1996) 'The Rise of the Network Society', Volume 1 of *The Information Age: Economy, Society and Culture*, Oxford: Blackwell.

Castells, M. (1997) 'The Power of Identity', Volume 2 of *The Information Age: Economy, Society and Culture*, Oxford: Blackwell.

CCCS. (1982) *The Empire Strikes Back: Race and Racism in 1970s Britain*, London: Hutchinson.

Chen, K.-H. and Morley, D. (eds.) (1996) *Stuart Hall: Critical Dialogues in Cultural Studies*, London: Routledge.

Chesters, G. (2004) 'Global Complexity and Global Civil Society', *Voluntas: The International Journal of Voluntary and Non-Profit Organizations*, 15, 4: 323–342.

Chesters, G. and Welsh, I. (2004) 'Rebel Colours: "Framing" in Global Social Movement', *Sociological Review*, 52, 3: 314–335.

Chesters, G. and Welsh, I. (2005) 'Complexity and Social Movement: Process and Emergence in Planetary Action Systems', *Theory, Culture and Society*, 22, 5: 187–211.

Chesters, G. and Welsh, I. (2006) *Complexity and Social Movements: Multitudes at the Edge of Chaos*, London: Routledge.

Churchill, W. (1998) *Pacifism as Pathology: Reflections on the Role of Armed Struggle in North America*, Winnipeg: Arbeiter Ring.

Clawson, D. (2008) 'Neo-Liberalism Guarantees Social Movement Unionism', *Employee Responsibilities and Rights Journal*, 20: 207–212.

Cleaver, H. (1998) 'The Zapatistas and the Electronic Fabric of Struggle', in J. Holloway and E. Pelaez, (eds.) *Zapatista! Reinventing Revolution in Mexico*, London: Pluto Press.

Clémençon, R. (2010) 'Preface: Copenhagen and After', in C. Lever-Tracey (ed.) *Handbook of Climate Change and Society*, London: Routledge, pp. xxv–xxx.

Cock, J. (2006) 'Connecting the Red, Brown & Green: The Environmental Movement in South Africa', in R. Ballard, A. Habib and I. Valodia (eds.) *Voices of Protest: Social Movement in Post-Apartheid South Africa*, Durban: University of KwaZulu Natal Press, pp. 203–224.

Cohen, R. and Rai, S. (2000) 'Global Social Movements: Towards a Cosmopolitan Politics', in R. Cohen and S. Rai (eds.) *Global Social Movements*, London: Athlone Press.

Cohn, C. (1987) 'Sex and Death in the Rational World of American Defense Intellectuals', *Signs*, 12, 4: 687–718.

Conway, J. (2004) *Identity, Place, Knowledge: Social Movements Contesting Globalization*, Halifax: Fernwood.

Cox, L. and Fominaya, C. F. (2009) 'Movement Knowledge: What do we Know, How do we Create Knowledge and What do we do with It?', *Interface: A Journal for and About Social Movements*, 1, 1: 1–20.

Crook, S., Pakulski, J. and Waters, M. (1992) *Postmodernization: Change in Advanced Society*, Cambridge: Polity Press.

Cross, T. (1984) *The Black Power Imperative*, New York: Faulkner.

Crossley, N. (2002) 'Repertoires of Contention and Tactical Diversity in the UK Psychiatric Survivors Movement: The Question of Appropriation', *Social Movement Studies*, 1, 1: 47–71.

Crossley, N. (2002a) *Making Sense of Social Movements*, London: McGraw-Hill.

Cruikshank, M. (1992) *The Gay and Lesbian Liberation Movement*, New York: Routledge.

Dalton, R. (1996) *Citizen Politics: Public Opinion and Political Parties in Advanced Industrial Democracies*, New Jersey: Chatham House.

Dalton, R. J., Kuechler, M. and Burklin, W. (1990) 'The Challenge of the New Movements', in R. J. Dalton and M. Kuechler (eds.) *Challenging the Political Order: New Social and Political Movements in Western Democracies*, New York: Oxford University Press.

Darnovsky, M., Epstein, B. L. and Flacks, R. (1995) *Cultural Politics and Social Movements*, Philadelphia: Temple University Press.

De Jong, W., Shaw, M. and Stammers, N. (eds.) (2005) *Global Activism, Global Media*, London: Pluto Press.

De Sousa Santos, B. (2003) 'The World Social Forum Towards a Counter Hegemonic Globalization', Presented at the XXIV International Congress of the Latin American Studies Association, Dallas, 27–27 March. Online at: http://www.duke.edu/%7Ewmignolo/publications/pubboa.html

Debord, G. (1967/1983) *Society of the Spectacle*, Michigan: Black and Red.

Debord, G. and Wolman, G. J. (1956) 'A User's Guide to Détournement', originally published in *Les Lèvres Nues*, 8. Online at: http://www.bopsecrets.org/SI/detourn.htm

Deleuze, G. (1992) 'Postscript on the Societies and Control', *October*, 59: 3–7. Online at: http://www.n5m.org/n5m2/media/texts/deleuze.htm, accessed 1 August 2009.

Deleuze, G. and Parnet, C. (2002) *Dialogues II*, London: Athlone.

della Porta, D. (1995) *Social Movements, Political Violence and the State: A Comparative Analysis of Italy and Germany*, Cambridge: Cambridge University Press.

della Porta, D. (1996) 'Social Movements and the State: Thoughts on the Policing of protest', in D. McAdam, J. D. McCarthy and M. N. Zald (eds.) *Comparative Perspectives on Social Movements: Political Opportunities, Mobilizing Structures, and Cultural Framings*, Cambridge: Cambridge University Press.

della Porta, D. and Reiter, H. (eds.) (1998) *Policing Protest: The Control of Mass Demonstrations in Western Democracies*, London: University of Minnesota Press.

della Porta, D. and Diani, M. (1999) *Social Movements: An Introduction*, London: Blackwell.

della Porta, D., Krien, H. and Rucht, D. (eds.) (1999) *Social Movements in a Globalizing World*, London: Palgrave.

Diani, M. (2000) 'Social Movement Networks Virtual and Real', *Information, Communication & Society*, 3, 3: 386–401.

Diani, M. and McAdam, D. (2003) *Social Movements and Networks: Relational Approaches to Collective Action*, Oxford: Oxford University Press.

Dobson, A. (1997) *Green Political Thought*, 2nd Ed., London: Routledge.

Dobson, A. (1998) *Justice and the Environment: Conceptions of Environmental Sustainability and Dimensions of Social Justice*, Oxford: Oxford University Press.

Doherty, B. (2002) *Ideas and Actions in the Green Movement*, London: Routledge.

Doherty, B. (2006) 'Friends of the Earth International: Negotiating a Transnational Identity', *Environmental Politics*, 15, 5: 860–880.

Dolgoff, S. (1972) *Bakunin on Anarchy*, New York: Random House.

Duberman, M. (1993) *Stonewall*, London: Penguin Books.

Dunning, E., Murphy, P. and Williams, J. (1988) *The Roots of Football Hooliganism: A Historical and Sociological Study*, London: Routledge.

Dryzek, J. S., Downes, D., Hunold, C., Scholsberg, D., with Hans-Kristian Hernes (2003) *Green States and Social Movements: Environmentalism in the United States, United Kingdom, Germany and Norway*, Oxford: Oxford University Press.

Emirbayer, M. and Goodwin, J. (1994) 'Network Analysis, Culture and the Problem of Agency', *American Journal of Sociology*, 99, 6: 1411–1454.

Engels, F. (1884/1972) *The Origins of the Family, Private Property and the State*, New York: Pathfinder Press.

Enloe, C. (1983) *Does Khaki Become You?*, London: Pluto Press.

Enloe, C. (1990) *Bananas Beaches & Bases: Making Feminist Sense of International Politics*, Berkeley CA: University of California Press.

Escobar, A. (1998) 'Whose Knowledge? Whose Nature? Biodiversity, Conservation and the Political Ecology of Social Movements', *Journal of Political Ecology*, 5: 53–82.

Escobar, A. (2009) *Territories of Difference: Place, Movements, Life, Redes*, Durham, NC: Duke University Press.

Esteves, A. M. (2008) 'Processes of Knowledge Production in Social Movements as Multi-Level Power Dynamics', *Sociology Compass*, 2, 6: 34–53.

Evans, S. (1978) *The Roots of Women's Liberation in the Civil Rights Movement and the New Left*, New York: Alfred A. Knopf.

Eyerman, R. and Jamison, A. (1991) *Social Movements: A Cognitive Approach*, Cambridge: Polity Press.

Eyerman, R. and Jamison, A. (1998) *Music and Social Movements*, Cambridge: Cambridge University Press.

Fairbrother, P. (2008) 'Social Movement Unionism or Trade Unions as Social Movements', *Employee Responsibilities and Rights Journal*, 20: 213–220.

Feldman, A. (2002) 'Making Space at the Nations' Table: Mapping the Transformative Geographies of the International Indigenous Peoples' Movement', *Social Movement Studies*, 1, 1: 31–46.

Fisher, W. F. and Ponniah, T. (eds.) (2003) *Another World is Possible: Popular Alternatives to Globalization at the World Social Forum*, London: Zed.

Flam, H. (ed.) (1994) *States and Anti-Nuclear Movements*, Edinburgh: Edinburgh University Press.

Flam, H. and King, D. (eds.) (2005) *Emotions and Social Movements*, London: Routledge.

Fleisher, D. Z. and Zames, F. (2001) *The Disability Rights Movement: From Charity to Confrontation*, Philadelphia: Temple University Press.

Foreman, D. (1991) *Confessions of an Eco-Warrior*, New York: Harmony.

Foreman, D. and Haywood, B. (1993) *Ecodefense*, Chicago: Abzug Press.

Foucault, M. (1975) *Birth of the Clinic,* London: Tavistock.

Foucault, M. (1977) *Discipline and Punish,* London: Penguin Press.

Foucault, M. (1979) *The History of Sexuality*, London: Penguin Press.

Fox-Piven, F. and Cloward R. A. (1977) *Poor People's Movements*: *Why They Succeed, How They Fail*, New York: Random House/Vintage.

Federici, S. (2010) 'Precarious Labor: A Feminist Viewpoint', *Variant*, Spring/Summer, 23–25.

Freeman, J. (1973) 'The Tyranny of Structurelessness', *Berkeley Journal of Sociology*, 17: 151–165. Online at: http://uic.edu/orgs/cwluherstory/jofreeman/joreen/tyranny.htm

Friedan, B. (2001) *The Feminine Mystique*, New York: W.W. Norton.

Gamson, W. A. and Meyer, D. S. (1996) 'Framing Political Opportunity', in D. McAdam, J. D. McCarthy and M. N. Zald (eds.) *Comparative Perspectives on Social Movements: Political Opportunities, Mobilizing Structures, and Cultural Framings*, Cambridge: Cambridge University Press.

Giddens, A. (2009) *The Politics of Climate Change*, Oxford: Polity.

Gilbert, D. (2002) *The SDS WUO: Students for a Democratic Society and the Weather Underground Organization*, Montreal: Abraham Guillen Press.

Gillis, S., Howie, G. and Munford, R. (2004) *Third Wave Feminism: A Critical Exploration*, London: Palgrave Macmillan.

Gilroy, P. (1987) *There Ain't No Black in the Union Jack: The Cultural Politics of Race and Nation*, London: Hutchinson.

Gitlin, T. (1980) *The Whole World is Watching: Mass Media in the Making and Unmaking of the New Left*, California: California University Press.

Goffman, E. (1974/1986) *Frame Analysis: An Essay on the Organization of Experience*, Boston: Northeastern Press.

Goodwin, J., Jasper, J. and Polletta, F. (eds.) (2001) *Passionate Politics*, Chicago: University of Chicago Press.

Gorz, A. (1980/1987) *Ecology as Politics*, London: Pluto.

Gorz, A. (1982) *Farewell to the Working Class: An Essay on Post-Industrial Socialism*, London: Pluto Press.

Graeber, D. (2002) 'The New Anarchists', *New Left Review*, 13: 61–73.

Graeber, D. (2009) *Direct Action: An Ethnography*, Oakland, CA: AK Press.

Graeber, D. and Shukaitis, S. (eds.) (2007) *Constituent Imaginations*, Edinburgh: AK Press.

Granovetter, M. S. (1973) 'The Strength of Weak Ties', *American Journal of Sociology*, 78, 6: 1360–1380.

Greenpeace International (2009) *Greenpeace International Annual Report 2007*. Online at: http://www.greenpeace.org/international/press/reports/gpi-annual-report-2007, accessed 28 September 2009.

Grubacic, A. (2003) 'Life After Social Forums: New Radicalism and the Question of Attitudes Towards Social Forums', *Znet*. Online at: http://www.zmag.org/content/showarticle.cfm?SectionID=41&ItemID=3010

Gurr, T. (1970) *Why Men Rebel*, Princeton, NJ: Princeton University Press.

Habermas, J. (1968/1971) *Towards a Rational Society: Student Protest, Science and Politics*, London: Heinemann.

Habermas, J. (1976) *Knowledge and Human Interests*, London: Heinemann.

Habermas, J. (1981) *The Theory of Communicative Action*, Cambridge: Polity.

Habermas, J. (1985) 'Civil Disobedience, the Litmus Test for the Democratic Constitutional State', *Berkeley Journal of Sociology*, XXX: 95–116.

Habermas, J. (1987) *Theory of Communicative Action, Vol II: The Critique of Functionalist Reason*, Cambridge: Polity Press.

Habermas, J. (2003) *The Future of Human Nature*, Oxford: Polity Press.

Hall, S., Chricher, C., Jefferson, T., Clarke, J. and Roberts, B. (1978) *Policing the Crisis*, London: Macmillan.

Haraway, D. (1989) *Primate Visions*, New York: Routledge.

Hardt, M. and Negri, A. (2000) *Empire*, Cambridge, MA: Harvard University Press.

Hardt, M. and Negri, A. (2004) *Multitude: War and Democracy in the Age of Empire*, New York: Penguin.

Hardt, M. and Negri, A. (2009) *Commonwealth*, Cambridge, MA: Harvard University Press.

Harford, B. and Hopkins, S. (eds.) (1984) *Greenham Women: Women at the Wire*, London: Women's Press.

Harvie, D., Milburn, K., Trott, B. and Watts, D. (eds.) (2005) *Shut them Down: G8, Gleneagles 2005 and the Movement of Movements*, London: Autonomedia.

Haywood, L. and Drake, J. (eds.) (1997) *Third Wave Feminism: Being Feminist, Doing Feminism*, Minnesota: University of Minnesota Press.

Hess, D., Breyman, S., Campbell, N. and Martin, B. (2008) 'Science, Technology & Social Movements', in E. J. Hacket, O. Amsterdamska, M. Lynch and J. Wajcman (eds.) *The Handbook of Science & Technology Studies*, 3rd Ed., Cambridge, MA: MIT Press, pp. 473–498.

Hetherington, K. (1996) 'Identity Formation, Space and Social Centrality', *Theory, Culture and Society*, 13, 4: 33–52.

Hetherington, K. (1998) *Expressions of Identity: Space, Performance, Politics*, London: Sage.

Holloway, J. (2002) *Change the World Without Taking Power*, London: Pluto Press.

Holloway, J. and Pelaez, E. (eds.) (1998) *Zapatista! Reinventing Revolution in Mexico*, London: Pluto Press.

hooks, b. (1981) *Ain't I a Woman*, Boston: South End Press.

Houtart, F. and Polet, F. (eds.) (2001) *The Other Davos: The Globalization of Resistance to the World Economic System*, London: Zed.

Huber, J. (1976) 'Towards a Socio-Technological Theory of the Women's Movement', *Social Problems*, 23, 3: 71–88.

Hurd, R., Milkman, R. and Turner, L. (2003) 'Reviving the American Labor Movement: Institutions and Mobilization', *European Journal of Industrial Relations*, 9, 1: 99–117.

Inglehart, R. (1977) *The Silent Revolution: Changing Values and Political Styles among Western Publics*, Princeton, NJ: Princeton University Press.

Inglehart, R. (1990) *Culture Shift in Advanced Industrial Society*, Princeton, NJ: Princeton University Press.

Inglehart, R. (1997) *Modernization and Postmodernization: Cultural, Economic and Political Change in 43 Societies*, Princeton, NJ: Princeton University Press.

Jamison, A. (2001) *The Making of Green Knowledge: Environmental Politics and Cultural Transformation*, Cambridge: Cambridge University Press.

Jamison, A., Eyerman R., Cramer J. with Laessoe, J. (1990) *The Making of the New Environmental Consciousness: A Comparative Study of the Environmental Movements in Sweden, Denmark and the Netherlands*, Edinburgh: Edinburgh University Press.

Jappe, A. (1999) *Guy Debord*, Berkeley, CA: University of California Press.

Jasper, J. (1997) *The Art of Moral Protest: Culture, Biography and Creativity in Social Movements*, Chicago: University of Chicago Press.

Jasper, J. (1998) 'The Emotions of Protest: Reactive and Affective Emotions in and around Social Movements', *Sociological Forum*, 13: 397–424.

Jasper, J. (2003) 'The Emotions of Protest', in J. Jasper and J. Goodwin *The Social Movements Reader: Cases and Concepts*, Oxford: Blackwell.

Johnston, H. (2009) 'Protest Cultures: Performances, Artefacts and Ideations', in H. Johnston (ed.) *Culture, Social Movements and Protest*, Aldershot: Ashgate.

Johnston, H. and Klandermans, B. (eds.) (1995) *Social Movements and Culture*, London: UCL Press.

Joppke, C. (1993) *Mobilizing Against Nuclear Energy*, Berkeley, CA: University of California Press.

Jordan, J. (1998) 'The Art of Necessity: The Subversive Imagination of Anti-Road Protest and Reclaim the Streets', in G. McKay (ed.) *DIY Culture: Parties and Protest in Nineties Britain*, Verso: London.

Junor, B. (1995) *Greenham Common Women's Peace Camp*, London: Working Press.

Kaldor, M. (2003) *Global Civil Society: An Answer to War?*, London: Polity.

Katsiaficas, G. (1997) *European Autonomous Social Movements and the Decolonization of Everyday Life*, New Jersey: Humanities Press International.

Keane, J. (2003) *Global Civil Society?*, Cambridge: Cambridge University Press.

Keck, M. E. and Sikkink, K. (1998) *Activists Beyond Borders: Advocacy Networks in International Politics*, New York: Cornell University Press.

Kenney, P. (2002) *A Carnival of Revolution*, Oxford: Princeton University Press.

Kirk, G. (1989) 'Our Greenham Common', in A. Harris and Y. King, *Rocking the Ship of State: Towards a Feminist Peace Politics*, Boulder, CO: Westview Press.

Kitschelt, H. (1986) 'Political Opportunity Structures and Political Protest: Anti-Nuclear Movements in Four Democracies', *British Journal of Political Science*, 16: 57–85.

Klandermans, B. (1997) *The Social Psychology of Protest*, Oxford: Blackwell.

Klandermans, B. (1991) 'New Social Movements and Resource Mobilization: The European and American Approach Revisited', in D. Rucht (ed.) (1991) *Research on Social Movements: The State of the Art in Western Europe and the USA*, Boulder, CO: Westview Press.

Klandermans, B., Kriesi, H. and Tarrow, S. (eds.) (1988) *From Structure to Action: Comparing Social Movement Research Across Cultures*, International Social Movement Research, 1, Greenwich, MA: JAI.

Klein, N. (2003) 'More Democracy – Not More Political Strongmen', *Znet*. Online at: http://www.zmag.org/content/showarticlecfm?SectionID=41&ItemID=2946

Kornhauser, A. (1959) *The Politics of Mass Society*, Glencoe: Free Press.

Kriesi, H., Koopmans, R., Duyvendak, J.-W. and Giugni, M. (1995) *New Social Movements in Western Europe*, London: University of Minnesota Press.

Kropotkin, P. (1998) *Fields, Factories and Workshops Tomorrow*, London: Freedom Press.

Laclau, E. and Mouffe, C. (1985) *Hegemony and Socialist Strategy*, London: Verso.

Lakey, G. (2001) *The Sword that Heals*, Edmonton: Training for Change. Online at: http://trainingforchange.org/nonviolent_action_sword_that_heals

Lassn, K. (1999) *Culture Jam – The Uncooling of America*, New York: Eagle Books.

Latour, B. (2007) *Reassembling the Social: An Introduction to Actor Network Theory*, Oxford: Oxford University Press.

Le Bon, G. (1895/2008) *The Crowd*, BiblioBazaar, LCC. Online at: http:// www.bibliobazaar.com/opensource

Leslie, E. (1999) 'Introduction to Adorno/Marcuse Correspondence on the German Student Movement', *New Left Review*, 233: 118–136.

Lichterman, P. (1996) *The Search for Political Community: American Activists Reinventing Community*, Cambridge: Cambridge University Press.

Lipsky, M. (ed.) (1970) *Law and Order: Police Encounters*, New York: Aldine.

Lotringer, S. (2004) 'Foreward', in P. Virno *A Grammar of the Multitude*, New York: Semiotext(e).

Lyotard, J.-F. (1984) *The Postmodern Condition*, Manchester: Manchester University Press.

McAdam, D. (1986) 'Recruitment to High-Risk Activism: The Case of Freedom Summer', *American Journal of Sociology*, 92, 64–90.

McAdam, D. (1988) *Freedom Summer*, Oxford: Oxford University Press.

McAdam, D., Tarrow, S. and Tilly, C. (2001) *Dynamics of Contention*, Cambridge: Cambridge University Press.

McBryde, H. and Johnson, H. (2005) *Too Late to Die Young: Nearly True Tales from a Life*, New York: Henry Holt.

McCarthy, J. D. and Zald, M. N. (1973) *The Trends of Social Movements in America: Professionalization and Resource Mobilization*, Morristown, NJ: General Learning Press.

McCarthy, J. D. and Zald, M. N. (1977) 'Resource Mobilization and Social Movements: A Partial Theory', *American Journal of Sociology*, 82, 6: 1212–1241.

McCarthy, J. D. and Zald, M. N. (1987) *Social Movements in an Organizational Society*, Oxford: Transaction Books.

McCaughey, M. and Ayers, M. (2003) *Cyberactivism: Online Activism in Theory and Practice*, London: Routledge.

McCormick, J. (1995) *The Global Environmental Movement*, 2nd Ed., Chichester: Wiley.

McDonald, K. (2006) *Global Movements: Action and Culture*, Oxford: Blackwell.

McKay, G. (1996) *Senseless Acts of Beauty: Cultures of Resistance since the Sixties*, London: Verso.

McKay, G. (1998) *DiY Culture: Party & Protest in Nineties Britain*, London: Verso.

McKechnie, R. and Welsh, I. (2002) 'When the Global Meets the Local: Critical Reflections on Reflexive Modernisation', in F. Buttel, P. Dickens,

R. Dunlap and A. Gijswijt (eds.) *Sociological Theory and the Environment: Classical Foundations, Contemporary Insights*, Boulder, CO: Rowan & Littlefield, pp. 286–310.

McLeish, P. and Welsh, I. (1996) 'The European Road to Nowhere: Anarchism and Direct Action Against the UK Roads Programme', *Anarchist Studies*, 4, 1: 27–44.

Maffesoli, M. (1995) *The Time of the Tribes*, London: Sage.

Maheu, L. (ed.) (1995) *Social Movements and Social Classes: The Future of Collective Action*, London: Sage.

Marcos, Subcomandante. (2001) *Our Word is our Weapon*, New York: Seven Stories Press.

Marcuse, H. (1964) *One-Dimensional Man: Studies in the Ideology of Advanced Industrial Society*, Boston: Beacon.

Marcuse, H. (1969) *An Essay on Liberation*, Boston: Beacon Press.

Marsh, P. (1979) *Aggro: The Illusion of Violence*, London: Dent.

Marx, K. (1852/1977) *The Eighteenth Brumaire of Louis Bonaparte*, Moscow: Progress.

Marx, K. (1859/1970) *A Contribution to the Critique of Political Economy*, Ed. M. Dobb, Trans. S. W. Ryazanskaya, London: Lawrence & Wishart.

Marx, K. and Engels, F. (1848/2002) *Manifesto of the Communist Party*, London: Penguin.

May, T. (1994) *The Political Philosophy of Poststructuralist Anarchism*, University Park: Pennsylvania University Press.

Mayer, M. (1999) 'Urban Movements and Urban Theory in the Late-20th-Century City', in R. A. Beauregard and S. Body-Gendrot (eds.) *The Urban Moment*, Thousand Oaks, CA: Sage.

Mayer, M. and Roth, R. (1995) 'New Social Movements and the Transformation to Post-Fordist Society', in M. Darnovsky *et al. Cultural Politics and Social Movements*, Philadelphia: Temple University Press.

Meikle, G. (2003) *Future Active: Media Activism and the Internet*, London: Routledge.

Melucci, A. (1980) 'The New Social Movements: A Theoretical Approach', *Social Science Information*, 19, 2: 199–226.

Melucci, A. (1981) 'Ten Hypotheses for the Analysis of New Movements', in D. Pinto (ed.) *Contemporary Italian Sociology*, New York: Cambridge University Press.

Melucci, A. (1985) 'The Symbolic Challenge of Contemporary Movements', *Social Research*, 52, 4: 789–816.

Melucci, A. (1989) *Nomads of the Present*, London: Radius Hutchinson.

Melucci, A. (1995) 'The New Social Movements Revisited: Reflections on a Sociological Misunderstanding', in L. Maheu (ed.) *Social Movements and Social Classes: The Future of Collective Action*, London: Sage.

Melucci, A. (1996) *Challenging Codes: Collective Action in the Information Age*, Cambridge: Cambridge University Press.

Melucci, A. (1996a) *The Playing Self: Person and Meaning in the Planetary Society*, Cambridge: Cambridge University Press.

Mertes, T. (ed.) (2004) *A Movement of Movements: Is Another World Really Possible*, London: Verso.

Merton, R. K. (1942) 'The Normative Structure of Science', in R. K. Merton, *The Sociology of Science: Theoretical and Empirical Investigations*, Chicago: University of Chicago Press.

Meyer, D. and Staggenborg, S. (1996) 'Movements, Countermovements, and the Structure of Political Opportunity', *American Journal of Sociology*, 101, 6: 1628–1660.

Meyer, D. and Tarrow, S. (eds.) (1998) *The Social Movement Society: Contentious Politics for a New Century*, Oxford: Rowman & Littlefield.

Middendorp, C. (1992) 'Left-Right Self-Identification and (Post) Materialism in the Ideological Space', *Electoral Studies*, 11: 249–260.

Mies, M. and Shiva, V. (1993) *Ecofeminism*, London: Routledge.

Milkman, R. and Voss, K. (2004) *Rebuilding Labor: Organizing and Organizers in the New Union Movement*, Ithaca, NY: Cornell University Press.

Miller, N. (2006) *Out of the Past: Gay and Lesbian History From 1869 to the Present*, New York: Alyson Books.

Millet, K. (2000) *Sexual Politics*, Champaign: University of Illinois Press.

Moaddel, M. (1992) *Class, Politics, and Ideology in the Iranian Revolution*, Columbia: Colombia University Press.

Moaddel, M. (1992a) 'Ideology as Episodic Discourse: The Case of the Iranian Revolution', *American Sociological Review*, 57: 353–379.

Moore, W. (1995) 'Rational Rebels: Overcoming the Free-Rider Problem', *Political Research Quarterly*, 48, 2: 417–454.

Mottl, T. L. (1980) 'The Analysis of Countermovements', *Social Problems*, 27, 5: 620–635.

Mouffe, C. (1984) 'Towards a Theoretical Interpretation of New Social Movements', *Rethinking Marx*, New York: International General/MMRC.

Murray, R. (1989) 'Fordism and Post-Fordism', in S. Hall and M. Jacques (eds.) *New Times*, London: Lawrence & Wishart.

Naess, A. (1989) *Ecology, Community and Lifestyle*, Trans. David Rothenburg, Cambridge: Cambridge University Press.

Nelkin, D. (1981) 'Nuclear Power as a Feminist Issue', *Environment*, 23, 1: 14–39.

Nelkin, D. and Pollak, M. (1982) *The Atom Besieged*, Cambridge, MA: MIT Press.

Newman, S. (2007) *Unstable Universalities: Poststructuralism and Radical Politics*, Manchester: Manchester University Press.

Nicholson, L. (ed.) (1997) *The Second Wave: A Reader in Feminist Theory*, London: Routledge.

Nilsen, A. G. (2009) 'The Authors and the Actors of their Own Drama: Towards a Marxist Theory of Social Movements', *Capital & Class*, 90: 109–139.

Nogueira, A. (2002) 'The Birth and Promise of the Indymedia Revolution', in B. Shepard and R. Hayduk (eds.) *From ACT UP to the WT: Urban Protest and Community Building in the Era of Globalization*, London: Verso.

Notes from Nowhere (eds.) (2003) *We are Everywhere: The Irresistible Rise of Global Anticapitalism*, London: Verso.

Oakley, A. (1974) *The Sociology of Housework*, London: Martin Robertson.

Oberschall, A. (1973) *Social Conflict and Social Movements*, Englewood Cliffs, NJ: Prentice Hall.

O'Connor, J. (1998) *Natural Causes: Essays in Ecological Marxism*, New York: Guildford Press.

Offe, C. (1985) 'New Social Movements: Changing Boundaries of the Political', *Social Research*, 52: 817–868.

Olson, M. (1968) *The Logics of Collective Action: Public Goods and the Theory of Groups*, Cambridge, MA: Harvard University Press.

Parkin, F. (1968) *Middle Class Radicalism*, Manchester: Manchester University Press.

Parks, R. and Haskins, J. (1992) *Rosa Parks: My Story*, London: Penguin.

Parsons, T. (1969) *Politics and Social Structure*, New York: Free Press.

Patel, S., Burra, S. and D'Cruz, C. (2001) 'Slum/Shack Dwellers International', *Environment and Urbanisation*, 13, 2: 45–59.

Pellow, D. N. and Brulle, R. J. (2005) *Power, Justice and the Environment: A Critical Appraisal of the Environmental Justice Movement*, Cambridge MA: MIT Press.

Pettit, A. (1983) *The Greenham Factor*, London: Greenham Print Shop.

Pickerill, J. (2003) *Cyberprotest: Environmental Activism On-Line*, Manchester: Manchester University Press.

Pickerill, J. (2006) 'Radical Politics on the Net', *Parliamentary Affairs*, 59, 2: 266–282.

Pickvance, C. (2003) 'From Urban Social Movements to Urban Movements: A Review and Introduction to a Symposium on Urban Movements', *International Journal of Urban and Regional Research*, 27, 1: 102–109.

Plant, S. (1992) *The Most Radical Gesture: The Situationist International in a Postmodern Age*, London: Routledge.

Polletta, F. (2009) 'Storytelling in Social Movements', in H. Johnston (ed.) (2009) *Culture, Social Movements and Protest*, Aldershot: Ashgate.

Porritt, J. (2005) *Capitalism as if the World Matters*, London: Earthscan.

Porritt, J. and Winner, D. (1988) *The Coming of the Greens*, London: Fontana.

Power, L. (1995) *No Bath but Plenty of Bubbles: An Oral History of the Gay Liberation Front 1970–7*, London: Cassell.

Purdue, D. A. (2000) *Anti-GenetiX: The Emergence of the Anti-GM Movement*, London: Ashgate.

Purdue, D., Dürrschmidt, J., Jowers, P. and O'Doherty, R. (1997) 'DIY Culture and Extended Milieux: LETS, Veggie Boxes and Festivals', *Sociological Review*, 45, 4: 645–667.

Puttnam, R. (1995) 'Bowling Alone: America's Declining Social Capital', *Journal of Democracy*, 6, 1: 65–78.

Randall, V. (1982) *Women and Politics*, London: Macmillan.

Randle, M. (1994) *Civil Disobedience*, London: Fontana Press.

Rathbone, E. (1920) *Utopia Calling: A Plea for Family Allowances*, London: NUSEC.

Rochon, T. R. (1988) *Mobilizing for Peace: The Anti-nuclear Movements in Western Europe*, Princeton, NJ: Princeton University Press.

Rochon, T. R. (1998) *Culture Moves: Ideas, Activism and Changing Values*, Princeton, NJ: Princeton University Press.

Rootes, C. (1995) 'A New Class? The Higher Educated and the New Politics', in L. Maheu (ed.) *Social Movements and Social Classes: The Future of Collective Action*, London: Sage.

Rootes, C. (2005) 'Facing South? British Environmental Movement Organisations and the Challenge of Globalisation', *Environmental Politics*, 15, 5: 768–786.

Roseneil, S. (1995) *Disarming Patriarchy: Feminism and Political Action at Greenham*, Buckingham: Open University Press.

Ross, A. (1991) *Strange Weather*, London: Verso.

Ross, A. (2009) *Nice Work if you Can Get it: Life and Labor in Precarious Times*, New York: New York University Press.

Ross, J. (2000) *The War Against Oblivion*, Monroe, LO: Common Courage Press.

Roszak, T. (1970) *The Making of a Counter Culture: Reflection on the Technocratic Society and Its Youthful Opposition*, London: Faber & Faber.

Roszak, T. (1972) *Where the Wasteland Ends: Politics and Transcendence in Post Industrial Society*, London: Faber & Faber.

Rotblat, J. (ed.) (1997) *World Citizenship: Allegiance to Humanity*, London: Macmillan.

Rothman, H. (2000) 'Disseminating the Principles of the Universal Declaration on the Human Genome and Human Rights', *New Genetics and Society*, 19, 1: 89–104.

Routledge, P. (2004) 'Convergence of Commons: Process Geographies of People's Global Action', *The Commoner*, 8. Online at: http://www .commoner.org.uk/previous_issues.htm#n8

Rowell, A. (1996) *Green Backlash: Global Subversion of the Environmental Movement*, London: Routledge.

Rucht, D. (1991) 'Sociological Theory as a Theory of Social Movements?: A Critique of Alain Touraine', in D. Rucht (ed.) *Research on Social Movements: The State of the Art in Western Europe and the USA*, Boulder, CO: Westview Press.

Rudig, W. (1990) *Anti-Nuclear Movements: A World Survey of Opposition to Nuclear Energy*, Harlow: Longman.

Ruggiero, V. and Montagna, N. (eds.) (2008) *Social Movements: A Reader*, London: Routledge.

Saad Filho (2003) *Anti-Capitalism: A Marxist Introduction*, London: Pluto.

Scarce, R. (1990) *Eco-Warriors*, Chicago: Barnes & Noble.

Schalit, J. (2002) *The Anti-Capitalism Reader*, New York: Akashic Books.

Schenk, C. (2003) 'Social Movement Unionism Beyond the Organising Model', in P. Fairbrother and C. Yates (eds.) *Trade Unions in Renewal: A Comparative Study*, London: Routledge, pp. 244–262.

Schlesinger, P. (1987) 'On National Identity: Some Conceptions and Misconceptions Criticized', *Social Science Information*, 26: 219–264.

Schudson, M. (1989) 'How Culture Works: Perspectives from Media Studies on the Efficacy of Symbols', *Theory & Society*, 18: 153–80.

Schuurman, F. and van Naerssen, T. (1989) *Urban Social Movements in the Third World*, London: Routledge.

Scotch, R. K. (1988) 'Disability as the Basis for a Social Movement: Advocacy and the Politics of Definition', *Journal of Social Issues*, 44, 1: 159–172.

Scotch, R. K. (1989) 'Politics and Policy in the History of the Disability Rights Movement', *The Milbank Quarterly*, 67, 2: 380–400.

Scotch, R. K. (2001) *From Goodwill to Civil Rights: Transforming Federal Disability Policy*, Philadelphia: Temple University Press.

Scott, A. (1990) *Ideology and the New Social Movements*, London: Unwin Hyman.

Scott, A. (1992) 'Political Culture and Social Movements', in J. Allen, P. Braham and P. Lewis (eds.) *Political and Economic Forms of Modernity*, Cambridge: Polity and OU Press.

Seel, B., Paterson, M. and Doherty, B. (eds.) (2000) *Direct Action in British Environmentalism*, London: Routledge.

Segal, L. (1987) *Is the Future Female? Troubled Thoughts on Contemporary Feminism*, London: Virago.

Sen, J., Anand, A., Escobar, E. and Waterman, P. (eds.) (2004) *World Social Forum: Challenging Empires*, New Delhi: Viveka Foundation.

Shakespeare, T. (2006) *Disability Rights and Wrongs*, London: Routledge.

Shapiro, J. (1993) *No Pity: People with Disabilities Forging a New Civil Rights Movement*, London: Random House.

Shukaitis, S. (2007) 'Whose Precarity is it Anyway', *Fifth Estate*, 3, 41: 374.

Shukaitis, S. and Graeber, D. (eds.) (2007) *Constituent Imagination: Militant Investigations, Collective Theorization*, Oakland, CA: AK Press.

Sitrin, M. (2006) *Horizontalism: Voices of Popular Power in Argentina*, London: AK Press.

Slater, D. (ed.) (1985) *New Social Movements and the State in Latin America*, Amsterdam: CEDLA.

Smelser, N. (1962) *Theory of Collective Behaviour*, New York: Free Press.

Smith, J., Chatfield, C. and Pagnucco, R. (eds.) (1997) *Transnational Social Movements and Global Politics: Solidarity Beyond the State,* Syracuse, NY: Syracuse University Press.

Smith, L. T. (1999) *Decolonizing Methodologies: Research and Indigenous Peoples*, London: Zed.

Snow, D. and Benford, R. (1988) 'Ideology, Frame Resonance and Participant Mobilization', in B. Klandermans, H. Kriesi and S. Tarrow (eds.) *From Structure to Action: Comparing Social Movement Research Across Cultures*, International Social Movement Research, 1, Greenwich, NJ: JAI.

Snow, D., Rochford, B., Worden, S. and Benford, R. (1986) 'Frame Alignment Processes, Micromobilization and Movement Participation', *American Sociology Review*, 51: 464–481.

Stallman, R. (1999) 'The GNU Operating System and the Free Software Movement', in *Open Sources: Voices from the Open Source Revolution*. Online at: http://www.oreilly.com/catalog/opensources/book/stallman.html

Starr, A. (2000) *Naming the Enemy: Anti-Corporate Movements Confront Globalization*, London: Zed.

Stephens, J. (1998) *Sixties Radicalism & Postmodernism*, Cambridge: Cambridge University Press.

Szerszynski, B. (1999) 'Performing Politics: The Dramatics of Environmental Protest', in L. Ray and A. Sayer (eds.) *Culture and Economy After the Cultural Turn*, London: Sage.

Tarrow, S. (1989) *Democracy and Disorder: Protest and Politics in Italy, 1965–1975*, Oxford: Oxford University Press.

Tarrow, S. (1991) *Struggle, Politics and Reform: Collective Action, Social Movements and Cycles of Protest*, Cornell University, NJ: Center for International Studies.

Tarrow, S. (1998) *Power in Movement: Social Movements and Contentious Politics*, Cambridge: Cambridge University Press.

Tarrow, S. (2005) *The New Transnational Activism*, Cambridge: Cambridge University Press.

Taylor, R. (1988) *The British Peace Movement 1958–1965*, Oxford: Clarendon Press.

Thorpe, C. and Welsh, I. (2008) 'Beyond Primitivism: Towards a Twenty-First Century Anarchist Theory and Praxis for Science and Technology', *Anarchist Studies*, 16, 1: 48–75.

Tickle, A. and Welsh, I. (eds.) (1998) *Environment and Society in Eastern Europe*, Harlow: Longman.

Tilly, C. (1978) *From Mobilization to Revolution*, Reading, MA: Addison-Wesley.

Tilly, C. (2004) *Social Movements, 1768–2004*, Boulder, CO: Paradigm.

Tormey, S. (2004) *Anti-Capitalism: A Beginners Guide*, Oxford: Oneworld.

Toscano, A. (2009) 'The War Against Pre-Terrorism: The Tarnac 9 and the Coming Insurrection', *Radical Philosophy*, 154: commentaries. Online at: http://www.radicalphilosophy.com/default.asp?channel_id=2187& editorial_id=27700

Touraine, A. (1971) *The Post-Industrial Society*, London: Wildwood House.

Touraine, A. (1977) *The Self-Production of Society*, Chicago: University of Chicago Press.

Touraine, A. (1981) *The Voice and the Eye*, Cambridge: Cambridge University Press.

Touraine, A. (1983) *Anti-Nuclear Protest: The Opposition to Nuclear Energy in France*, Cambridge: Cambridge University Press.

Touraine, A. (1995) *Critique of Modernity*, Oxford: Blackwell.

Turner, R. and Killian, L. (1987) *Collective Behaviour*, 3rd Ed, Englewood Cliffs, NJ: Prentice Hall.

Turner, V. (1974) *Drama, Fields and Metaphors: Symbolic Action in Human Societies*, Ithaca, NY: Cornell University Press.

Umansky, I. and Umansky, L. (eds.) (2001) *The New Disability History: American Perspectives*, New York: New York University Press.

Urry, J. (2003) *Global Complexity*, London: Routledge.

Urry, J. (2007) *Mobilities*, Cambridge: Polity.

US House of Representatives. (2005) *Anatomy of a Revolutionary Movement: 'Students for a Democratic Society'*, Washington, DC: University Press of the Pacific.

Van De Donk, W., Loader, B., Nixon, P. and Rucht, D. (2003) *Cyberprotest: New Media, Citizens and Social Movements*, London: Routledge.

Van Deburg, W. L. (1992) *New Day in Babylon: The Black Power Movement and American Culture*, Chicago: University of Chicago Press.

Vaneigem, R. (1967/1994) *The Revolution of Everyday Life*, London: Left Bank Books and Rebel Press.

Varese, S. (1996) 'The New Environmentalist Movement of Latin American Indigenous Peoples', in S. B. Brush and D. Stabinsky (eds.) *Valuing Local Knowledge: Indigenous People and Intellectual Property Rights*, Washington, DC: Island Press, pp. 122–138.

Virno, P. (2004) *A Grammar of the Multitude*, New York: Semiotext(e).

Voss, K. and Sherman, R. (2000) 'Breaking the Iron Law of Oligarchy: Union Revitalization in the American Labor Movement', *American Journal of Sociology*, 106, 2: 303–349.

Waddington, D., Jones, K., and Critcher, C. (1989) *Flashpoints: Studies in Public Disorder*, London: Routledge.

Walby, S. (1990) *Theorising Patriarchy*, Oxford: Blackwell.

Wall, D. (1994) *Green History*, London: Routledge.

Wall, D. (1999) *Earth First! and the Anti-Roads Movement*, London: Routledge.

Waterman, P. (2003) *First Reflections on the 3rd World Social Forum*. Online at: http://www.nadir.org/nadir/initiativ/agp/free/wsf/waterman_poa.htm

Weiviorka, M. (1995) *The Arena of Racism*, London: Sage.

Welsh, I. (2000) *Mobilising Modernity: The Nuclear Moment*, London: Routledge.

Welsh, I. (2001) 'Anti Nuclear Movements: Failed Projects or Heralds of a Direct Action Milieu?', *Sociological Research Online*, 6, 3. Online at: http://www.socresonline.org.uk/6/3/welsh.html

Welsh, I. (2007) 'Social Movements, Innovation and Efficiency: The New Genetics in Germany and the UK', in I. Bluhdorn and J. Uwe (eds.) (2007) *Economic Efficiency & Democratic Empowerment: Contested Modernization in Britain and Germany*, Lanham, MD: Lexington, pp. 275–295.

Welsh, I. (2007a) 'In Defence of Civilisation: Terrorism and Environmental Politics in the 21st Century', *Environmental Politics*, 16, 2: 359–378.

Welsh, I. (2010) 'Climate Change, Complexity and Collaboration Between the Sciences', in C. Lever-Tracey (ed.) *Handbook of Climate Change and Society*, London: Routledge.

Welsh, I., Evans, R. and Plows, A. (2007) 'Human Rights & Genomics: Science, Genomics and Social Movements at the 2004 London Social Forum', *New Genetics and Society*, 26, 2: 123–135.

Wettergren, A. (2009) 'Fun and Laughter: Culture Jamming and the Emotional Regime of Late Capitalism', *Social Movement Studies*, 8, 1: 1–16.

Williams, R. (1989) *Resources of Hope: Culture, Democracy, Socialism*, London: Verso.

Wissenberg, M. and Levy, Y. (eds.) (2004) *Liberal Democracy and Environmentalism: The End of Environmentalism?*, London: Routledge.

Wright, S. (2002) *Storming Heaven: Class Composition and Struggle in Italian Autonomist Marxism*, London: Pluto Press.

Yearley, S. (1988) *Science, Technology & Social Change*, London: Unwin Hyman.

Yinger, J. M. (1982) *Countercultures*, New York: Freedom Press.

Young, J. (1990) *Post Environmentalism*, London: Belhaven.

Young, N. (ed.) (2010) *The Oxford International Encyclopaedia of Peace*, Oxford: Oxford University Press.

Zack, N. (2005) *Inclusive Feminism: A Third Wave Theory of Women's Commonality*, Lanham, MD: Rowman & Littlefield.

Zald, M. (1996) 'Culture, Ideology and Strategic Framing', in D. McAdam, J. D. McCarthy and M. N. Zald (eds.) *Comparative Perspectives on Social Movements: Political Opportunities, Mobilizing Structures, and Cultural Framings*, Cambridge: Cambridge University Press.

Zald, M. N. and Ash, R. (1966) 'Social Movement Organizations: Growth, Decay and Change', *Social Forces*, 44, 3: 327–341.

Zald, M. N. and Useem, B. (1987) 'Movement and Countermovement Interaction: Mobilization, Tactics and State Involvement', M. N. Zald and J. D. McCarthy (eds.) *Social Movements in an Organizational Society: Collected Essays*, New Brunswick, NJ: Transaction Books.

INDEX

Page numbers in **bold** indicate the main entries for key concepts.

**Fifty Key Contemporary Thinkers: From Structuralism
to Post-Humanism**

John Lechte

Now in a fully updated second edition, with a new introduction
and new sections covering Phenomenology and the Post-Human,
Fifty Key Contemporary Thinkers surveys the lives and ideas of
the most influential thinkers of the twentieth and twenty-first
centuries including:

- Agamben
- Bergson
- Butler
- Haraway
- Heidegger
- Husserl

With full cross-referencing and up-to-date lists of major primary
and secondary texts, this book is essential reading for students
seeking a guide to hard-to-grasp theoretical ideas.

978-0-415-32694-0

Available from all good bookshops

For ordering and further information please visit

http://www.routledge.com

Globalization: The Key Concepts

Annabel Mooney and Betsy Evans

'This book provides masterful, non-technical definitions of major globalization-related concepts. It is an impressive piece of interdisciplinary work on globalization.'

Dr. Alessandra Guariglia, *University of Nottingham*

Viewed as a destructive force or an inevitability of modern society, globalization is the focus of a multitude of disciplines. A clear understanding of its processes and terminology is imperative for anyone engaging with this ubiquitous topic. *Globalization: The Key Concepts* offers a comprehensive guide to this cross-disciplinary subject and covers concepts such as:

- Homogenization
- Neo-Liberalism
- Risk
- Knowledge Society
- Time–space compression
- Reflexivity

With extensive cross-referencing and suggestions for further reading, this book is an essential resource for students and interested readers alike as they navigate the literature on globalization studies.

978–0–415–36860–5

Available from all good bookshops

For ordering and further information please visit

http://www.routledge.com

Politics: The Basics

4th edition

Stephen D. Tansey and Nigel Jackson

This highly successful introduction to the world of politics has been fully revised and updated to explore the systems, movements and key issues in modern politics. The new edition builds on the reputation for clarity and comprehensive coverage of the previous editions, and includes:

- A greater range of international examples
- Discussion of non-Western political structures
- Issues of trust and apathy in voting systems
- Analysis of the 'war on terror'
- The role of the internet in politics

Accessible in style and topical in content, this book assumes no prior knowledge in politics, and is ideal reading for new undergraduates and all those interested in how politics operates.

978–0–415–42244–4

Available from all good bookshops

For ordering and further information please visit

http://www.routledge.com